New and Old Wars

Third Edition

New and Old Wars

Third Edition

MARY KALDOR

polity

First published in 2012 by Polity Press

Polity Press
65 Bridge Street
Cambridge CB2 1UR, UK

Polity Press
350 Main Street
Malden, MA 02148, USA

ISBN-13: 978-0-7456-5562-8
ISBN-13: 978-0-7456-5563-5(pb)

A catalogue record for this book is available from the British Library.

Typeset in 11 on 13 pt Berling
by Toppan Best-set Premedia Limited
Printed and bound in Great Britain by the MPG Books Group

For further information on Polity, visit our website: www.politybooks.com

Contents

Preface to the Third Edition

In recent years, a number of scholars have remarked on what they describe as the decline of war in the twenty-first century, as well as the decline of combat-related casualties. These include the celebrated book by Steve Pinker, *The Better Angels of Our Nature*, the Human Security Report and John Mueller's book, *The Remnants of War*.[1]

What these studies show is a decline in what I call in this book 'old war' – that is to say, war involving states in which battle is the decisive encounter. Indeed, all these scholars base their conclusions on the Uppsala Conflict Data Program in which conflict is defined as involving states and is characterized by a certain minimum number of battle deaths. New wars involve networks of state and non-state actors and most violence is directed against civilians. Some critics of the 'new war' thesis conflate new wars with civil wars and argue that both inter-state and civil wars are declining. But new wars, as I explain in the introduction, are wars in which the difference between internal and external is blurred; they are both global and local and they are different both from classic inter-state wars and classic civil wars.

This tendency to define war as 'old war' obscures the reality of new wars. I do not know whether the number of new wars is increasing or not. Nor do we know the scale of casualties in new wars, although they are almost certainly lower than in 'old wars'. But my point is rather that we need to understand and analyse this new type of violence. While we should celebrate the decline of 'old war', we cannot rest on our laurels; we need to be able to address the main contemporary sources of insecurity. In large parts of the world – Central Asia, East Africa or Central Africa – people experience great suffering, and this matters whether it is more or less than in the past. Moreover, new wars are associated with state weakness, extremist identity politics and transnational criminality, and there is a danger that this type of violence will spread as the world faces a growing economic crisis. In the context of spending cuts, there is a tendency for governments to cut the very capabilities most suitable for addressing new wars and to protect their capabilities for fighting 'old wars'.

This is why it is important to present a new edition of this book. I have updated the book in places and included new material. The first edition of the book was published before 9/11 and I have included a new chapter on the wars in Iraq and Afghanistan. I argue that the 'old war' mindset of the United States greatly exacerbated the conditions for what was to become in both countries a new war. In fact, the experience of the wars led to new thinking in the Pentagon; the revamped counter-insurgency doctrine included ideas such as nation-building and population security and bringing together military and civilian capabilities. But it turned out to be very difficult to change the culture of the military and now the United States has reverted to an 'old war' campaign of defeating terrorists, using, in particular, long-distance air strikes in places such as Afghanistan, Pakistan, Yemen and Somalia. Even though precision has greatly improved and civilian casualties from air strikes are lower than in the past, as I argue in chapter 7, this further worsens the insecurity in these places.

The first edition of this book generated a lively debate about new wars and I have also included a new afterword that deals with this debate. Most of the criticisms question whether 'new wars' are really new or whether they are really war. My point is that they may not really be new and we may decide not to call them war but something is happening that is different from 'old war' and we need to understand it. It is the preoccupation with old war that prevents us from developing policy-relevant analysis.

Since writing the book, much of my work has focused on policy-oriented research and, in particular, developing the concept of human security as a way of addressing 'new wars'. I have not included this research in the book, even though I have updated chapter 6 'Towards a Cosmopolitan Approach', which represented an early version of my ideas on human security. Those who wish to learn more about human security can refer to two more recent books: *Human Security: Reflections on Globalisation and Intervention* and *The Ultimate Weapon is No Weapon: Human Security and the New Rules of War and Peace*, which I co-authored with a serving American army officer.[2]

Like Pinker and others, I greatly welcome the decline of 'old war'. But 'old war' can always be reinvented. Many of the critics point out, rightly, that the wars of the early modern period were similar to 'new wars' before states became as strong as they are today. The process of pacification and of eliminating brigands, highwaymen, pirates, warlords and other private wars was associated with the development of what I call 'old wars' – the wars of modernity of the nineteenth and twentieth centuries, as I describe in chapter 2. It was through war that states were able to centralize and control violence. If we fail to address the new wars of today, something along the same lines could always happen again.

The most important reason for optimism at the moment is the wave of peaceful protest that started in the Middle East and has become worldwide. It is the rise of civil society that has marginalized Al Qaeda and other extremist militant groups. It is the kind of cosmopolitan politics that I argue, in this book, is key to finding an answer to new wars. Much depends, therefore, on how far this new awakening, as it is often described, produces an institutional response. There is, of course, a huge risk that failure to produce an institutional response will have the opposite consequence. Indeed, at the time of writing, 'old war' thinking, that is to say geopolitical or realist approaches that focus on the security of Israel or the threat of Iranian nuclear weapons, could exacerbate 'new wars' in places like Syria and Iraq. The current brutal repression in Syria is not a civil war; it is a war against civilians and against cosmopolitan politics.

In preparing this third edition, I would like to thank Iavor Rangelov, Sabine Selchow and Yahia Said for discussions about the debate on new wars; Marika Theros for help with the new material on Afghanistan; Anouk Rigterink for help in the debate about data, especially displacement data; Tom Kirk for assistance in collecting the recent new wars literature; and Domenika Spyratou for general support.

Abbreviations

ABiH	Army of Bosnia–Herzegovina
ANC	African National Congress
AU	African Union
BRA	Bougainville Revolutionary Army
BSA	Bosnian Serb Army
CIA	Central Intelligence Agency
CIS	Commonwealth of Independent States
CLC	Concerned Local Citizens
CPA	Coalition Provisional Authority
DDR	Disarmament, Demobilization and Reintegration
DRC	Democratic Republic of Congo
ECHO	European Community Humanitarian Office
ECOMOG	Economic Community of West African States Ceasefire Monitoring Group
ECOWAS	Economic Community of West African States
EU	European Union
EUFOR	European Force
GDP	Gross Domestic Product
GPS	Global Positioning System
HCA	Helsinki Citizens' Assembly
HDZ	Croatian Democratic Party
HOS	Paramilitary wing of HSP
HSP	Croatian Party of Rights
HSR	Human Security Report
HV	Croatian Army

HVO	Croatian Defence Council
ICC	International Criminal Court
ICFY	International Conference on Former Yugoslavia
ICRC	International Committee of the Red Cross
IDP	Internally displaced person
IDMC	Internal Displacement Monitoring Centre
IED	Improvised explosive device
IFOR	Implementation Force
IFP	Inkatha Freedom Party
IGO	Intergovernmental organization
IISS	International Institute for Strategic Studies
IMF	International Monetary Fund
IRA	Irish Republican Army
IRC	International Rescue Committee
ISAF	International Security Assistance Force
ISCI	Islamic Supreme Council in Iraq
JAM	Jaish al-Mahdi (often known as Sadrists)
JNA	Yugoslav National Army
KLA	Kosovo Liberation Army
MIME-NET	Military-Industrial-Entertainment Network
MOS	Muslim Armed Forces
MPRI	Military Professional Resources Incorporated
NACC	NATO Coordination Council
NATO	North Atlantic Treaty Organization
NGO	Non-governmental organization
OAU	Organization of African Unity
OHR	Office of the High Representative in Bosnia–Herzegovina
OSCE	Organization for Security and Cooperation in Europe
PASOK	Panhellenic Socialist Movement (Greece)
PGM	Precision-guided missile
RENAMO	Resistência Nacional Moçambiçana
RMA	Revolution in Military Affairs
RPA	Remotely piloted vehicle
SCR	Security Council Resolution
SDA	(Muslim) Party of Democratic Action
SDS	Serbian Democratic Party
SFOR	Stabilization Force
SIPRI	Stockholm International Peace Research Institute

SPLA	Sudan People's Liberation Army
SRT	Serb Radio and Television station
TO	Territorial Defence Units
UAV	Unmanned aerial vehicle
UCDP	Uppsala Conflict Data Program
UN	United Nations
UNDP	United Nations Development Programme
UNHCR	United Nations High Commissioner for Refugees
UNICEF	United Nations Children's Fund
UNPROFOR	United Nations Protection Force
UNU	United Nations University
WEU	Western European Union
WIDER	World Institute for Development Economics Research
WMD	Weapons of mass destruction

1
Introduction

In the summer of 1992, I visited Nagorno-Karabakh in the Transcaucasian region in the midst of a war involving Azerbaijan and Armenia. It was then that I realized that what I had previously observed in the former Yugoslavia was not unique; it was not a throwback to the Balkan past but rather a contemporary predicament especially, or so I thought, to be found in the post-communist part of the world. The Wild West atmosphere of Knin (then the capital of the self-proclaimed Serbian republic in Croatia) and Nagorno-Karabakh, peopled by young men in home-made uniforms, desperate refugees and thuggish, neophyte politicians, was quite distinctive. Later, I embarked on a research project on the character of the new type of wars and I discovered from my colleagues who had first-hand experience of Africa that what I had noted in Eastern Europe shared many common features with the wars taking place in Africa and perhaps also other places, for example South Asia. Indeed, the experience of wars in other places shed new light on my understanding of what was happening in the Balkans and the former Soviet Union.[1]

My central argument is that, during the last decades of the twentieth century, a new type of organized violence developed, especially in Africa and Eastern Europe, which is one aspect of the current globalized era. I describe this type of violence as 'new war'. I use the term 'new' to distinguish such wars from prevailing perceptions of war drawn from an earlier era, which

I outline in chapter 2. I use the term 'war' to emphasize the political nature of this new type of violence, even though, as will become clear in the following pages, the new wars involve a blurring of the distinctions between war (usually defined as violence between states or organized political groups for political motives), organized crime (violence undertaken by privately organized groups for private purposes, usually financial gain) and large-scale violations of human rights (violence undertaken by states or politically organized groups against individuals).

In most of the literature, the new wars are described as internal or civil wars or else as 'low-intensity conflicts'. Yet, although most of these wars are localized, they involve a myriad of transnational connections so that the distinction between internal and external, between aggression (attacks from abroad) and repression (attacks from inside the country), or even between local and global, are difficult to sustain. The term 'low-intensity conflict' was coined during the Cold War period by the US military to describe guerrilla warfare or terrorism. Although it is possible to trace the evolution of the new wars from the so-called low-intensity conflicts of the Cold War period, they have distinctive characteristics which are masked by what is in effect a catch-all term. Some authors describe the new wars as privatized or informal wars;[2] yet, while the privatization of violence is an important element of these wars, in practice, the distinction between what is private and what is public, state and non-state, informal and formal, what is done for economic and what for political motives, cannot easily be applied. A more appropriate term is perhaps 'post-modern', which is used by several authors.[3] Like 'new wars', it offers a way of distinguishing these wars from the wars which could be said to be characteristic of classical modernity. However, the term is also used to refer to virtual wars and wars in cyberspace;[4] moreover, the new wars involve elements of pre-modernity and modernity as well. A more recent term used by Frank Hoffman, which has gained widespread currency, particularly in the military, is 'hybrid wars'[5] – the term nicely captures the blurring of public and private, state or non-state, formal and informal that is characteristic of new wars; it is also used to refer to a mixture of different types of war (conventional warfare, counter-insurgency, civil war, for example) and, as such, may miss the specific logic of new wars. Finally, Martin

Shaw uses the term 'degenerate warfare', while John Mueller talks about the 'remnants' of war.[6] For Shaw, there is a continuity with the total wars of the twentieth century and their genocidal aspects; the term draws attention to the decay of the national frameworks, especially military forces. Mueller argues that war in general (what I call old wars) has declined and that what is left is banditry often disguised as political conflict.

Critics of the 'new war' argument have suggested that many features of the new wars can be found in earlier wars and that the dominance of the Cold War overshadowed the significance of 'small wars' or 'low-intensity' conflicts.[7] There is some truth in this proposition. The main point of the distinction between new and old wars was to change the prevailing perceptions of war, especially among policy makers. In particular, I wanted to emphasize the growing illegitimacy of these wars and the need for a cosmopolitan political response – one that put individual rights and the rule of law as the centrepiece of any international intervention (political, military, civil or economic). Nevertheless, I do think that the 'new war' argument does reflect a new reality – a reality that was emerging before the end of the Cold War. Globalization is a convenient catch-all to describe the various changes that characterize the contemporary period and have influenced the character of war.[8]

Among American strategic writers, there has been much discussion about what is variously known as the Revolution in Military Affairs, or Defence Transformation.[9] The argument is that the advent of information technology is as significant as was the advent of the tank and the aeroplane, or even as significant as the shift from horse power to mechanical power, with profound implications for the future of warfare. In particular, it is argued that these changes have made modern war much more precise and discriminate. However, these apparently new concepts are conceived within the inherited institutional structures of war and the military. They envisage wars on a traditional model in which the new techniques develop in a more or less linear extension from the past. Moreover, they are designed to sustain the imagined character of war which was typical of the Cold War era and utilized in such a way as to minimize own casualties. The preferred technique is spectacular aerial bombing or rapid and dramatic ground manoeuvres and most recently the use of robots and UAVs (unmanned aerial vehicles) especially drones, which reproduce the appearance of classical war for public consumption but which turn out to be rather clumsy as an instrument and, in some cases, outright counterproductive, for influencing the reality on the ground. Hence Baudrillard's famous remark that the Gulf War did not take place.[10] These complex sophisticated techniques were initially applied in the Gulf War of 1991, developed further in the last phases of the war in Bosnia–Herzegovina and in Kosovo, and, most recently, in the wars in Iraq and Afghanistan, and also Pakistan, Yemen and Somalia.

I share the view that there has been a revolution in military affairs, but it is a revolution in the social relations of warfare, not in technology, even though the changes in social relations are influenced by and make use of new technology. Beneath the spectacular displays are real wars, which, even in the case of the 1991 Iraq war in which thousands of Kurds and Shi'ites died, are better explained in terms of my conception of new wars. In this third edition, I have added a new chapter on the wars in Iraq and Afghanistan to show the clash between what I call technology-updated 'old war' and the 'new war' in both places.

The new wars have to be understood in the context of the process known as globalization. By globalization, I mean the intensification of global interconnectedness – political, economic, military and cultural – and the changing character of political authority. Even though I accept the argument that globalization has its roots in modernity or even earlier, I consider that the globalization of the 1980s and 1990s was a qualitatively new phenomenon which can, at least in part, be explained as a consequence of the revolution in information technologies and dramatic improvements in communication and data processing. This process of intensifying interconnectedness is a contradictory one involving both integration and fragmentation, homogenization and diversification, globalization and localization. It is often argued that the new wars are a consequence of the end of the Cold War; they reflect a power vacuum which is typical of transition periods in world affairs. It is undoubtedly true that the consequences of the end of the Cold War – the availability of surplus arms, the discrediting of socialist ideologies, the disintegration of totalitarian empires, the withdrawal of superpower support to client regimes – contributed in important ways to the new wars. But equally, the end of the Cold War could be viewed as the way in which the Eastern bloc succumbed to the inevitable encroachment of globalization – the crumbling of the last bastions of territorial autarchy, the moment when Eastern Europe was 'opened up' to the rest of the world.

The impact of globalization is visible in many of the new wars. The global presence in these wars can include international reporters, mercenary troops and military advisers, and diaspora volunteers as well as a veritable 'army' of international agencies ranging from non-governmental organizations (NGOs) such as Oxfam, Save the Children, Médecins Sans Frontières, Human Rights Watch and the International Red Cross to international institutions such as the United Nations High Commissioner for Refugees (UNHCR), the European Union (EU), the United Nations Children's Fund (UNICEF), the Organization for Security and Cooperation in Europe (OSCE), the African Union (AU) and the United Nations (UN) itself, including peacekeeping troops. Indeed, the wars epitomize a new kind of global/local divide between those members of a global class who can speak English, have access to the Internet and satellite television, who use dollars or euros or credit cards, and who can travel freely, and those who are excluded from global processes, who live off what they can sell or barter or what they receive in humanitarian aid, whose movement is restricted by roadblocks, visas and the cost of travel, and who are prey to sieges, forced displacement, famines, landmines, etc.

In the literature on globalization, a central issue concerns the implications of global interconnectedness for the future of territorially based sovereignty – that is to say, for the future of the modern state.[11] The new wars arise in the context of the erosion of the autonomy of the state and, in some extreme cases, the disintegration of the state. In particular, they occur in the context of the erosion of the monopoly of legitimate organized violence. This monopoly is eroded from above and from below. It has been eroded from above by the transnationalization of military forces which began during the two world wars and was institutionalized by the bloc system during the Cold War and by innumerable transnational connections between armed forces that developed in the post-war period.[12]

The capacity of states to use force unilaterally against other states has been greatly weakened. This is partly for practical reasons – the growing destructiveness of military technology and the increasing interconnectedness of states, especially in the military field. It is difficult to imagine nowadays a state or group of states risking a large-scale war which could be even more destructive than what was experienced during the two world wars. Moreover, military alliances, international arms production and trade, various forms of military cooperation and exchanges, arms control agreements, etc., have created a form of global military integration. The weakening of states' capacity to use unilateral force is also due to the evolution of international norms. The principle that unilateral aggression is illegitimate was first codified in the Kellogg–Briand pact of 1928, and reinforced after World War II in the UN Charter and through the reasoning used in the war crimes trials in Nuremberg and Tokyo.

At the same time, the monopoly of organized violence is eroded from below by privatization. Indeed, it could be argued that the new wars are part of a process which is more or less a reversal of the processes through which modern European states evolved. As I argue in chapter 2, the rise of the modern state was intimately connected to war. In order to fight wars, rulers needed to increase taxation and borrowing, to eliminate 'wastage' as a result of crime, corruption and inefficiency, to regularize armed forces and police and to eliminate private armies, and to mobilize popular support in order to raise money and men. As war became the exclusive province of the state, so the growing destructiveness of war against other states was paralleled by a process of growing security at home; hence the way in which the term 'civil' came to mean internal. The modern European state was reproduced elsewhere. The new wars occur in situations in which state revenues decline because of the decline of the economy as well as the spread of criminality, corruption and inefficiency, violence is increasingly privatized both as a result of growing organized crime and the emergence of paramilitary groups, and political legitimacy is disappearing. Thus the distinctions are breaking down between external barbarity and domestic civility, between the combatant as the legitimate bearer of arms and the non-combatant, or between the soldier or policeman and the criminal. The barbarity of war between states may have become a thing of the past. In its place is a new type of organized violence that is more pervasive and long-lasting, but also perhaps less extreme.

In chapter 3, I use the example of the war in Bosnia–Herzegovina to illustrate the main features of the new wars, mainly because it is the war with which I was most familiar when I originally wrote this book. The war in Bosnia–Herzegovina shares many of the characteristics of wars in other places. But in one sense it is exceptional; it became the focus of global and European attention during the 1990s. More resources – governmental and non-governmental – have been concentrated there than in any other new war up until the current wars in Iraq and Afghanistan. On the one hand, this means that, as a case study, it has atypical features. On the other hand, it also means that it became the paradigm case from which different lessons were drawn in the post-Cold War period, the example which has been used to argue out different general positions, and, at the same time, a laboratory in which experiments in the different ways of managing the new wars have taken place.

The new wars can be contrasted with earlier wars in terms of their goals, the methods of warfare and how they are financed. The goals of the new wars are about identity politics in contrast to the geo-political or ideological goals of earlier wars. In chapter 4, I argue that, in the context of globalization, ideological and/or territorial cleavages of an earlier era have increasingly been supplanted by an emerging political cleavage between what I call cosmopolitanism, based on inclusive, universalist, multicultural values, and the politics of particularist identities.[13] This cleavage can be explained in terms of the growing divide between those who are part of global processes and those who are excluded, but it should not be equated with this division. Among the global class are members of transnational networks based on exclusivist identity, while at the local level there are many courageous individuals who refuse the politics of particularism.

By identity politics, I mean the claim to power on the basis of a particular identity – be it national, clan, religious or linguistic. In one sense, all wars involve a clash of identities – British against French, communists against democrats. But my point is that these earlier identities were linked either to a notion of state interest or to some forward-looking project – ideas about how society should be organized. Nineteenth-century European nationalisms or post-colonial nationalisms, for example, presented themselves as emancipatory nation-building projects. The new identity politics is about the claim to power on the basis of labels – in so far as there are ideas about political or social change, they tend to relate to an idealized nostalgic representation of the past. It is often claimed that the new wave of identity politics is merely a throwback to the past, a resurgence of ancient hatreds kept under control by colonialism and/or the Cold War. While it is true that the narratives of identity politics depend on memory and tradition, it is also the case that these are 'reinvented' in the context of the failure or the corrosion of other sources of political legitimacy – the discrediting of socialism or the nation-building rhetoric of the first generation of post-colonial leaders. These backward-looking political projects arise in the vacuum created by the absence of forward-looking projects. Unlike the politics of ideas which are open to all and therefore tend to be integrative, this type of identity politics is inherently exclusive and therefore tends towards fragmentation.

There are two aspects of the new wave of identity politics which specifically relate to the process of globalization. First, the new wave of identity politics is both local and global, national as well as transnational. In many cases, there are significant diaspora communities whose influence is greatly enhanced by the ease of travel and improved communication. Alienated diaspora groups in advanced industrial or oil-rich countries provide ideas, funds and techniques, thereby imposing their own frustrations and fantasies on what is often a very different situation. Second, this politics makes use of the new technology. The speed of political mobilization is greatly increased by the use of the electronic media. The effect of television, radio or videos on what is often a non-reading public cannot be overestimated. The protagonists of the new politics often display the symbols of a global mass culture – Mercedes cars, Rolex watches, Ray-Ban sunglasses – combined with the labels that signify their own brand of particularistic cultural identity. The use of mobiles and/or the Internet and social media hugely contribute to the construction of political networks.

The second characteristic of the new wars is the changed mode of warfare[14] – the means through which the new wars are fought. The strategies of the new warfare draw on the experience of both guerrilla warfare and counter-insurgency, yet they are quite distinctive. In conventional or regular war, the goal is the capture of territory by military means; battles are the decisive encounters of the war. Guerrilla warfare developed as a way of getting round the massive concentrations of military force which are characteristic of conventional war. In guerrilla warfare, territory is captured through political control of the population rather than through military advance, and battles are avoided as far as possible. The new warfare also tends to avoid battle and to control territory through political control of the population, but whereas guerrilla warfare, at least in theory as articulated by Mao Tse-tung or Che Guevara, aimed to capture 'hearts and minds', the new warfare borrows from counter-insurgency techniques of destabilization aimed at sowing 'fear and hatred'. The aim is to control the population by getting rid of everyone of a different identity (and indeed of a different opinion) and by instilling terror. Hence the strategic goal of these wars is to mobilize extremist politics based on fear and hatred. This often involves population expulsion through various means such as mass killing and forcible resettlement, as well as a range of political, psychological and economic techniques of intimidation. This is why all these wars are characterized by high levels of refugees and displaced persons, and why most violence is directed against civilians. Behaviour that was proscribed according to the classical rules of warfare and codified in the laws of war in the late nineteenth century and early twentieth century, such as atrocities against non-combatants, sieges, destruction of historic monuments, etc., constitutes an essential component of the strategies of the new mode of warfare. The terrorism experienced in places such as New York, Madrid or London, as well as in Israel or Iraq, can be understood as a variant of the new strategy – the use of spectacular, often gruesome, violence to create fear and conflict.

In contrast to the vertically organized hierarchical units that were typical of 'old wars', among the units that fight these wars is a disparate range of different types of groups, such as paramilitary units, local warlords, criminal gangs, police forces, mercenary groups and also regular armies, including breakaway units from regular armies. In organizational terms, they are highly decentralized and they operate through a mixture of confrontation and cooperation even when on opposing sides. They make use of advanced technology even if it is not what we tend to call 'high technology' (stealth bombers or cruise missiles, for example). In the last fifty years, there have been significant advances in lighter weapons – undetectable landmines, for example, or small arms which are light, accurate and easy to use so that they can even be operated by children. Modern communications – cellular phones or computer links – are also used in order to coordinate, mediate and negotiate among the disparate fighting units.

The third way in which the new wars can be contrasted with earlier wars is what I call the new 'globalized' war economy, which is elaborated in chapter 5 along with the mode of warfare. The new globalized war economy is almost exactly the opposite of the war economies of the two world wars. The latter were centralized, totalizing and autarchic. The new war economies are decentralized. Participation in the war is low and unemployment is extremely high. Moreover, these economies are heavily dependent on external resources. In these wars, domestic production declines dramatically because of global competition, physical destruction or interruptions to normal trade, as does tax revenue. In these circumstances, the fighting units finance themselves through plunder, hostage-taking and the black market or through external assistance. The latter can take the following forms: remittances from the diaspora, 'taxation' of humanitarian assistance, support from neighbouring governments, or illegal trade in arms, drugs or valuable commodities such as oil or diamonds or human trafficking. All of these sources can only be sustained through continued violence so that a war logic is built into the functioning of the economy. This retrograde set of social relationships, which is entrenched by war, has a tendency to spread across borders through refugees or organized crime or ethnic minorities. It is possible to identify clusters of war economies or near war economies in places such as the Balkans, the Caucasus, Central Asia, the Horn of Africa, Central Africa or West Africa.

Because the various warring parties share the aim of sowing 'fear and hatred', they operate in a way that is mutually reinforcing, helping each other to create a climate of insecurity and suspicion – indeed, it is possible to find examples in both Eastern Europe and Africa, as well as Iraq and Afghanistan, of mutual cooperation for both military and economic purposes.[15] Often, among the first civilians to be targeted are those who espouse a different politics, those who try to maintain inclusive social relations and some sense of public morality. Thus, although the new wars appear to be between different linguistic, religious or tribal groups, they can also be presented as wars in which those who represent particularistic identity politics cooperate in suppressing the values of civility and multiculturalism. In other words, they can be understood as wars between exclusivism and cosmopolitanism.

This analysis of new wars has implications for the management of conflicts, which I explore in chapter 6. There is no possible long-term solution within the framework of identity politics. And because these are conflicts with extensive social and economic ramifications, top-down approaches are likely to fail. In the early 1990s there was great optimism about the prospects for humanitarian intervention to protect civilians. The concept of 'Responsibility to Protect' developed by the Canadian-sponsored International Commission on Intervention and State Sovereignty in 2001 was approved by the United Nations General Assembly in 2005 and has received considerable emphasis within the United Nations.[16] However, the practice of humanitarian intervention was, on the one hand, subverted by what happened in New York on 11 September 2001 and the subsequent War on Terror. And, on the other hand, the development of Responsibility to Protect is, I would argue, constrained by a kind of myopia about the character of the new warfare. The persistence of inherited mandates and the tendency to interpret these wars in traditional terms, has been the main reason why humanitarian intervention has often failed to prevent the wars and may actually have helped to sustain them in various ways – for example, through the provision of humanitarian aid, which is an important source of income for the warring parties, or through the legitimation of war criminals by inviting them to the negotiating table, or through the effort to find political compromises based on exclusivist assumptions. Even in cases where the goals are clearly humanitarian, as in the Kosovo and Libya wars, the means are often those of updated old war with problematic consequences.

The key to any long-term solution is the restoration of legitimacy, the reconstitution of the control of organized violence by public authorities, whether local, national or global. This is both a political process – the rebuilding of trust in, and support for, public authorities – and a legal process – the re-establishment of a rule of law within which public authorities operate. This cannot be done on the basis of particularistic politics. An alternative forward-looking cosmopolitan political project which would cross the global/local divide and reconstruct legitimacy around an inclusive, democratic set of values has to be counterposed against the politics of exclusivism. In all the new wars there are local people and places that struggle against the politics of exclusivism – the Hutus and Tutsis who called themselves Hutsis and tried to defend their localities against genocide; the non-nationalists in the cities of Bosnia–Herzegovina, particularly Sarajevo and Tuzla, who kept alive civic multicultural values; the elders in Northwest Somaliland who negotiated peace; the civil society groups in both Iraq and Afghanistan who insist on the idea of Afghanistan and Iraq. What is needed is an alliance between local defenders of civility and transnational institutions which would guide a strategy aimed at controlling violence. Such a strategy would include political, military and economic components. It would operate within a framework of international law, based on that body of international law that comprises both the 'laws of war' and human rights law, which could perhaps be termed cosmopolitan law, and it would put emphasis on various forms of transitional justice. In this context, peacekeeping could be reconceptualized as cosmopolitan law-enforcement. Since the new wars are, in a sense, a mixture of war, crime and human rights violations, so the agents of cosmopolitan law-enforcement have to be a mixture of soldiers and police. I also argue that a new strategy of reconstruction, which includes the reconstruction of social, civic and institutional relationships, should supplant the current dominant approaches of structural adjustment or humanitarianism.

The wars in Iraq and Afghanistan are good illustrations of the way in which misperceptions about the character of war exacerbate 'new wars'. The fall of the Taliban in December 2001 seemed to offer a new model of how to defeat authoritarian regimes. In Iraq, the Bush administration believed that they could apply this model and defeat Saddam Hussein rapidly, using new technology to substitute for manpower, and install a new regime, along the lines of the occupation of post-war Germany and Japan. But in both countries, they found themselves caught up in an ever-worsening new war spiral, involving both state and non-state actors, identity politics, a criminalized war economy and growing numbers of civilian casualties. This is the subject of chapter 7, which has been written especially for this new edition.

In the final chapter of the book, I discuss the implications of the argument for global order. Although the new wars are concentrated in Africa, Eastern Europe and Asia, they are a global phenomenon not just because of the presence of global networks, or because they are reported globally. The characteristics of the new wars I have described are to be found in North America and Western Europe as well. The right-wing militia groups in the United States are not so very different from the paramilitary groups in other places. Indeed, in the United States it is reported that private security officers outnumber police officers by two to one. Nor is the salience of identity politics and the growing disillusionment with formal politics just a Southern and Eastern phenomenon. The violence in the inner cities of Western Europe and North America can, in some senses, be described as new wars. The suicide bombers responsible for the attacks of 7 July 2005 on London were, after all, home-grown. It is sometimes said that the advanced industrial world is integrating and the poorer parts of the world are fragmenting. I would argue that all parts of the world are characterized by a combination of integration and fragmentation even though the tendencies to integration are greater in the North and the tendencies to fragmentation may be greater in the South and East.

Since 9/11 it has become clear that it is no longer possible to insulate some parts of the world from others. Neither the idea that we can re-create some kind of bipolar or multipolar world order on the basis of identity – Christianity versus Islam, for example – nor the idea that the 'anarchy' in places such as Africa and Eastern Europe can be contained is feasible if my analysis of the changing character of organized violence has some basis in reality. This is why the cosmopolitan project has to be a global project even if it is, as it must be, local or regional in application.

The book was originally based on direct experience of the new wars, especially in the Balkans and the Transcaucasian region. As one of the chairs of the Helsinki Citizens' Assembly (HCA), I travelled extensively in these areas and learned much of what I know from the critical intellectuals and activists involved in local branches of the HCA. In particular, in Bosnia–Herzegovina, the HCA was given the status of an implementing agency of the UNHCR, which enabled me to move around the country during the war in support of local activists. I was also lucky enough to have access to the various institutions responsible for carrying out the policies of the international community; as chair of the HCA, it was one of my tasks, along with others, to present the ideas and proposals of local branches to governments and international institutions such as the EU, NATO, the OSCE and the UN. More recently, I have been involved in projects aimed at supporting civil society in Iraq and Afghanistan. As an academic, I was able to supplement and put into context this knowledge through reading, through exchanges with colleagues working in related fields and through research projects undertaken for the United Nations University (UNU), the European Commission and the United Nations Development Programme (UNDP).[17] In particular, I have been greatly helped by the newsletters, news digests, pleas for help and monitoring reports that now can be received daily on the Internet.

The aim of this book is not simply to inform, although I have tried to provide information and to back my assertions with examples. The aim is to offer a different perspective, the perspective derived from the experiences of critically minded individuals on the ground, tempered by my own experience in various international forums. It is a contribution to the reconceptualization of patterns of violence and war that has to be undertaken if the tragedies that are encroaching in many parts of the world are to be halted. I am not an optimist, yet my practical suggestions may seem utopian. I offer them in hope, not in confidence, as the only alternative to a grim future.

2

Old Wars

As Clausewitz was fond of pointing out, war is a social activity.[1] It involves the mobilization and organization of individual men, almost never women, for the purpose of inflicting physical violence; it entails the regulation of certain types of social relationships and has its own particular logic. Clausewitz, who was arguably the greatest exponent of modern war, insisted that war could not be reduced either to art or to science. Sometimes he likened war to business competition, and he often used economic analogies to illustrate his points.

Every society has its own characteristic form of war. What we tend to perceive as war, what policy makers and military leaders define as war, is, in fact, a specific phenomenon which took shape in Europe somewhere between the fifteenth and eighteenth centuries, although it has passed through several different phases since then. It was a phenomenon that was intimately bound up with the evolution of the modern state. It went through several phases, as I have tried to show in table 2.1, from the relatively limited wars of the seventeenth and eighteenth centuries associated with the growing power of the absolutist state, to the more revolutionary wars of the nineteenth century such as the Napoleonic Wars or the American Civil War, both of which were linked to the establishment of nation-states, to the total wars of the early twentieth century, and the imagined Cold War of the late twentieth century, which were wars of alliances and, later, blocs.

Table 2.1 *The evolution of old wars*

	17th and 18th centuries	*19th century*	*Early 20th century*	*Late 20th century*
Type of polity	absolutist state	nation-state	coalitions of states; multinational states; empires	blocs
Goals of war	reasons of state; dynastic conflict; consolidation of borders	national conflict	national and ideological conflict	ideological conflict
Type of army	mercenary/professional	professional/conscription	mass armies	scientific-military elite/professional armies
Military technique	use of firearms, defensive manoeuvres, sieges	railways and telegraph, rapid mobilization	massive firepower; tanks and aircraft	nuclear weapons
War economy	regularization of taxation and borrowing	expansion of administration and bureaucracy	mobilization economy	military-industrial complex

Each of these phases was characterized by a different mode of warfare, involving different types of military forces, different strategies and techniques, different relations and means of warfare. But, despite these differences, war was recognizably the same phenomenon: a construction of the centralized, 'rationalized', hierarchically ordered, territorialized modern state. As the centralized, territorialized modern state gives way to new types of polity emerging out of new global processes, so war, as we presently conceive it, is becoming an anachronism.

This chapter aims to provide a stylized description of old wars. Actual warfare never exactly fitted the stylized description. This type of war was predominantly European. There were always rebellions, colonial wars or guerrilla wars, both in Europe and elsewhere, which were sometimes given the description of 'irregular warfare' or else not called wars at all. Instead, they were called uprisings, insurgencies or, more recently, low-intensity conflicts. Nevertheless, it is the stylized notion of war that still profoundly affects our thinking about war and dominates, even today, the way policy makers conceive of national security.

War and the Emergence of the Modern State

Clausewitz defined war as 'an act of violence intended to compel our opponent to fulfill our will'.[2] At the time, this definition implied that 'we' and 'our opponent' were states, and the 'will' of one state could be clearly defined. Hence the kind of war that Clausewitz analysed, even though he did devote some writing to small wars, was predominantly war between states for a definable political end, i.e. state interest.

The notion of war as state activity was firmly established only towards the end of the eighteenth century. The only precedent for this type of war was ancient Rome, although even in this case it was one-sided; the state, i.e. Rome, fought against barbarians who had no notion of the separation of state and society. Van Creveld argues that war between the Greek city-states did not count as state warfare since there was no clear distinction between the state and the citizens. Wars were fought by citizen militias, and contemporary

accounts of warfare tended to refer to war between 'the Athe-
nians' and 'the Spartans' rather than to war between 'Athens'
and 'Sparta'.[3] Between the fall of the Roman Empire and the
late Middle Ages, war was fought by a variety of actors – the
Church, feudal barons, barbarian tribes, city-states – each with
its own characteristic military formations. Hence, the barbarian mode of fighting was generally based on warrior cults, the
individual warrior being the key military unit. Feudal barons
depended on knights, with their codes of honour and chivalry,
supported by serfs. The city-states of Northern Italy typically
depended on citizen militias, much like the earlier Greek
city-states.

In the early stages of European state formation, monarchs
raised armies to fight wars from coalitions of feudal barons
rather as the UN Secretary-General, today, has to mobilize
voluntary contributions from individual states in order to raise
a peacekeeping force. Gradually, they were able to consolidate
territorial borders and to centralize power by using their
growing economic assets, derived from customs duties, various
forms of taxation and borrowing from the emergent bourgeoisie, to raise mercenary armies which gave them a certain
degree of independence from the barons. However, mercenary
armies turned out to be unreliable; their loyalty could not be
counted on. Moreover, they were disbanded after wars or for
the winter. The cost of disbandment and of re-enlistment was
often prohibitive and, in the closed seasons, the mercenaries
could always find other less savoury ways of making a living.
Thus, mercenary armies came to be replaced by standing
armies which enabled monarchs to create specialized, professional military forces. The introduction of drill and exercise,
pioneered by Gustavus Adolphus of Sweden and Prince
William of Orange, kept the army occupied in periods
when there was no open warfare. According to Keegan, the
establishment of permanent infantry troops, the creation of
compagnies d'ordonnance or regiments, became the 'device
for securing the control of armed force by the state'. They
were kept in garrison towns which became 'schools of the
nation'.[4] Uniforms were introduced to distinguish soldiers
from civilians. As Michael Roberts puts it, 'the soldier
became the King's man for he wore the King's coat'[5] – literally, as it turned out, because kings increasingly tended to

wear military uniforms to exhibit their roles as military commanders.

The new type of military organization was to become typical of the emerging administrative arrangements that were associated with modernity. The soldier was the agent of what Max Weber called rational-legal authority:

> The modern military officer is a type of appointed official who is clearly marked out by certain class distinctions ... In this respect, such officers differ radically from elected military leaders; from charismatic condottieri; from the type of officers who recruit and lead mercenary armies as a capitalistic enterprise; and finally from the incumbents of commissions which have been purchased. There may be gradual transitions between these types. The patrimonial 'retainer' who is separated from the means of carrying out his function and the proprietor of a mercenary army for capitalistic purposes, have along with the private capitalistic entrepreneur, become pioneers of the modern type of bureaucracy.[6]

The establishment of standing armies under the control of the state was an integral part of the monopolization of legitimate violence which was intrinsic to the modern state. State interest became the legitimate justification for war, supplanting concepts of justice, *jus ad bellum*, drawn from theology. The Clausewitzean insistence that war is a rational instrument for the pursuit of state interest – 'the continuation of politics by other means' – constituted a secularization of legitimacy that paralleled developments in other spheres of activity. Once state interest had become the dominant legitimation of war, then claims of just cause by non-state actors could no longer be pursued through violent means.

In the same vein, there developed rules about what constituted legitimate warfare which were later codified in the laws of war. All types of warfare are characterized by rules; the very fact that warfare is a socially sanctioned activity, that it has to be organized and justified, requires rules. There is a thin dividing line between socially acceptable killing and what is ostracized by society. But that dividing line is defined differently in different periods. In the Middle Ages, the rules of warfare, *jus in bello*, were derived from papal authority. Under the modern state, a new set of secular rules had to be evolved. According to van Creveld:

> To distinguish war from mere crime, it was defined as something waged by sovereign states and by them alone. Soldiers were defined as personnel licensed to engage in armed violence on behalf of the state ... To obtain and maintain their license, soldiers had to be carefully registered, marked and controlled to the exclusion of privateering. They were supposed to fight only when in uniform, carrying their arms 'openly' and obeying a commander who could be held responsible for their actions. They were not supposed to resort to 'dastardly' methods such as violating truces, taking up arms again after they had been taken prisoner, and the like. The civilian population was supposed to be left alone, 'military necessity' permitting.[7]

In order to finance standing armies, administration, taxation and borrowing had to be regularized. Throughout the eighteenth century, military spending accounted for around three-quarters of state budgets in most European states. Administrative reform had to be undertaken to improve tax-raising capacities; corruption had to be limited, if not eliminated, to prevent 'leakage'.[8] War offices and secretaries of war had to be established to organize and improve the efficiency of expenditure. To extend borrowing, it was necessary to regularize the banking system and the creation of money, to separate the king's finance from the finance of the state and, ultimately, to establish central banks.[9]

Likewise, other means had to be found to establish law and order and justice within the territory of the state, both to provide a secure basis for taxation and borrowing and for legitimacy. A kind of implicit contract was established whereby kings offered protection in exchange for funds. The elimination and/or outlawing of brigands, privateers and highwaymen removed private forms of 'protection', thus swelling the king's revenue-raising capacity, and created a basis for legitimate economic activity. Hence, parallel to the redefinition of war as war between states, as an external activity, was the process Anthony Giddens calls internal pacification, which included the introduction of monetary relations – e.g. wages and rent – in place of more direct coercion, the phasing out of violent forms of punishment such as flogging and hanging, and the establishment of civilian agencies for tax collection and domestic law-enforcement. Particularly important was the emerging distinction between the military and the civilian police responsible for domestic law and order.[10]

The process of monopolization of violence was by no means smooth and uninterrupted, nor did it take place at the same time or in the same way in different European states. The Prussian state, created after the Treaty of Westphalia out of the various pieces of territory held by the House of Hohenzollern, is often considered a model. This state, which was an entirely artificial creation, was able in the eighteenth century to match the military strength of France with only one-fifth of the population, owing to the vigorous combination of military reform and rational administration introduced by Frederick William, the Great Elector, and his successors. In contrast, French kings faced continual rebellions by the nobility and had enormous difficulty in regularizing administration and tax collection. Skocpol argues that a central consideration in explaining the French Revolution was the inability of the *ancien régime* to develop the administrative and financial capacity necessary to realize its military ambitions.[11]

Nor was the process as rational or as functional as this stylized description suggests. Michael Roberts insisted that it was military logic that led to the formation of standing armies. But it is difficult to distinguish the exigencies of war from the demands of domestic consolidation. Cardinal Richelieu favoured the establishment of a standing army because he saw it as a way to bring the nobles under control. Rousseau consistently argued that war was directed as much against subjects as against other states:

Again, anyone can understand that war and conquest without and the encroachments of despotism within give each other mutual support; that money and men are habitually taken at pleasure from a people of slaves to bring others beneath the same yoke; and that conversely war furnishes a pretext for exactions of money and another, no less plausible, for keeping large armies constantly on foot, to hold people at awe. In a word, anyone can see that aggressive princes wage war at least as much on their subjects as on their enemies, and that the conquering nation is left no better off than the conquered.[12]

While rational state interest was claimed to be the goal of war, more emotive causes have always been required to instil loyalty and to persuade men to risk their lives. It was, after all, religious fervour that inspired Cromwell's New Model Army, which was the earliest example of a modern professional force. Prussian success is often attributed to the force of Lutheranism.

By the end of the eighteenth century, it was possible to define the specific socially organized activity which we perceive as war. It could be situated in the context of a whole series of new distinctions which were characteristic of the evolving state. These included:

- the distinction between public and private, between the sphere of state activity and non-state activity;
- the distinction between internal and external, between what took place within the clearly defined territory of the state and what took place outside;
- the distinction between the economic and the political which was associated with the rise of capitalism, the separation of private economic activity from public state activities, and the removal of physical coercion from economic activities;
- the distinction between the civil and the military, between domestic non-violent legal intercourse and external violent struggle, between civil society and barbarism;
- the distinction between the legitimate bearer of arms and the non-combatant or the criminal.

Above all, there emerged the distinction between war and peace itself. In place of more or less continuous violent activity, war became a discrete event, an aberration in what appeared to be a progressive evolution towards a civil society, not in today's sense of active citizenry and organized NGOs, but in the sense of day-to-day security, domestic peace, respect for law and justice. It became possible to conceive of 'perpetual peace'. Even though many of the great liberal thinkers understood the connection between state consolidation and war, they also anticipated that increasing interchange between states and growing accountability of states towards an informed public could usher in a more integrated Europe and a more peaceful world, an extension of civil society beyond national borders. It was Kant, after all, who pointed out in 1795 that the global community had shrunk to the point where a 'right violated anywhere could be felt everywhere'.[13]

Clausewitz and the Wars of the Nineteenth Century

Clausewitz began to write *On War* in 1816, one year after the ending of the Napoleonic Wars. He had participated in the wars on the losing side and had been taken prisoner, and the book is profoundly influenced by his experience. The Napoleonic Wars constituted the first people's war. Napoleon introduced conscription, the *levée en masse*, in 1793, and in 1794 he had 1,169,000 men under arms – the largest military force ever before created in Europe.

The central thesis of *On War*, particularly the first chapter, which was the only chapter Clausewitz considered to be completed, is that war tends towards extremes. War is a social activity that brings together different tendencies or emotions – reason, chance and strategy, and passion that can be linked, respectively, to the state or the political leaders, the army or the generals, and the level of the people. From this trinitarian depiction of war, Clausewitz derived his concept of absolute war. Absolute war is best interpreted as a Hegelian abstract or ideal concept; it is the inner tendency of war that can be derived from the logic of the three different tendencies. It has its own existence, which is in tension with empirical realities.

The logic was expressed in terms of three 'reciprocal actions'. At a political or rational level, the state always meets resistance in achieving its objectives and therefore has to press harder. At a military level, the aim has to be disarmament of the opponent in order to achieve the political objective, otherwise there is always a danger of counter-attack. And, finally, the strength of will depends on popular feelings and sentiments; war unleashes passion and hostility that may be uncontrollable. For Clausewitz, war was a rational activity even though emotions and sentiments were mobilized in its service. In this sense, it is also a modern activity based on secular considerations and not confined by prohibitions derived from pre-rational conceptions of the world.

Real war differs from abstract war for two main reasons – political and military. First, the political objective may be limited and/or popular backing may be insufficient:

> The more violent the excitement which precedes a War, by so much nearer will the War approach to its abstract form, so much the more will it be directed to the destruction of the enemy, so much the nearer will the military and political ends coincide; so much the more purely military and less political the War appears to be, but the weaker the motives and the tensions, so much the less will the natural direction of the military element – that is force – be coincident with the direction which the political element indicates; so much the more must, therefore, the War become diverted from its natural direction.[14]

Second, war is always characterized by what Clausewitz calls 'friction' – problems of logistics, poor information, uncertain weather, indiscipline, difficult terrain, inadequate organization and so on – all of which slow down war and make it different in reality from paper plans. War, says Clausewitz, is a 'resistant medium' in which uncertainty, inflexibility and unforeseen circumstance all play their part. Real war is the outcome of the tension between political and practical constraints and the inner tendency for absolute war.

As forces increased in scale, it became more and more difficult for organization and command to be carried out by a single person. Hence there was a growing need for a strategic theory which could provide the basis for a shared discourse about war through which war could be organized. As Simpkin puts it, there was a need for a 'jargon' which could guide common military doctrines and what later became known as standard operating procedures.[15]

Clausewitz provided the basic building blocks of a body of strategic thinking that was developed during the nineteenth and twentieth centuries. The two main theories of warfare – attrition theory and manoeuvre theory – were initially developed in *On War* along with his discussion of offence and defence and of concentration and dispersion. Attrition theory means that victory is achieved by wearing down the enemy, by imposing on the enemy a higher casualty rate or 'attrition rate'; it is usually associated with defensive strategies and with high concentrations of force. Manoeuvre theory depends on surprise and pre-emption. In this case, mobility and dispersion are important to create uncertainty and to achieve speed. As Clausewitz pointed out, these two theories are necessarily complementary. It is very difficult to achieve a decisive victory through attrition. Yet, at the same time, a strategy based on manoeuvre ultimately needs a superiority of force to be successful.

The most salient conclusion of *On War* is the importance of overwhelming force and a readiness to use force – the combination of physical and moral forces. This apparently simple point was not obvious in the early nineteenth-century context in which Clausewitz was writing. In the eighteenth century wars were fought, by and large, prudently, in order to conserve professional forces. There was a tendency to avoid battle; defensive sieges were preferred to offensive assaults; campaigns were halted for the winter and strategic retreats were frequent – Clausewitz referred to these wars as 'half and half' wars. For Clausewitz, battle was the 'single activity of war'; it was the decisive moment, which he compared to cash payment in the marketplace. The mobilization of force and the application of force were the most important factors in determining the outcome of war:

> As the use of physical power to the utmost extent by no means excludes the cooperation of the intelligence, it follows that he who uses force unsparingly, without reference to the bloodshed involved, must obtain a superiority if his adversary uses less vigour in its application. The former then dictates the law to the latter and both proceed to extremities to which the only limitations are those imposed by the amount of counteracting force on each side.[16]

The Napoleonic model in which all citizens were mobilized was not to be repeated until World War I. However, several developments during the nineteenth century brought the Clausewitzean version of modern war closer to reality. One was the dramatic advance in industrial technology which began to be applied to the military field. Particularly important was the development of the railway and the telegraph, which enabled much greater and faster mobilization of armies; these techniques were used to great effect in the Franco-Prussian War, which ended with the unification of Germany in 1871. The mass production of guns, particularly small arms, was pioneered in the United States so that the American Civil War is often described as the first industrialized war. The development of military technology was one reason for the extension of state activity into the industrial sphere. The late nineteenth-century naval arms race marked the emergence of what was later to be described as the military-industrial complex in both Germany and Britain.

A second development was the growing importance of alliances. If overwhelming force was what mattered in war, then force could be augmented through alliances. By the end of the nineteenth century, alliances began to solidify – an important reason why the major powers were all drawn into World War I.

A third important development was the codification of the laws of war which began in the mid-nineteenth century with the Declaration of Paris (1856), which regulated maritime commerce in wartime. In the American Civil War, a prominent German jurist was employed to draw up the so-called Lieber Code, which laid down the rules and basic principles for war on land and treated the rebels as an international opponent. The Geneva Convention of 1864 (inspired by Henri Dunant, who founded the International Red Cross), the St Petersburg Declaration of 1868, the Hague Conferences of 1899 and 1907, and the London Conference of 1908 all contributed to a growing body of international law concerning the conduct of war – the treatment of prisoners, the sick and wounded, and non-combatants, as well as the concept of 'military necessity' and the definition of weapons and tactics that do not conform to this concept. While these rules were not always followed, they contributed importantly to a delineation of what constitutes legitimate warfare and the boundaries within which unsparing force could be applied. In a sense, they were an attempt to preserve the notion of war as a rational instrument of state policy in a context where the logic of war and the extremist tendencies of war, combined with growing technological capacities, were leading to ever-increasing levels of destructiveness.[17]

To sum up, modern war, as it developed in the nineteenth century, involved war between states with an ever-increasing emphasis on scale and mobility, and an increasing need for 'rational' organization and 'scientific' doctrine to manage these large conglomerations of force.

The Total Wars of the Twentieth Century

In Clausewitz's work, there was always a tension between his insistence on reason and his emphasis on will and emotion. Men of genius and military heroes are central characters in *On War*; sentiments such as patriotism, honour and bravery are part of the fabric of the book. Equally significant, however, are his conclusions about the instrumental nature of war, the importance of scale and the need for an analytical conceptualization of war. Indeed, the tensions between reason and emotion, art and science, attrition and manoeuvre, defence and offence, instrumentalism and extremism constitute the key components of Clausewitzean thought. These tensions can be said to have reached breaking point in the twentieth century.

First of all, the wars of the first half of the twentieth century were total wars involving a vast mobilization of national energies both to fight and to support the fighting through the production of arms and necessities. Clausewitz could not possibly have envisaged the awesome combination of mass production, mass politics and mass communications when harnessed to mass destruction. Nevertheless, war in the twentieth century came as close as can be conceived to Clausewitz's notion of absolute war, culminating in the discovery of nuclear weapons which, in theory, could wreak total destruction without 'friction'. But at the same time, some of the characteristics of the new wars were foreshadowed in the total wars of the twentieth century. In a total war, the public sphere tries to incorporate the whole of society, thus eliminating the distinction between public and private. The distinction between the military and the civil, between combatants and non-combatants, correspondingly starts to break down. In World War I, economic targets were considered legitimate military targets. In World War II, the term 'genocide' entered into legal parlance as a result of the extermination of the Jews.[18] On the Allied side, the indiscriminate bombing of civilians, creating a scale of devastation of genocidal proportions (even if it did not match the scale of extermination carried out by the Nazis), was justified on the grounds of breaking enemy morale – as 'military necessity', to use the language of the laws of war.

Second, as war involved more and more people, the justification of war in terms of state interest became increasingly hollow, if it ever had any convincing validity. War, as van Creveld points out, is a proof that men are not selfish. No individualistic utilitarian calculation can justify risking death. The main reason why mercenary armies were so unsatisfactory is that economic incentive is, of its nature, inadequate as a motivation for warfare. The same is true of 'state interest' – a concept that derives from the same school of positivistic thinking that gave rise to modern economics. Men go to war for a variety of individual reasons – adventure, honour, fear, comradeship, protection of 'home and hearth' – but socially organized legitimate violence needs a common goal in which the individual soldier can believe and which he shares with others. If soldiers are to be treated as heroes and not as criminals, then heroic justification is needed to mobilize their energies, to persuade them to kill and risk being killed.

In World War I, patriotism seemed sufficiently powerful to demand sacrifice, and millions of young men volunteered to fight in the name of King and Country. The terrible experience of that war led to disillusion and despair and an attraction to more powerful abstract causes – what Gellner calls secular religions.[19] For the Allied nations, World War II was literally a war against evil; whole societies were mobilized, knowing what war entailed in a way that their predecessors in World War I did not: the fight against Nazism and the protection of their own ways of life. They fought in the name of democracy and/ or socialism against fascism. In the Cold War, the same ideologies were called upon to justify the ever-continuing arms race. To justify the threat of mass destruction, the Cold War was presented as a struggle of good against evil along the lines of the wartime experience. But the Cold War was only a war in the imagination; actual wars like the Americans in Vietnam or the Soviet Union in Afghanistan called into question the belief in the importance of that struggle.

In fact, the idea that war is illegitimate already began to gain acceptance after the trauma of World War I. The Kellogg–Briand Pact of 1928 renounced war as an 'instrument of policy' except in self-defence. This prohibition was reinforced by the Nuremberg and Tokyo trials, in which German and Japanese leaders were prosecuted for 'planning aggressive war', and codified in the UN Charter. Nowadays, it does seem to have become widely accepted that the use of force is only justifiable either in self-defence or if it is sanctioned by the international community – in particular, the UN Security Council. Even the US administration, under George W. Bush, felt the need to justify the war in Iraq in terms of a new doctrine of 'pre-emptive self-defence' and to have at least the appearance of a 'coalition of the willing'.

Third, the techniques of modern war have developed to a point of sharply diminishing utility. The great battleships of the late nineteenth century turned out to be more or less irrelevant in World War I. What mattered was mass-produced firepower. World War I was a defensive war of attrition in which rows of young men, directed by generals schooled in nineteenth-century strategic thought to use force unsparingly, were mowed down by machine guns. Towards the end of the war, the introduction of tanks and aircraft enabled an offensive breakthrough which made possible the type of manoeuvre warfare which was to characterize World War II. In the post-war period, the increase in the lethality and accuracy of all munitions, due at least in part to the revolution in electronics, has greatly increased the vulnerability of all weapons systems. The weapons platforms of World War II have become extraordinarily complex and expensive, thus diminishing their utility because of cost and logistical requirements, combined with ever-diminishing improvements in performance.[20] The problems of mobilization and inflexibility, and the risks of attrition, have been magnified in the post-war period, making it almost prohibitive to mount a major operation against a symmetrical opponent.

The logical end point of the technological trajectory of modern war is, of course, weapons of mass destruction, particularly nuclear weapons. A nuclear war would be one in which force is applied in the extreme in a matter of minutes. But what rational purpose could ever justify their use? In the post-war period, many strategic thinkers have grappled with this problem. Do not nuclear weapons nullify the premise of modern warfare – state interest?[21]

Finally, in the post-war period, alliances were rigidified so that the distinction between what is internal and what is external is also eroded. Already in World War II, it became apparent that individual nation-states could not fight wars unilaterally. This lesson was applied in the construction of the post-war alliances – NATO and the Warsaw Pact. Integrated command systems established a military division of labour in which only the superpowers had the independent capacity to wage full-scale wars. Essentially, European countries, in the post-war period, abandoned one of the essential attributes of sovereignty – the monopoly of legitimate organized violence – and, at least in Western Europe, what was effectively a transnational civil society was extended to a group of nations. There is a widespread discussion about the social-science finding that democracies do not go to war with each other.[22] One explanation for this finding, which interestingly is rarely discussed in the literature, is the integration of military forces on a transnational basis which provides a practical constraint against war. Claus Offe makes a similar point about the 1989 revolutions in Eastern Europe; the reason they were so peaceful, he argues, was because of the integration of military forces in the Warsaw Pact, and this also explains the Romanian exception.[23]

Outside the European alliances, a network of military connections was established through looser alliances, the arms trade, the provision of military support and training, creating a set of patron–client relationships which also inhibited the capacity to wage war unilaterally. Since 1945, there have been very few inter-state wars, and these (India and Pakistan, Greece and Turkey, Israel and the Arab states) were generally restrained by superpower intervention. The exception, which proves the rule, was the Iran–Iraq War. This war lasted for eight years and could be waged unilaterally because of the availability of oil revenues. Both sides learned the disutility of modern conventional warfare. To quote van Creveld again:

A million or so casualties later, the belligerents found themselves back at their starting points. The Iranians were taught that, in the face of massive firepower assisted by gas, their fanatic young troops would not be able to achieve a break-through except on the road to heaven. The Iraqis learnt that conventional superiority alone was incapable of inflicting a meaningful defeat on a large country with almost three times their own population.[24]

The erosion of the distinctions between public and private, military and civil, internal and external, also calls into question the distinction between war and peace itself. World War II was a total war, representing a fusion between war, state and society – a fusion which continued to characterize totalitarian socie-ties. The Cold War sustained a kind of permanent war psycho-sis based on the theory of deterrence which is best encapsulated in the slogan 'War is Peace' in Orwell's *Nineteen Eighty-Four*. The Cold War kept alive the idea of war while avoiding its reality. The maintenance of large standing armies integrated in military alliances, the continued technological arms race, and the levels of military spending hitherto never experienced in peacetime were supposed to have guaranteed peace because no war of the stylized type described in this chapter broke out on European soil. At the same time, many wars took place all over the world, including Europe, in which more people died than in World War II. But because these wars did not fit our concep-tion of war, they were discounted.

The irregular, informal wars of the second half of the twen-tieth century, starting with the wartime resistance movements and the guerrilla warfare of Mao Tse-tung and his successors, represent the harbingers of the new forms of warfare. The actors, techniques and counter-techniques which emerged out of the cracks of modern warfare were to provide the basis for new ways of socially organizing violence. During the Cold War, their character was obscured by the dominance of the East–West conflict; they were conceived as a peripheral part of the central conflict. Even before the end of the Cold War, when the threat of another 'modern war' really began to recede, we began to become aware of what Luttwak calls the new bellicosity.[25]

3

Bosnia–Herzegovina: A Case Study of a New War

The war in Bosnia–Herzegovina lasted from 6 April 1992 until 12 October 1995, when a ceasefire agreement, brokered by the US Assistant Secretary of State Richard Holbrooke, came into effect. Around two-thirds of the population were displaced from their homes and between 100,000 and 260,000 people died. Violations of human rights took place on a massive scale, including forced detention, torture, rape and castration. Many historic monuments of incalculable value were destroyed.

The war in Bosnia–Herzegovina became the archetypal example, the paradigm of the new post-Cold War type of warfare. There were many other wars in the world happening at the same time, as Boutros Boutros-Ghali insensitively pointed out to Sarajevans when he visited the city on 31 December 1992. If human tragedies can be measured in numbers, it can even be asserted, as Boutros-Ghali did, that more terrible things have happened in other places.[1] But the war in Bosnia–Herzegovina impinged on global consciousness more than any other war in the last decade of the twentieth century.

The war mobilized a huge international effort, including high-level political talks involving all the major governments and the humanitarian efforts of international institutions and NGOs, as well as far-ranging media attention. Individual careers were made or broken, world status in the post-Cold War era was, at least partially, determined – the dismal inadequacy of the EU foreign policy-making capacity, the floundering of the UN, the US comeback, the redefinition of Russia's role, even the origin of the widespread belief that Muslims are the world's victims. Both the initial large-scale deployment of troops from NATO and Partnership for Peace countries and the subsequent EU military mission have had far-reaching implications for the role of NATO and for the institutional framework of European security as well as for the way in which we conceive of peacekeeping.

For these reasons, the war in Bosnia–Herzegovina could be considered one of those defining events in which entrenched political assumptions, strategic thinking and international arrangements are both challenged and reconstructed. While the 1991 Gulf War was significant as the first post-Cold War international crisis, the Bosnian crisis lasted longer and was more representative of wars of the 1990s. When the war began, the central actors in the so-called international community had not had time to adjust their inherited mindsets either about the character of war or about their perception of Yugoslavia. The international reaction was at best confused and sometimes stupid, at worst culpable for what happened. But during the war some attitudes changed, especially among those operating on the ground. A few far-sighted individuals, both from Bosnia itself and from within international institutions, were, in perhaps marginal ways, able to influence and encourage new ways of thinking. In particular, the experience of the war in Bosnia–Herzegovina helps to explain some of the profound differences between the United States and Europe on security issues.

This chapter traces the deficiencies of inherited ways of perceiving the war and sets out the need for a new type of analysis in relation to political and military assumptions about why and how wars are fought in the new century and the implications for international involvement.

Why the War was Fought – Political Goals

Bosnia–Herzegovina was the most ethnically mixed republic of former Yugoslavia; according to the 1991 census, the population consisted of Muslims (43.7 per cent), Serbs (31.4 per cent) and Croats (17.3 per cent), with the balance being made up of Yugoslavs, Jews, Roma and people who described themselves in a variety of other ways, such as 'giraffes' or 'lampshades'. In fact, around a quarter of the population were intermarried and, in urban areas, a secular pluralistic culture flourished. The main difference between the ethnic groups was religion – the Serbs were Orthodox and the Croats were Catholic. In the first democratic elections of November 1990, parties which claimed to represent the different ethnic groups received over 70 per cent of the votes and controlled the National Assembly. These parties were the SDA (the Party of Democratic Action), which was the Muslim nationalist party, the SDS (the Serbian Democratic Party) and the HDZ (the Croatian Democratic Party). Although they promised during the election campaign that their aim was for the three communities to live peacefully together, these three groups became the parties to the conflict.

The political goal of the Bosnian Serbs and the Bosnian Croats, backed by Serbia and Croatia, respectively, was 'ethnic cleansing'. This phenomenon has been defined by the UN Commission of Experts as 'rendering an area ethnically homogeneous by using force or intimidation to remove from a given area persons from another ethnic or religious group.'[2] They wanted to establish ethnically homogeneous territories which would eventually become part of Serbia and Croatia, and to divide the ethnically mixed Bosnia–Herzegovina into a Serbian and a Croat part. To justify these goals, they used the language of self-determination which was drawn from the earlier communist rhetoric about wars of national liberation in the third world. The goal of the Bosnian government, which was controlled by the Bosnian Muslims, was the territorial integrity of Bosnia–Herzegovina, since Muslims were a majority in Bosnia–Herzegovina and had most to lose from partition; from time to time, the Bosnian government was prepared to consider a rump Muslim state or ethnic cantonization.

Ethnic cleansing was a characteristic of East European nationalism in the twentieth century. The term was first used to describe the expulsion of Greeks and Armenians from Turkey in the early 1920s. Ethnic cleansing takes a variety of forms, ranging from economic and legal discrimination to appalling forms of violence. The milder form was practised by Croatia after the elections of 1990 when Serbs began to lose their jobs and when Serb policemen in Serb majority areas were replaced. The form of violent ethnic cleansing that was to be typical of the war in Bosnia–Herzegovina was initiated by the Serbs in Croatia together with the JNA (the Yugoslav National Army) and sundry paramilitary groups, systematized by the Bosnian Serbs and their allies in Bosnia–Herzegovina, and copied by the Croats both in Bosnia–Herzegovina and in Croatia.

How is this form of virulent ethnic nationalism to be explained? The dominant perception of the war is expressed in the terms 'Balkanization' or 'tribalism'. The Balkans, it is argued, situated at the confluence of civilizations and caught historically between the shifting borders of the Ottoman and Austro-Hungarian empires, has always been characterized by ethnic divisions and rivalries, by ancient hatreds that persist just beneath the surface. These divisions were temporarily suppressed during the communist period, only to burst forth again in the first democratic elections. 'A Letter from 1920', a short story written by Ivo Andrić between the two world wars, is widely quoted as evidence for this view. In the story, a young man decides to leave Bosnia forever, because it is 'a country of fear and hate'.[3]

This perception of the war, evident, for example, in David Owen's book, pervaded European policy-making circles and the high-level negotiations.[4] It was deliberately fostered by some of the parties to the conflict themselves. Thus Karadžić, the Bosnian Serb leader, said that Serbs, Croats and Muslims were like 'cats and dogs', while Tudjman, the Croatian president, repeatedly emphasized that Serbs and Croats could not live together because Croats were Europeans while Serbs were Easterners, like Turks or Albanians.[5] (Interestingly enough, he seems, at least from time to time, to think it is possible to live with Muslims since, in his view, they are really Croats, and Croatia and Bosnia–Herzegovina were traditionally united. On the other hand, the Serbs consider Muslims to be like Turks, in other words, like themselves, according to Croat conceptions! Indeed, yet another argument prevalent among Serb intellectuals was that Muslims were in fact Serbs who had converted to Islam under the Ottomans.)

It is a view which corresponds to the primordial view of nationalism, that nationalism is inherent and deeply rooted in human societies deriving from organically developed 'ethnies'.[6] What it does not explain is why there are long periods of co-existence of different communities or nationalities, or why waves of nationalism take place at particular times. It does not explain the undoubted existence of alternative conceptions of Bosnian and indeed Yugoslav society as a rich unified culture, as opposed to multiculturalism, which includes the various religious communities and languages and also important elements of secularity.[7] Undoubtedly, Bosnia–Herzegovina has a grim history, especially during the twentieth century, but so do other parts of Europe. The view that aggressive nationalism is somehow peculiar to the Balkans allows us to assume that the rest of Europe is immune to the Bosnian phenomenon. The former Yugoslavia, despite the fact that it was earlier considered to be the most liberal of the communist regimes and first on the list of potential new members of the EU, has become a black spot in the middle of Europe surrounded by other supposedly more 'civilized' societies – Greece to the south, Bulgaria and Romania to the east, Austria, Hungary and Italy to the north and west. But what if the current wave of nationalism has contemporary causes? Does not the primordial view amount to a kind of myopia, an excuse for inaction, or worse?

There is an alternative view which holds that nationalism has been reconstructed for political purposes. This view corresponds more closely to the 'instrumentalist' conception of nationalism, according to which nationalist movements reinvent particular versions of history and memory to construct new cultural forms that can be used for political mobilization.[8] What happened in Yugoslavia was the disintegration of the state both at a federal level and, in the case of Croatia and Bosnia–Herzegovina, at a republican level. If we define the state in the Weberian sense as the organization which 'successfully upholds the monopoly of legitimate organized violence', then it is possible to trace, first, the collapse of legitimacy and, second, the collapse of the monopoly of organized violence. The emergence of virulent nationalism, which did indeed construct itself on the basis of certain traditional social divisions and prejudices – divisions which by no means encompassed the whole of contemporary Yugoslav society – has to be understood in terms of the struggle, on the part of increasingly desperate (and corrupt) elites, to control the remnants of the state combined with growing economic insecurity and the loss of self-worth associated with that insecurity that made people vulnerable to ideas about national identity. Moreover, in a post-totalitarian society, control is much more extensive than in more open societies, extending to all major social institutions – enterprises, schools, universities, hospitals, media and so forth.

To understand why the state ruptured along national lines can best be explained in terms of the recent history of Yugoslavia rather than by delving into the pre-communist past. The Titoist regime was a totalitarian regime in the sense of centralized control over all aspects of social life. It was more liberal than other regimes in Eastern Europe and allowed a certain degree of economic pluralism: from the 1960s Yugoslav citizens were allowed to travel and hold foreign currency accounts; artistic and intellectual freedom was much greater than in other communist countries. The political identity of the Yugoslav regime was derived, in part, from the struggle of the partisans during World War II; in part, from its capacity to provide reasonable living standards for the population; and, in part, from its special international position as a bridge between East and West, with its own indigenous brand of socialism, and its role as leader of the non-aligned movement. As the memory of World War II faded and as the economic and social gains of the post-war period began to disappear, it was inevitable that its legitimacy would be called into question. The fall of the Berlin Wall, the democracy movements in the rest of Eastern Europe, and the end of the East–West division added a final blow to former Yugoslav identity.

Although the Yugoslav partisans had fought on the slogan 'Brotherhood and Unity' and the aim was to develop a new socialist Yugoslav man or woman, as in the Soviet Union, the regime had built into its functioning a complicated system of checks and balances to ensure that no ethnic group became dominant; in effect, it institutionalized ethnic difference. In order to counterbalance the numerical dominance of Serbs, six republics were established, each (with the exception of Bosnia–Herzegovina) with a dominant nationality – Serbia, Montenegro, Croatia, Bosnia–Herzegovina, Slovenia and Macedonia. In addition, there were two autonomous provinces inside Serbia: Kosovo (where there was an Albanian majority) and Vojvodina (with a mixed population of Serbs, Croats and Hungarians).

Despite this, polls consistently showed, up until the 1980s, growing support for Yugoslavism. This system was augmented by the 1974 constitution which devolved power to republics and autonomous provinces and established a mechanism for elite rotation based on ethnic arithmetic. Although the League of Communists retained its monopoly position, after 1974 the party itself increasingly divided along national lines. In a situation in which other political challenges were disallowed, a nationalist political discourse became the only form of legitimate debate. In effect, there were ten communist parties – one for each republic and autonomous province, one for the federation and one for the JNA. As Ivan Vejvoda points out, the 1974 constitution empowered collective actors, notably *nomenklatura* at the republican and provincial levels, while further disenfranchising individual citizens. It was decentralization of totalitarianism.[9] In this context, national communitarian identities were the obvious candidates to fill the vacuum created by the loss of Yugoslavism.

Yugoslavia experienced the strains of economic transition some ten years earlier than other East European countries.[10] During the 1950s and 1960s, the country experienced fast economic growth based on a model of rapid defence-oriented heavy industrialization that was typical of centrally planned economies. In the Yugoslav case, this was somewhat modified by the self-management model and the fact that agriculture, for the most part, remained in private hands. During this period, Yugoslavia received substantial amounts of foreign assistance because it was seen as a buffer against a possible Soviet attack on Southeast Europe. In the 1970s, Western aid began to decline and was replaced by commercial loans, which were relatively easy to acquire following the oil crisis. As in the case of other centrally planned economies, Yugoslavia had great difficulty restructuring its economy; this was compounded by the slowdown in growth in Western countries, which inhibited the growth of exports and reduced the earnings from remittances from Yugoslavs working abroad, and by the growing autonomy of the republics and self-governing provinces who felt no responsibility for the balance of payments and competed with each other to create money.

By 1979, the debt had reached crisis proportions – some $US20 billion. An International Monetary Fund (IMF) Recovery Plan was agreed in 1982 which included both liberalization and austerity. The main effect of this plan was to intensify the competition for resources at the level of the republics and to contribute to the growing criminalization of the economy. The federation was unable to control the creation of money, and by December 1989 the monthly inflation rate had reached 2,500 per cent. Unemployment averaged 14 per cent throughout the decade; particularly hard hit were urban middle classes, largely dependent on state salaries and pensions, and rurally based industrial workers, who were forced to survive on what they could produce from their small agricultural plots. A series of corruption scandals in the late 1980s, especially in Bosnia–Herzegovina, revealed the growing links between the degenerate ruling elite and a new class of mafia types. Typical in this respect was the Agromerc scandal, which revealed the nefarious activities of Fikret Abdić, long-time party boss in Bihać, who was later to become a key figure in the war. Nationalist arguments were a way of coping with economic discontent, appealing to the victims of economic insecurity and concealing the growing *nomenklatura*–mafia alliance.

By the end of the 1980s the unravelling of Yugoslav statehood had gathered pace. The last federal prime minister, Antje Marković, tried to reimpose control at a federal level with a programme of 'shock therapy' introduced in January 1990. Despite the success of the programme in reducing inflation, it caused immense resentment at the level of republics because it effectively removed their 'license to print money'.[11] By November 1990, Yugoslavia as a single economic space was challenged by various unilateral economic actions – above all, massive Serbian borrowing to pay for the imposition of Serbian rule in Kosovo, known as the 'Great Bank Robbery', but also the Slovene refusal to contribute to the Fund for Underdeveloped Regions and the unilateral Croatian abolition of excise tax on cars, effectively bribing voters with the promise of cheaper foreign cars.

Yugoslavia as a single communicative space also unravelled. By the 1970s, each republic and province controlled its own television and radio. There was occasional rotation of news programmes on the first channel and news from other republics and autonomous provinces could be seen (by rotation) on the second channel. This broke down in the late 1980s.[12] Despite the last-ditch attempt by Marković to establish an all-Yugoslav television, *Yutel*, the media were effectively nationalized, providing a powerful basis for nationalist propaganda.

By 1990 federal legitimacy had been challenged, at the level both of legislatures and of the judiciary. The first democratic elections were held in the republics and not at a federal level. When the federal constitutional court challenged decisions taken by the newly elected republican parliaments, such as the Slovene decision not to contribute to the Fund for Underdeveloped Regions or the Slovene and Croatian declarations of sovereignty, these legal opinions were ignored. A similar disregard for constitutional decisions taken at a republican level was shown by those Serbs in Croatia who wanted to declare a 'Serbian Autonomous Region'.

Finally, the last vestige of Yugoslav statehood was removed in 1991, when the monopoly of organized violence broke down. The JNA had been the bastion of Yugoslavism.[13] Already by the 1970s Territorial Defence Units (TOs) were established in the republics as a result of a new 'Generalized Popular Defence System' introduced after the Soviet invasion of Czechoslovakia in 1968. By 1991 the JNA was increasingly being used as a tool of Slobodan Milošević, the president of Serbia, while the Slovenes and Croats were secretly organizing and arming their own independent forces based on the TOs and the police through the growing black market for surplus arms then emerging in Eastern Europe. At the same time, the Serbs were creating their own paramilitary groups. In particular, they initiated their plan 'RAM' (Frame), secretly to arm and organize the Serbs in Croatia and Bosnia–Herzegovina. The JNA utterly failed in its efforts to disarm the paramilitaries (the Croats and Slovenes claimed that their forces were not paramilitary groups but legal defence forces) and ended up siding with the Serb paramilitary groups in Croatia and Bosnia.[14]

The emergence of a new form of nationalism paralleled the disintegration of Yugoslavia. It was new in the sense that it was associated with the disintegration of the state, in contrast to earlier 'modern' nationalisms which aimed at state-building, and that, unlike earlier nationalisms, it lacked a modernizing ideology. It was also new in terms of the techniques of mobilization and the forms of organization. It was Milošević who was the first to make extensive use of the electronic media to propagate the nationalist message. His 'anti-bureaucratic revolution', which aimed to remove the Titoist system of checks and balances perceived as discriminating against Serbs, provided the basis for a populist political appeal over the heads of the existing communist hierarchy. Through mass rallies, he legitimized his hold on power. The victim mentality often characteristic of majorities who feel themselves minorities was nurtured with an electronic diet of tales of 'genocide' in Kosovo, first by the Turks in 1389 and more recently by the Albanians, and of holocaust in Croatia and Bosnia–Herzegovina, with clips of World War II interspersed with current developments. In effect, the Serbian public experienced a virtual war long before the real war was to take place – a virtual war that made it difficult to distinguish truth from fiction so that war became a continuum in which the 1389 battle of Kosovo, World War II and the war in Bosnia were all part of the same phenomenon. David Rieff describes how Bosnian Serb soldiers, after a day of shooting from the hills around Sarajevo, would ring their Muslim friends in the town. This extraordinarily contradictory behaviour made perfect sense to the soldiers because of the psychological dissonance produced by this virtual reality. They were not shooting at their private friends, but at Turks. 'Before the summer ends', one soldier told Rieff, 'we will have driven the Turkish army out of the city, just as they drove us from the field of Kosovo in 1389. That was the beginning of Turkish domination of our lands. This will be the end of it, after all these cruel centuries ... We Serbs are saving Europe even if Europe does not appreciate our efforts.'[15]

If Milošević perfected the media technique, it was Tudjman who developed the horizontal transnational form of organization. Unlike Milošević, he came from a dissident background, having spent time in prison in the early 1970s for his nationalist views, although formerly he had been a JNA general. His party – the HDZ – had little time to prepare for the first democratic elections, and did not control the media. Tudjman, however, had been mobilizing support among the Croatian diaspora in North America. He claimed that the HDZ had branches in thirty-five North American cities, each with fifty to several hundred members and some with up to two thousand members. The diaspora was always regarded with great suspicion by the communist authorities; émigrés were largely considered to be former *Ustashe* (the wartime Croatian fascists). Tudjman said later that the most crucial political decision he had ever made was to invite the émigrés back for the HDZ Congress in February 1990.[16] This transnational form of organization was a highly significant source of funds and election techniques and, subsequently, arms and mercenaries. It induced another form of virtual reality arising from the time–space distantiation of diaspora party members, who were, in effect, imposing on a contemporary situation an image of Croatia which dated from when they had left.

The process of disintegration and the rise of a new form of virulent nationalism was encapsulated in Bosnia–Herzegovina, which had always been a mixed society. The differentiation of communities along religious lines (Orthodox, Catholic, Muslim and Jewish) had been institutionalized during the latter part of Ottoman rule through the millet system and, in various forms, this 'institutionalized communitarianism', as Xavier Bougarel calls it,[17] was sustained throughout Austro-Hungarian rule (1878–1914) and during the first and second Yugoslavias. Nevertheless, in the post-war period there were many mixed marriages and, particularly in cities, the communitarian logic was supplanted by a modern secular culture. Yugoslavism was particularly strong in Bosnia–Herzegovina. It was in this republic that *Yutel* was most popular and that Marković was to choose to launch his reform party.

Bougarel distinguishes 'institutionalized communitarianism' from political and territorial nationalism. The former depends on a balance between communities, which is known as *komsiluk* (good neighbourliness) and which is threatened by political or military mobilization, as happened during the two world wars. The re-emergence of political nationalism in the late 1980s occurred, as was the case earlier, for instrumental reasons. It was a response, according to Bougarel, to discontent arising from uneven development and to the growing divide between the economic and scientific elite and backward rural regions. This divide was especially acute in Bosnia–Herzegovina and was exacerbated during the 1980s. It was also a response to the loss of legitimacy of the ruling party.

Six months before the 1990 elections, a poll conducted in Bosnia–Herzegovina showed that 74 per cent of the population favoured the banning of nationalist parties. Yet, when the election did take place, 70 per cent of the voters supported these parties. This discrepancy can be explained in terms of Bougarel's argument. Most people feared the threat to *komsiluk* represented by the nationalist parties. But once political mobilization took place, they found it necessary to rally to their community. Even so, other factors also need to be taken into account. On the one hand, the League of Communists in Bosnia–Herzegovina was traditionally considered hard line and slow to adapt to the wave of democracy that was affecting the rest of Eastern Europe – the nationalist parties represented the most obvious alternative to the communists. Moreover, it was discredited by a series of corruption scandals in the late 1980s. On the other hand, the speed of nationalist mobilization is explained partly by the role of Croatia and Serbia. The HDZ, the Croat nationalist party, was actually a branch of Tudjman's party, and the SDS, the Serb nationalist party, was a branch of the Serbian nationalist party that was established in the Krajina, the Serb-dominated part of Croatia. In addition, *Matica Hrvatska*, the Croatian cultural centre in Zagreb, and the Serbian Academy of Sciences, responsible for the notorious 1986 memorandum which first set out a Serb nationalist programme, both played an active role in mobilizing nationalist sentiment, together with the religious institutions.

The elections were won by the nationalist parties and they formed an uneasy coalition – not surprisingly, given the conflicting nature of their political goals. In particular, the SDS members of the Assembly were repeatedly outvoted by the SDA and the HDZ. The non-nationalist civic parties won 28 per cent of the vote; they were supported largely by urban intellectuals and industrial workers. The war was precipitated by the decision of the international community to recognize Slovenia and Croatia and any other former Yugoslav republic provided it held a referendum and recognized minority rights (something that was ignored in the Croatian and Bosnian cases). The SDA and HDZ favoured independence; the Serbs did not.

Bougarel concludes that the contradictory portrayals of Bosnia–Herzegovina as a land of tolerance and coexistence and as a country of fear and hate are, in fact, both true. Fear and hate are not endemic but, in certain periods, are mobilized for political purposes. This mobilization of 'fear and hate' takes specific forms in specific periods and has to be explained in terms of specific causes. In other words, the new nationalism is a contemporary phenomenon arising from recent history and shaped by the current context. Indeed, the very scale of the violence can be interpreted not as a consequence of 'fear and hate', but rather as a reflection of the difficulty of reconstructing 'fear and hate'. As Živanović, an independent-minded liberal who remained in Serb-controlled areas throughout the war, put it: 'The war had to be so bloody because the ties between us were so strong.'[18]

It is sometimes argued that Muslim nationalism is a different phenomenon from Serb and Croatian nationalism. Those who oppose the dominant perception of the war as a civil war often argue that this was a war of Serbian and, to a lesser extent, Croatian aggression. It is certainly true that Bosnian Serb nationalists, aided and abetted by the Serbian and Yugoslav governments, were the aggressors in this war, and it was they who initiated and applied most systematically and extensively the policy of ethnic cleansing. Likewise, Croat nationalists, backed by the Croatian government, followed their example, albeit on a lesser scale. It is also the case that the SDA, the Muslim nationalist party, was always in favour of a unified multicultural Bosnia–Herzegovina. However, multiculturalism, for the Muslim nationalists, meant political organization along communitarian lines – hence, Izetbegović's attempts to organize 'acceptable' ethnic groupings such as the Serb Civic Council or the Croat Peasants' Party. Moreover, the SDA did display some of the inclinations of other nationalist parties – such as the tendency to impose rigid political control over all institutions, or the use of the media to generate a virtual war against other communities: the SDA magazine, *Dragon of Bosnia*, was especially shrill in its calls for nationalist violence.[19] The UN Commission of Experts says that Bosnian forces did not engage in ethnic cleansing, although they committed war crimes. However, Croatians were certainly expelled or chose to leave from parts of Central Bosnia captured by Bosnian forces during the Muslim–Croat conflict, and this was also true of Serbs in areas captured during the last days of the war. In other words, this was a war of Serbian and Croatian aggression, but it was a new nationalist war as well.

That fear and hate were not endemic to Bosnian society became apparent in the outburst of civic activism during the run-up to the war.[20] A mass peace movement developed with

strong support from the Bosnian media, trade unions, intellectuals, students and women's groups. Tens of thousands of
people formed a human chain across every single bridge in
Mostar in July 1991. A *Yutel*-organized rally in Sarajevo in
August 1991 was attended by 100,000 people. In September,
400 European peace activists, travelling as the Helsinki Citizens Assembly Peace Caravan, joined thousands of Bosnians in
a human chain which linked the mosque, the Orthodox church,
the Catholic church and the synagogue in Sarajevo. Similar
demonstrations were organized in Tuzla and in Banja Luka and
other towns and villages.

The high point and the end of the movement came in March
and April 1992. On 5 March, peace activists succeeded in
pulling down barricades erected by Muslim and Serb nationalist groups after a Serb bridegroom had been shot at his wedding.
On 5 April, 50,000 to 100,000 demonstrators marched
through Sarajevo to the parliament building to demand the
resignation of the government and to ask for an international
protectorate. Thousands more came in busloads from Tuzla,
Zenica and Kakanj but could not enter the city because of Serb
and Muslim barricades. The war began when Serb snipers fired
on the demonstrators from the Holiday Inn – the first person
to die was a twenty-one-year-old medical student from
Dubrovnik, Croatia.[21] The following day, Bosnia–Herzegovina
was recognized by European states and the Serbs left the
Bosnian Assembly. The state was recognized at the very
moment of its disintegration.

According to Bougarel, the Bosnian war was a civil war in
the sense that it was a war *against* the civilian population and
against civil society.[22] And Tadeusz Mazowiecki, the Special
Rapporteur for the UN Commission on Human Rights, reports
the belief of some observers that 'the attacking forces are
determined to "kill" the city [Sarajevo] and the tradition of
tolerance and ethnic harmony that it represents'.[23] Or to put
it another way, the war could be viewed as a war of exclusivist
nationalists against a secular multicultural pluralistic society.

How the War was Fought – Military and Economic Means

Yugoslavia was probably the most militarized country in Europe
outside the Soviet Union. Until 1986, military spending

amounted to 4 per cent of GNP – more than any other non-Soviet European country except Greece.[24] The JNA itself consisted of some 70,000 regular officers and staff, plus around 150,000 conscripts. In addition, each republic and autonomous province was responsible for organizing and equipping the TOs, largely reserve forces, which were reportedly 1 million strong.

The JNA remained a Yugoslav entity up to 1991. The army controlled a network of interconnected bases, weapons stores and enterprises, which, in contrast to the rest of the economy, were organized on a Yugoslav-wide basis. Even though the partisan strategy which informed JNA organization was based on decentralized local combat formations, control remained centralized at a Yugoslav level. Among JNA officers, 70 per cent of whom were Serbian or Montenegrin, Yugoslavism continued to grow at a time when it was declining in other spheres of social life. The JNA accounted for the bulk of the federal budget and, by 1991, it seemed as though the JNA and the League of Communists were virtually all that was left of the Yugoslav idea – hence, Yugoslavism came to be associated with totalitarianism and militarism.

From 1986 to 1991 military spending fell dramatically, from $US2,491 million in constant 1988 prices to $US1,376 million,[25] thus contributing to a growing sense of victimization and paranoia about internal and external enemies within the JNA. (The arrest of young Slovenian journalists who had criticized arms exports to the third world in 1988, and the subsequent notorious trial, was an expression of this paranoia.) The story of the wars in Slovenia, Croatia and, above all, Bosnia–Herzegovina is also the story of the break-up of the Yugoslav military-industrial complex. The JNA and the TOs disintegrated into a combination of regular and irregular forces augmented by criminals, volunteers and foreign mercenaries competing for control over the former Yugoslavia's military assets.

At the outset of the war in Bosnia–Herzegovina, there was a bewildering array of military and paramilitary forces. In theory, there were three parties to the conflict – the Serbs, Croats and Bosnians. In practice, different forces cooperated with each other in differing combinations throughout the war. Thus, in the early stages of the war, the Croats and Bosnians cooperated against the Serbs. Then, after the publication of the Vance–Owen Plan in 1993, which was based on ethnic cantonization, the Croats and Muslims started fighting each other, since the Croats wanted to establish control of 'their' cantons. Then came the Washington Agreement between the Muslims and Croats, imposed by the Americans, and, in the final stages of the war, the Muslims and Croats cooperated again, at least officially. During the course of the war, the forces of each party to the conflict were increasingly centralized and regularized. By the end of the war, the main regular forces were the Bosnian Serb Army (BSA), the Croatian Defence Council (HVO) and the Army of Bosnia–Herzegovina (ABiH).

After the ten-day war in Slovenia in June 1991, the JNA withdrew to Croatia (leaving their weapons behind). By mid-July 1991, the JNA had moved an estimated 70,000 troops into Croatia. Together with some 12,000 irregular Serb forces, both local volunteers and (often criminal) groups imported from Serbia proper, they experimented with the strategies that were to be used in Bosnia–Herzegovina. After the ceasefire in Croatia the JNA withdrew to Bosnia–Herzegovina, taking with them their equipment. In May 1992, the JNA formally withdrew from Bosnia–Herzegovina. In practice, only some 14,000 troops withdrew to Serbia and Montenegro; approximately 80,000 troops transferred to the Bosnian Serb Army.

The HVO was formed out of the militia attached to the HDZ. It operated together with the Croatian Army (HV), which was formed on the basis of Croatian territorial defence forces and built up during the course of the war with training assistance from a private company formed by American retired generals called Military Professional Resources Incorporated (MPRI).[26]

There was no Bosnian army when the war broke out. Essentially, the defence of Bosnian territory was locally organized. Sarajevo was defended by a motley crew of patriotic leagues and other paramilitary groups, largely organized by the Sarajevo underground. Tuzla was defended by the local police force augmented by a locally organized patriotic league. Although Izetbegović announced the formation of a regular army in May 1992, it was not until Silajdžić became prime minister in the autumn of 1993 that the various gangster groups were controlled and the army command was centralized. Even at that time,

Table 3.1   *Regular forces in Bosnia–Herzegovina 1995*

	Armed forces	Main battle tanks	Artillery	Multiple rocket launchers	Mortars
ABiH	92,000	31	100	2	200
HVO	50,000	100	200	30	300
BSA	75,000	370	700	70	900

Source: *Military Balance 1995–6*, International Institute for Strategic Studies, London, 1996.

the UN Commission of Experts estimated that, of 70,000 troops, only 44,000 were armed.[27]

The BSA was much better equipped than the other regular forces, as can be seen from table 3.1. In particular, it had a considerable advantage in heavy weapons – tanks, artillery, rocket launchers and mortars. It inherited the JNA's equipment and, more importantly, it controlled most of the JNA's weapons stores; these had been situated in the hills of Bosnia–Herzegovina, because this was envisaged to be the heartland of any guerrilla-based defence of Yugoslavia, and had been well stocked in anticipation of a long war. The ABiH, which was the least well equipped and suffered, in particular, from a dearth of heavy weapons, was dependent on Croatian supply routes to acquire arms.[28] The HVO received equipment from Croatia. In addition to equipment taken from weapons stocks in Croatia, various black-market sources were used to acquire mainly surplus ex-Warsaw Pact equipment. (Interestingly, there was some evidence that ex-JNA enterprises in Croatia, Slovenia and Serbia continued to cooperate to produce spare parts and equipment.[29])

It is possible to identify, in addition to the regular forces, three main types of irregular force: paramilitary organizations, generally under the control of an individual; foreign mercenary groups; and local police augmented by armed civilians. The UN Commission of Experts identified eighty-three paramilitary groups on the territory of former Yugoslavia – some fifty-six were Serbian, thirteen were Croatian and fourteen were Bosnian. The estimated size of these forces was 20,000 to 40,000, 12,000 to 20,000 and 4000 to 6000, respectively. The vast majority of these acted locally, but certain groups operated much more widely in conjunction with regular forces and gained considerable notoriety.

On the Serb side, the two most well-known groups were Arkan's 'Tigers' and Šešelj's Chetniks or 'White Eagles'. Arkan, whose real name was Željko Ražnjatović, was a big figure in the Belgrade underworld. He owned a string of ice-cream parlours, allegedly a cover for his smuggling activities, which expanded considerably during the war. Before the war, he had apparently been recruited by a special unit in the Yugoslav government in order to assassinate émigrés. He also owned the fan club of the Belgrade Red Star football team and his Tigers were recruited from the club. The Tigers initially operated in Croatia; in Bosnia–Herzegovina they were reported as operating in twenty-eight counties. According to reports collected by the UN Commission: 'Their hair was cut short and they wore black woollen caps, black gloves cut off mid-finger, and black badges on the upper arm. According to other reports, they wore multicoloured uniforms, red arrows, knit caps, a badge showing the Serbian flag on the right arm, and an emblem showing a tiger and the words "Arkanove delije" on the shoulder.'[30] The Tigers were well armed, including tanks and mortars. Šešelj had been a dissident. He had taught at the University of Sarajevo and, reportedly, spent a year at the University of Michigan.[31] He was imprisoned in the early 1980s for his anticommunist writings. After he was released, he moved to Belgrade, where he joined the Serbian nationalists. His party, the Serbian National Renewal Party, gained seats in the 1990 elections and was particularly successful in the federal elections of May 1992, when his party won 33 out of 138 seats. Like the Tigers, the Chetniks were initially active in Croatia. In Bosnia–Herzegovina, they were reported to operate in thirty-four counties. The Šešeljovci were 'bearded men'. They wore Serbian military berets with a Serbian military flag on the front, or black fur hats with a Serbian cockade. They were reportedly always drunk and they recruited additional 'weekend fighters'.

Both Arkan and Šešelj seem to have operated together with the JNA. According to the UN Commission: 'In many of these counties, Šešelj and Arkan exercised control over other forces operating in the area. These forces consisted of local paramilitary groups, and sometimes the JNA. In some counties, Šešelj's and Arkan's forces operated under the command of the JNA.'[32] Šešelj always insisted that his forces were armed and equipped by Milošević.

The most well-known Croatian paramilitary group was HOS, a wing of the Croatian Party of Rights (HSP). Its members wore black uniforms and the Croatian chequered shield like the wartime *Ustashe*. Up to 1993, when their leader Dobroslav Paraga was arrested for trying to overthrow the Croatian government, HOS operated in conjunction with the HVO. Another Croatian paramilitary group was the 'Wolves' led by Jusuf Prazina, known as Juka. He was an underworld figure from Sarajevo before the war broke out and had been in prison five times. The Wolves wore 'crew-cuts, black jump-suits, sun glasses and sometimes masks'.[33] They operated together with the ABiH until August 1992 and then worked with the HVO.

The two notorious gangsters, Caco and Celo, operated in Sarajevo up until the autumn of 1993. Caco had been a club musician called Musan Topalović, and Celo was a criminal who had just come out of prison after serving eight years for rape. Most paramilitary groups on the Bosnian side were referred to as Green Berets or Muslim Armed Forces (MOS) and reportedly operated under the command of the ABiH.

The names of other paramilitary groups include Black Swans, Yellow Ants (which referred to their looting abilities), Mečet's Babies, Mosque Pigeons, Knights, Serbian Falcons, and so on. Among mercenaries, the most well known were the *Mujahidiin*, mostly veterans from the Afghan wars. They were supposed to have been expelled under the Dayton Agreement. They reportedly operated in Zenica, Travnik, Novi Travnik, Mostar and Konjic. According to Croat intelligence, they were organized by a man named Abdulah, who owned the 'Palma' video shop in Travnik. The UN Commission suggests that the *Mujahidiin* acted more or less independently of the ABiH. Other mercenaries included the Garibaldi Unit (Italians fighting alongside the Croats) and Russians fighting on the Serbian side, as well as mercenaries from Denmark, Finland, Sweden, Britain and the United States. British soldiers made redundant in the post-Cold War cuts took up positions training both Bosnian and Croatian forces.

Local militia were organized by municipalities, as in Tuzla, or by big enterprises, as in Velika Kladusa, in Fikret Abdić's Agrokomerc, or in Zenica, where the former communists still controlled the steelworks.

During the war, the formal economy collapsed. This was the result of a combination of factors: physical destruction, impossibility of acquiring inputs, and loss of markets. Industrial production was estimated at 10 per cent of its pre-war level and unemployment was between 60 and 90 per cent. The currency collapsed; exchange was based on a combination of barter and Deutschmarks. For the most part, people faced a painful choice: they could live insufficiently off humanitarian aid; they could volunteer for the army or become a criminal or both; or they could try to leave. Many people left, especially the young and educated, so that the population decline was even more dramatic than the figures on ethnic cleansing suggest.

The various military forces were totally dependent on outside sources of assistance. These included direct support from outside governments, 'taxation' of humanitarian assistance, and remittances from individuals. The regular forces were largely funded and equipped by sponsor governments. The BSA was funded by the Serbian government up to the embargo, imposed by Milošević in August 1994. The HVO was funded by Croatia, and the ABiH received support from Islamic states and, covertly, from the United States. The paramilitaries were funded from loot and extortion of expelled people, as well as confiscation of equipment, etc., from conquered territories, 'taxation' of humanitarian aid, which they collected at many checkpoints, and the black market. The local militia were funded by municipalities who received the 'taxes' from humanitarian assistance collected on their territory and also continued to tax citizens, including those who were abroad, and enterprises on their territory. All three types of force cooperated with each other both militarily and economically.

The strategy adopted by this combination of regular and irregular forces – a strategy practised most consistently and systematically by the Bosnian Serbs as well as by the Bosnian Croats – was territorial gain through political control rather than military offence. Violence was used to control populations rather than to capture territory. The difficulty of acquiring territory through military offence was made plain quite early on in the war in Croatia. The JNA experienced the classic problems of offence which have become typical of modern war, as was illustrated by the Iran–Iraq War. The two-month siege of Vukovar, a town in East Slavonia, Croatia, from September to October 1991, showed how massive superiority in both firepower and manpower was insufficient to capture a relatively small town. When Vukovar eventually fell, on 20 November 1991, it had been reduced to rubble. The attempt to take Dubrovnik, which, according to the memoirs of the then minister of defence, General Kadijević, was part of a plan to occupy Split and the Dalmatian Coast, failed.[34] A characteristic feature of the war in Bosnia was the siege of the main Bosnian cities. Although they could not be captured, they could be shelled continuously and cut off from supplies.

Except in the early stage of the war in Bosnia–Herzegovina, when the Bosnian Serbs faced very little opposition, and in the last stages of the war, when they had become very weak, little territory changed hands. Essentially, the war was directed not against opposing sides, but against civilian populations. This explains why there was no continuous front. Instead, different areas were controlled by different parties, and forces were interspersed in what the UN Commission describes as a 'chequered' military map, with confrontation lines in and around cities encircling the areas of control. Indeed, in late 1993, before the Washington Agreement between Muslims and Croats, territory under Bosnian control basically consisted of a few enclaves surrounded by hostile forces, what some described as a 'leopard skin' territory. With the exception of Banja Luka, which was under Serb control, and Mostar, which was divided between Croats and Muslims, most towns remained under Bosnian control while the countryside was divided between Serbs and Croats.

Apart from a few strategic points, e.g. the Brčko corridor, which connected Serb territories and which potentially provided a communication route from Northern Bosnia to Zagreb, there was relatively little fighting between the opposing sides. There were, indeed, various examples of cooperation, mostly in the black market, but also differing short-term and local military cooperation between different parties. On one occasion, UNPROFOR (the United Nations Protection Force) intercepted a telephone conversation between the local Muslim commander in Mostar and the local Serb commander discussing the price in German marks to be paid if the Serbs would shell the Croats. The nadir was reached when the Serbs took Mount Igman, overlooking Sarajevo, in July 1993; the paramilitary groups at that time defending Mount Igman were ready to 'sell' their positions in order to control the black-market routes. Most of the violence was directed against civilians – the shelling of cities and towns combined with sniper fire and various forms of atrocity within the towns and villages – and became, in effect, what was known as ethnic cleansing.

The Bosnian Serbs wanted to create an autonomous Bosnian Serb territory. But since there were almost no areas except Banja Luka where Serbs were numerically dominant and, perhaps more importantly, where extremist Serbs were numerically dominant, this had to be brought about through ethnic cleansing. The areas seem to have been chosen for strategic reasons, to link the Serb-held territories in Krajina with Serbia and to control JNA bases and weapons stores. The tactic of establishing 'Serb autonomous areas' seems to have followed a consistent pattern first worked out in the war in Croatia. Descriptions of the process can be found in numerous reports of journalists, UN agencies and independent NGOs such as Helsinki Watch.

The typical pattern applied to rural areas – villages and small towns. First, the regular forces would shell the area and issue frightening propaganda so as to instil a mood of panic. Reports of terror in neighbouring villages would add to the panic. Then the paramilitary forces would close in and terrorize the non-Serb residents with random killing, rape and looting. Control over local administration would then be established. In the more extreme cases, non-Serb men were separated from the women and killed or taken to detention centres. Women were robbed and/or raped and allowed to go or taken to special rape detention centres. Houses and cultural buildings such as mosques were looted, burned or blown up. The paramilitary groups also seem to have had lists of prominent people – community leaders, intellectuals, SDA members, wealthy people – who were separated from the rest and executed. 'It was the conscious elimination of an articulate opposition and of political moderation. It was also the destruction of a community from the top down.'[35] The television journalist Michael

Nicholson refers to this process as 'elitocide' and the mayor of Tuzla talked about 'intellectual cleansing'.

The existence of detention centres became known in August 1992. The UN Commission of Experts identified some 715, of which 237 were operated by Bosnian Serbs, 89 by the ABiH and government and 77 by Bosnian Croats. According to the Commission, they were the scene of 'the worst inhumane acts', including mass executions, torture, rape and other forms of sexual assault. (Although grave breaches of the Geneva Conventions were reported in the Bosnian camps, the allegations were fewer and less systematic than in the Serbian and Croatian camps.) A specific aspect of the process of ethnic cleansing has been widespread rape. Although mass rape has taken place in other wars, its systematic character, in detention centres and in particular places and at particular times, suggests that it may have been part of a deliberate strategy.[36]

In urban areas, in particular Banja Luka, ethnic cleansing was a slower, more legalistic process. The lives of non-Serbs were made untenable. For example, they were removed from their jobs, with no access to medical care; communication was cut off; they were not allowed to meet in groups of more than four. In many towns, variously described Bureaux for Population Exchange were established through which non-Serbs or non-Croats could surrender their property and pay large sums to be allowed to leave.[37]

Similar techniques were adopted in Croat-controlled areas. In Bosnian-controlled areas the evidence does not suggest deliberate ethnic cleansing, although many non-Muslims, especially Serbs, left for a variety of reasons, including psychological pressure, discrimination and forced recruitment in the army.[38] By the end of 1995, ethnic cleansing was almost complete, as can be seen from table 3.2. Only 13,000 Muslims remained in Northern Bosnia, according to UNHCR estimates, out of an original population totalling around 350,000, and only 4,000 Muslims and Croats remained in East Bosnia and South Herzegovina, out of an original population totalling 300,000. Many Serbs and Croats had also left Tuzla and Zenica.

The worst atrocities, certainly in the early stages of the war, seem to have been committed by paramilitary groups. According to the UN Commission: 'There is a ... strong correlation between reports of para-military activity and reports of rape

Table 3.2 *Ethnic cleansing in Bosnia–Herzegovina*

	1991 census				Estimates November 1995[a]			
	Serbs	*Croats*	*Muslims*	*Total*	*Serbs*	*Croats*	*Muslims*	*Total*
Bihac	29,398	6,470	202,310	238,178	1,000	5,000	174,000	180,000
Northern Bosnia–Herzegovina	624,840	180,593	355,956	1,161,389	719,000	9,000	13,000 [38,000 in Dec 94]	741,000
Zenica	79,355	169,657	328,644	577,656	16,000	115,000	439,000	570,000
Tuzla	82,235	38,789	316,000	437,024	15,000	19,000	659,000 [629,000]	693,000
Sarajevo	157,526	35,867	259,085	432,478	n/a	n/a	n/a	455,000
Enclaves	20,000		80,000	100,000			50,000 [115,000]	50,000
West Herzegovina/West-Central Bosnia	43,595	245,586	111,128	400,309	5,000	320,000	160,000	485,000
East Bosnia/South Herzegovina	304,017	40,638	261,003	605,658	450,000	4,000[b]	see previous column	454,000
Total	1,340,966	717,600	1,655,300	3,972,692	1,206,000 (−Sarajevo)	470,000	1,497,000	3,628,000

Notes: Figures in square brackets show numbers in November 1994.

[a] These figures are almost certainly overestimates, since more than a million Bosnian refugees left the country.

[b] This figure refers to both Croat and Muslim communities.

n/a Not available.

Source: UNHCR, Information Notes on Former Yugoslavia 11/95, Zagreb, 1995.

and sexual assault, detention facilities and mass graves. These types of activity (i.e. paramilitary activity and grave breaches of the Geneva Conventions) tended to occur in the same counties and evidence the localised nature of the activity.'[39] On the Serbian side, the activities of Arkan and Šešelj are well known; the UN Commission suggests that these were coordinated with the activities of the JNA (BSA), whereas, on the Croatian and Bosnian sides, the paramilitary groups acted more independently of regular forces. On the Croatian side, Paraga is said to have organized the detention camps at Capljina and Dretelj, while Juka was reported to have killed some 700 Muslims in Mostar and was responsible for the detention camp at the heliport.[40] On the Bosnian side, the worst atrocities seem to have been committed by the *Mujahidiin*.

The motivation of the paramilitary groups seems to have been largely economic, although there were clearly nationalist fanatics among them. According to Vasić, around 80 per cent of the paramilitaries were common criminals and 20 per cent were fanatical nationalists: 'The latter did not last long (fanaticism is bad for business).'[41] Arkan, reportedly, had lists of rich Muslims in possession of gold and money. The 'right to be the first to loot' was viewed as a form of payment.[42] Many former criminal groups were able to expand their pre-war rackets; most of the paramilitary groups were involved in black-market activities and, indeed, cooperated with each other across supposed confrontation lines in order to profit from the situation in besieged enclaves. Effectively, paramilitary groups were 'hired' to do the dirty work necessary to instil the 'fear and hate' which was not yet endemic in Bosnian society. Thus, the mafia economy was built into the conduct of warfare, creating a self-sustaining logic to the war both to maintain lucrative sources of income and to protect criminals from legal processes which might come into effect in peacetime.

The situation was better in a few places where the local state apparatus survived. One example was Tuzla, where the non-nationalists had won the 1990 elections. Tuzla was defended by the local police and local volunteers, who later became a local brigade of the Bosnian army, and an ideology of multicultural civic values was vigorously promoted. Throughout the war, the city maintained local energy sources and some local production, including mining. At the height of the war, when the town was completely cut off, the people lived off humanitarian assistance and rent in kind from UNPROFOR. By the end of the war, taxes raised in Tuzla accounted for 60 per cent of the total tax revenue of the Bosnian government. Nevertheless, it has proved very difficult for these islands of relative civility to survive in what Bougarel calls the communitarianized predatory economy.[43]

Towards the end of the war, the local militia and paramilitary groups were absorbed into the regular armies. The former became local brigades and the latter became 'Special Units'. The capture of Srebrenica, a classic ethnic-cleansing operation, in July 1995 was carried out entirely by the BSA. On the third day, the Special Units were sent in to undertake the most gruesome task – the massacre of 8,000 men and boys. On all sides, there were failed attempts to create a mobilization economy. In particular, after Serbia imposed a blockade on the Bosnian Serbs in August 1994, the BSA was reduced to self-finance. The Bosnian Serb government tried to centralize finance and take control of key sectors, but this was rejected by the so-called Serb parliament, whose members were linked in to the criminal economy. On all sides, but especially the Serb side, morale was very low at the end of the war. Vasić suggests that the BSA had only 30,000 effective troops. Many people, especially young people, had left; poverty, criminality and indiscipline were rife.

How far was the strategy of ethnic cleansing planned in advance? Or was it chanced upon by Serb forces in Croatia? The UN Commission says that the JNA's Department of Psychological Operations was reported to 'have had several plans for local provocation by special forces controlled by the Ministry of the Interior and "ethnic cleansing"'.[44] It quotes an article in the Slovenian newspaper *Delo* which claimed that, along with the plan 'RAM' (to arm the Serbs in Croatia and Bosnia–Herzegovina), the JNA had an additional plan for mass killings of Muslims and mass rapes as a weapon of psychological warfare: 'Analysis of the Muslims' behaviour showed their morale, desire for battle, and will could be crushed most easily by raping women, especially minors and even children, and by killing members of the Muslim nationality inside their religious facilities.'[45]

It is sometimes suggested that the JNA drew on its history as a partisan movement. It is certainly true that the localized and decentralized nature of the war has many parallels with guerrilla warfare. The organization of TOs meant that many trained reservists could be drawn into the war at a local level and that small arms in local weapons caches were easily available. However, in many ways, ethnic cleansing is the exact opposite of guerrilla warfare, which depended on the support of the local population; the guerrilla was supposed to be the 'fish in the sea', to use Mao's words. The aim of ethnic cleansing was the wholesale destruction of communities, the manufacture of 'fear and hate'. One speculation is that JNA thinking was perhaps influenced by counter-insurgency doctrines, as developed by the Americans in Vietnam and tried out in the low-intensity conflicts of the 1980s. Alex de Waal has suggested that African military strategists were influenced by these doctrines, and this may, in part, explain the similarities of the Bosnian War to the wars in Africa.[46] Undoubtedly, JNA staff would have studied these wars. The last Yugoslav minister of defence, General Kadijević, had spent six months at West Point Military Academy, although counter-insurgency was only a minor part of the curriculum there, and other JNA officers had also studied in the United States. It is probably more convincing to argue that the strategy of ethnic cleansing was developed on the ground, although prior discussions and experience must have had some relevance.

It was not only members of other ethnic groups who were targeted in the strategy of ethnic cleansing. It was moderates as well, those who refused to hate. This was first learned in Croatia when Babić and Martić, the leaders of the Krajina Serbs, seized control of the town of Pakrac and removed Serbs as well as people of other nationalities in positions of authority. Throughout the war, there were people on all sides who refused to be drawn into the mire of 'fear and hate'. The reports of the Special Rapporteur for the UN Commission on Human Rights consistently note the actions of brave Serbs who tried to protect their Muslim and Croat neighbours. *The Guardian* newspaper reported a Serb 'Schindler' living in Prijedor who organized his friends and neighbours to protect Muslims. The Jewish community in Mostar organized itself to help Muslims escape. Even though their ranks have been greatly depleted by death and flight, non-nationalist groups and parties still exist in different parts of Bosnia–Herzegovina.

The Nature of International Involvement

From the beginning, international involvement in the war in Bosnia–Herzegovina, and indeed in all the conflicts on the territory of former Yugoslavia, was extensive. This involvement took place both at an official level and at the level of civil society. The war became the focus of media attention and of peace, humanitarian and human rights groups, as well as of civic institutions such as churches or universities. Within the former Yugoslavia, great hopes were vested in the role of the international community. For many people, the term 'Europe' had an almost mystical significance; it was considered synonymous with civilized behaviour and emblematic of an alternative 'civic' outlook to which those who opposed nationalism aspired. What actually happened was deeply disappointing, giving rise to cynicism and despair.

In fact, there were two quite distinct forms of international involvement. One was the high-level political talks and missions. The other was, in effect, a new form of humanitarian intervention. The latter, I would argue, did in fact represent a considerable innovation in international action both in its goals and in its scale and in the way it fostered cooperation between international institutions and civil society. But it was fatally thwarted by the contradictions between what was happening at a humanitarian level and what was happening at the level of high politics, and, connectedly, by misconceptions about the political and military nature of the war.

There have been many explanations for the failure of the international community to prevent or stop the wars in the former Yugoslavia – lack of cohesion in the EU, unwillingness of governments to provide adequate resources, the short-termism of politicians. All these explanations have something in them. But the fundamental problem was conceptual, the failure to understand why or how the war was fought and the character of the new nationalist political formations that emerged after the collapse of Yugoslavia. Both politically and militarily, the war was perceived as a conflict between competing nationalisms of a traditional essentialist type, and this was true both of the Europeans who, like the Serbs, argued that the nationalisms were all equally to blame, and of the Americans, who tended to see the Serbs as bad 'totalitarian' nationalists and the Croats and Muslims as good 'democratic' nationalists. While Serbian and Croatian nationalism was definitely bad nationalism and Muslim nationalism was not quite so bad, such an analysis missed the point that this was a conflict between a new form of ethnic nationalism and civilized values. The nationalists had a shared interest in eliminating an internationalist humanitarian outlook, both within the former Yugoslavia and globally. Both politically and militarily, their war was not against each other but, to repeat the argument of Bougarel, against the civilian population and against civil society.

The so-called international community fell into the nationalist trap by taking on board and legitimizing the perception of the conflict that the nationalists wished to propagate. In political terms, the nationalists had a common totalitarian goal: to re-establish the kind of political control the Communist Party had once enjoyed on the basis of ethnic communities. To this end, they had to partition society along ethnic lines. By assuming that 'fear and hate' were endemic to Bosnian society and that the nationalists represented the whole of society, the international negotiators could see no other solution but the kind of compromise which the nationalists themselves aimed to achieve. By failing to understand that 'fear and hate' were not endemic but were being manufactured during the war, they actually contributed to the nationalist goals and helped to weaken the internationalist humanitarian outlook.

In military terms, it was assumed that the main violence was between the so-called warring parties and that civilians were, so to speak, caught in the crossfire. While the evidence of ethnic cleansing was plain to see, this was treated as a side-effect of the fighting, not as the goal of the war. The UN troops that were sent to Bosnia–Herzegovina to protect the civilian population were hamstrung because their masters were so fearful of being dragged into a conventional war. A sharp distinction was drawn between peacekeeping and war-fighting. Peacekeeping meant that the troops operated on the basis of consent between the warring parties. War-fighting would have meant taking sides. Throughout the war, the fear that any use of force would mean taking sides and would escalate the international military involvement prevented UN troops from effectively carrying out the humanitarian tasks they were sent to perform. What was not understood was that there was rather little fighting between the sides in the conventional sense and that the main problem was the continuing violence against civilians. The UN troops were supposed to be peacekeeping troops; they operated on the basis of consent. The consequence was that they were unable to protect aid convoys or safe havens; instead, they stood by, as one Sarajevan wag put it, 'like eunuchs at the orgy'.

The predominant approach in the high-level talks was an approach 'from above', a *realpolitik* approach, in which it was assumed that the leaders of political parties spoke for the people they represented. The problem of how to deal with the debris of Yugoslavia was thus understood as a problem of reaching a compromise with those leaders. Essentially, it was conceived as a problem of borders and territory, not as a problem of political and social organization. Since ethnic cleansing was seen as a side-effect of the war, the main concern was to stop the fighting by finding a political compromise acceptable to the warring parties. If the political leaders in the former Yugoslavia insisted that they could not live together, then some new set of territorial arrangements had to be found for the post-Yugoslav political space. Hence, the answer was partition. But partition was a cause of war as much as a solution. It was self-perpetuating since, as everyone knew, there was no way to create ethnically pure territories without population displacement. Since ethnic cleansing was the goal of the war, the only possible solution was one which accepted the results of ethnic cleansing. Thus, the very principle of partition legitimized nationalist claims.

The first partition was that of Yugoslavia, when Slovenia and Croatia, and later Bosnia–Herzegovina, were recognized.[47] At the same time, Croatia was partitioned after the ceasefire negotiated by Cyrus Vance, the UN envoy, in December 1991. The recognition of Bosnia–Herzegovina took place on the day that war broke out. In the efforts to halt the fighting, a series of doomed plans to partition Bosnia–Herzegovina were put forward, culminating in the Dayton Agreement. The first plan was the Carrington–Cutileiro Plan of the spring of 1992, which proposed to divide the country into three parts. After the failure of this plan, Lord Carrington resigned as EU negotiator and was replaced by David Owen, who became joint chairman with Cyrus Vance of the International Conference on Former

Yugoslavia (ICFY), established after the London Conference in August 1992. The Vance–Owen Plan was considered to be an improvement on the Carrington–Cutileiro Plan because it divided Bosnia–Herzegovina into ten cantons, nine of which were based on the domination of one or other of the ethnic groups. The plan was eventually rejected by the Bosnian Serb Assembly in May 1993, but not before it had provided the legitimation for the Croats to ethnically cleanse the regions they were awarded under the plan: this marked the beginning of the Croat–Muslim conflict. (It was said that HVO stands for 'Hvala Vance Owen' – 'Thank you Vance Owen'.) Under pressure from the Americans, a Muslim–Croat ceasefire was negotiated in the spring of 1994; essentially, the Washington Agreement, as the ceasefire agreement was known, established a Bosnian–Croat federation partitioned into even smaller ethnically dominated cantons. Meanwhile, the Vance–Owen Plan was replaced by the Owen–Stoltenberg Plan (Cyrus Vance having been replaced by Thorvald Stoltenberg), which was in turn supplanted by the Contact Group Plan – the Contact Group being a new negotiating forum involving the major outside players (the USA, Russia, Britain, France and Germany). Both these plans and the Dayton Agreement that eventually succeeded in halting the fighting were very similar to the original Carrington–Cutileiro Plan.

The Dayton Agreement finally succeeded in bringing about a ceasefire, partly because of military pressure (NATO finally undertook air strikes and an Anglo-French Rapid Reaction Force was sent to Bosnia), partly because of the collapse of Bosnian Serb morale, and perhaps most importantly because the military situation on the ground had been 'rationalized', with the Serb capture of two of the Eastern enclaves and the Croatian capture of the Krajina.[48] In other words, ethnic cleansing was virtually complete. Such was the ease of the military endgame that it has been suggested that there may have been some tacit understanding between Serbia and Croatia, perhaps even encouraged by outside players.[49] Certainly, the eventual partition was close to what Milošević and Tudjman had discussed way back in March 1991, at a famous meeting in Karadjordjevo.[50]

The negotiators were strongly criticized for even talking to the warring parties. How could they be seen to shake hands with people named as war criminals? How could they treat Izetbegović, the president of a recognized country, on a par with the Bosnian Serbs and the Bosnian Croats?[51] Those engaged in the negotiations make the point that those who make the war are the only ones who can stop it and therefore there are no alternatives to talks between the warring parties. There is something in this argument, but these talks should not have been given the priority they received in the overall policy. There were ways in which the non-nationalist political and civic parts of Bosnian society could have been given access to governments and international institutions, in which their ideas and proposals, including proposals for alternatives to partition, could have been heard and taken seriously and in which they were publicly seen to have the respect of the international community. They represented the hope for international values; they should have been seen as the main partners in the search for peace. There was an utter failure to understand that the nationalists did not and could not, because of the nature of their goals and the way in which they were pursued, appeal to 'hearts and minds', and that it was of vital importance to foster a political alternative.

In parallel with the high-level talks was the humanitarian intervention. At an early stage in the conflict, Sadako Ogata, the High Commissioner for Refugees, put forward a seven-point humanitarian response plan which was accepted by governments and international agencies in July 1992. The seven points were: 'respect for human rights and humanitarian law, preventive protection, humanitarian access to those in need, measures to meet special humanitarian needs, temporary protection measures, material assistance, and repair and rehabilitation'.[52] UNHCR took the lead role in a massive humanitarian effort providing aid to around two-thirds of the population of Bosnia–Herzegovina, and it coordinated the activities of a range of international humanitarian agencies and NGOs. Many courageous individuals contributed to this effort as aid workers, medical personnel, convoy drivers, etc. In addition to the aid effort, a series of measures was adopted by the UN aimed at protecting the civilian population and upholding international humanitarian law. These included the decision to protect humanitarian convoys, by force, if necessary (Security Council Resolution (SCR) 770 (1992)); the declaration of safe areas

(SCR 836 (1993)); the appointment of a Special Rapporteur for Human Rights by the Commission on Human Rights (August 1992); the appointment of a Commission to investigate war crimes (October 1992) and, in particular, rape (December 1992); and the establishment of 'an international tribunal for the prosecution of persons responsible for serious violations of international humanitarian law' (SCR 808 (1993)). The International Committee of the Red Cross (ICRC) was charged with gaining access to detention camps and organizing prisoner releases. And in the Washington Agreement, an EU administration was established to administer Mostar with the aim of reuniting the city.

These measures, at least in theory, represented a very significant innovation in international practice. Adopted under pressure from the international media, which exposed the reality of the war, and from campaigning groups, they constituted a potential new form of international humanitarianism. Although elements of the package had been introduced in previous conflicts – the safe haven/area concept in Iraq, the protection of humanitarian convoys in Somalia – this was the most ambitious deployment of UN peacekeeping troops designed to assist and protect the civilian population and to uphold humanitarian law. Moreover, the wording of the relevant Security Council resolutions was strong. Both SCR 770 (1992), which called for protection for humanitarian convoys and unimpeded access for the ICRC and other humanitarian organizations to 'camps, prisons and detention centres', and SCR 836 (1993), which established safe areas, were under Chapter VII of the UN Charter, which authorizes the use of force.[53] Some 23,000 UNPROFOR troops were sent to Bosnia–Herzegovina.

In addition to the UNPROFOR troops, NATO and the Western European Union (WEU) maintained naval forces in the Adriatic monitoring the arms embargo, and NATO was responsible for enforcing the no-fly zone over Bosnian air space, which was also authorized under Chapter VII (SCR 816 (1993)).

However, almost none of these measures was effectively implemented. Humanitarian aid was constantly obstructed and 'taxed' by the warring parties. The safe areas became vast insecure refugee camps constantly subjected to shelling;

humanitarian supplies were controlled sadistically by the Bosnian Serbs. War crimes continued to be committed, despite the efforts of Mazowiecki, the UN Commission of Experts and the Tribunal, the ICRC and other humanitarian organizations – indeed some of the worst instances of ethnic cleansing occurred in the last few months of the war. The no-fly zone was violated on countless occasions and the arms embargo was never strictly maintained. Despite the EU administration, Mostar continued to be divided, freedom of movement was still restricted and numerous violations of human rights were recorded. Many UN personnel themselves engaged in black-market activities, and allegations of crimes committed by UN personnel, especially rape, were never properly investigated. The nadir for the UN came in July 1995, when the so-called safe areas of Srebrenica and Zepa were overrun by Bosnian Serb forces.

Was any other approach possible once the war had begun? In political terms, David Owen argues that the first priority was to stop the fighting. But even now, after Dayton, it can be asked whether an agreement would ever have been reached before the parties were ready for it and whether the role of the international negotiators was anything more than a way of facilitating and legitimizing an agreement which, at least, the Serbs and the Croats wanted to reach. The consequence is that it is now extremely hard, as has already become clear, to dislodge the nationalists and war criminals from power, making long-term peace or normality a distant prospect.

Had the war been understood as, first and foremost, a war of genocide, then the first priority would have been the protection of the civilian population. Negotiations and political pressure could have focused on concrete goals on the ground to ease the humanitarian situation – such as the opening of Tuzla airport or the Mount Igman route to Sarajevo, or the release of prisoners – rather than on partition. The inclusion of non-nationalist parties and groups in the negotiation process could have assisted this task and made possible other 'take it or leave it' overall solutions not based on partition, such as an international protectorate.[54] At the very least, such an approach would have strengthened the alternatives to nationalism, thus obstructing the manufacture of 'fear and hate', and would have left the legitimacy of international organizations more intact.

On several occasions, Mazowiecki complained about the lack of cooperation with ICFY: 'The Special Rapporteur requested that human rights concerns should have priority in the peace process, and pointed out that peace negotiations should not have been conducted without ensuring the cessation of massive and gross human rights violations.'[55]

Militarily, a different perception might have led to a tougher, more 'robust' approach to peacekeeping. The belief that this was a war with 'sides' led to an extreme timidity about the use of force for fear that this would escalate and drag the international community into the war on one side or another. General Michael Rose was obsessive about crossing what he called the 'Mogadishu line', in reference to the failure of the UN mission in Somalia. It can, with equal justice, be argued that a tougher approach would have made the task easier and UN forces and personnel much less vulnerable than they were to hostage-taking or sporadic attacks. When in 1993 British soldiers, escorting a relief convoy to Tuzla from Kladanj, started to shoot back at Serbs firing from the hills, harassment was dramatically reduced. Yet General Morillon, the then Commander of UNPROFOR troops in Bosnia–Herzegovina, was reprimanded by the UN Secretary-General for 'exceeding his mandate'. A similar story can be recounted when a Danish officer in Tuzla ordered a tank to fire on the Serbs in retaliation for shelling.

For those on the ground, the frustration was immense, both for the UNPROFOR personnel themselves who were being ordered to appear to be cowards and for the personnel of humanitarian organizations who found their task as difficult as it had been before the arrival of the UN troops. Since humanitarian passage had to be negotiated anyway, this could as easily be done by the sheer willpower of people such as UNHCR's Larry Hollingsworth or Gerry Hulme than by a toothless UNPROFOR. As Larry Hollingsworth pointed out when leaving Bosnia:

> If you send in an army but don't allow it to be aggressive, why send in firepower and tanks? I'm left sadly with the conclusion that the troops were sent in not to be tough but to look tough ... We should have been much tougher from the beginning. The UN missed the chance to seize the initiative and be forceful, and we have seen a gradual chipping away of authority ever since.[56]

Owen himself argues that tougher peacekeeping was impossible because there were insufficient troops. He points out that it is not feasible, for example, to defend the 55-mile route from Sarajevo to Goradze, which crosses two mountain ranges, forty-four bridges and two narrow ravines: 'Calls for "robust" or "muscular" action from politicians, retired generals and commentators in television studios were greeted with hollow laughs from the men on the ground.'[57] But the argument can be put the other way round. The troops were equally, if not more, vulnerable if they were not prepared to use force, and this was clearly understood by the warring parties; hence, the temptation to expose this and to humiliate the international community by, for example, hostage-taking. Tougher action would have required regrouping and refusal to undertake certain tasks, for example monitoring as opposed to destroying heavy weaponry.

For similar reasons, Owen is very dismissive of the safe haven/area concept. It is true that UNPROFOR originally asked for 30,000 troops to defend the safe areas and argued that, at a pinch, they could make do with 10,000. In the end the Security Council authorized 7,500 troops, but money was appropriated only for 3,500 troops. The problem was that this argument was used to explain why nothing could be done, instead of intensifying the pressure for more troops. Towards the end of the war, increasing pressure from individuals such as General Morillon or Mazowiecki as well as public opinion did lead eventually to the deployment of the Rapid Reaction Force on Mount Igman and the toughening of the rules of engagement for the Implementation Force (IFOR).

In the end, the main use of force was air strikes, which had always been advocated by the Americans because they are a way of using force without risking casualties. Operation Deliberate Force lasted from 29 August to 14 September 1995; in all, 3,515 sorties were flown and more than 1,000 bombs were dropped.[58] Air strikes did help to put pressure on the Bosnian Serbs as a prelude to the Dayton Agreement and, supposedly, they deterred an attack on the last eastern enclave, Goradze. But air strikes are a cumbersome instrument for protecting civilians on the ground, and it was the protection of civilians that was needed above all else. Many people argue that the deployment of the Rapid Reaction Force was more effective.

What was needed, in effect, was not peacekeeping but humanitarian law-enforcement. This does represent a considerable challenge. It requires new strategic thinking about how to counter strategies of population control through ethnic cleansing – how to develop support and promote alternative sources of legitimacy among the local population, new rules of engagement and norms of behaviour, appropriate equipment, forms of organization and command structures.

After Dayton

The longest and most destructive war in Europe since 1945 ended after three-and-a-half years. The international operation mounted to implement the agreement involved an array of institutions – the UN, the EU, the Council of Europe, the OSCE, NATO and the WEU. For NATO, IFOR and its successors, the Stabilization Force (SFOR) and the European Force (EUFOR), was the largest operation ever undertaken by the alliance. Moreover, NATO was joined by Partnership for Peace countries, formerly members of the Warsaw Pact. Since December 2004, the EU has taken over NATO's role; even though this is not the first autonomous EU military mission, it marks a significant step forward in the development of a common European security policy. The process of implementation has been an important learning experience for the international community, exposing many of the same contradictions that dogged international involvement from the start of the war.

Indeed, the Dayton Agreement could be viewed as a product of those contradictions. It was primarily an agreement born of the *realpolitik* approach of high-level negotiators who perceived the world as divided into primordial nations. It was an agreement which partitioned Bosnia–Herzegovina into three statelets[59] and in which the parties to the agreement – i.e. the nationalists – were primarily responsible for its implementation. Nevertheless, the agreement also contained clauses which commit the parties, including the international community, to a humanitarian approach – clauses about human rights, the prosecution of war criminals, the return of refugees, freedom of movement, economic and social reconstruction. The agreement granted considerable power to the NATO commander and to the high representative responsible for civilian implementation.

Initially, the military side was much more effective than the civilian side. But the tasks that the military undertook – maintaining the ceasefire, separating the warring parties, controlling weapons stores – conformed to the logic of partition. The lack of capacity for public security as well as lack of will permitted the displacement of large numbers of Serbs from Sarajevo in the immediate aftermath of Dayton and continued low-level ethnic cleansing for months after the agreement was signed. Gradually, however, the civilian side has become stronger under successive high representatives. Various measures have been taken to integrate the three communities and to build a common state. These include the integration of the three armies and police reform; the common currency, flag, and licence plate; property laws, which facilitate refugee return; dismissal of extremist politicians and support for moderate democratic or civic politicians; and freedom of movement. Moreover, during this period, military forces deployed in Bosnia have begun to develop a capacity for humanitarian law-enforcement. From 1997, they began, together with local forces, to arrest war criminals, to redeploy forces in such a way as to protect returning refugees, and to act in support of the police in controlling criminality, ensuring freedom of movement, and preventing the worst manifestations of nationalist defiance. For example, in 1997, SFOR seized the transmitter of SRT (the Serb radio and television station which had been broadcasting anti-SFOR propaganda) and, in April 2001, the Office of the High Representative (OHR) and SFOR seized control of the Hercegovacka Banka in Mostar and in other towns, which was the main source of HDZ finances.

Despite all these efforts, nationalist politicians remain popular and democratic structures are very weak. Essentially, in today's Bosnia, the choice is between imperialist humanitarianism and extreme nationalism. The high representative between 2002 and 2006, Paddy Ashdown, was accused of acting like a 'European Raj'.[60] Yet the alternative to a strong international protectorate is nationalist partition and perhaps renewed warfare. The casualty of the war was democratic politics. The nationalist politicians who were responsible for starting the war succeeded in creating a genuine grass-roots nationalism that had hardly existed before the war. The trauma of the war left a trail of fear and insecurity, guilt and mistrust – emotions that cannot easily be allayed but which seek reassurance in the apparent certainties of ethnic identification. Moreover, the economy has never recovered from the impact of the war and the disintegration of Yugoslavia. Unemployment remains at 40 per cent, and many people are still dependent on a variety of illegal or informal activities which, up to now, have received 'protection' from the nationalist parties.

In other words, the nationalists won the war. The top-down realist approach of the international community during the war, unwittingly perhaps, legitimized their position. The humanitarian approach, which was exemplified by the efforts to establish safe havens and international administrations, was never strong enough to protect cosmopolitan politics. By the time the international community had learned from its mistakes, many of their potential partners in Bosnian civil society and politics had been killed or terrorized or had left the country. Moreover, even now, the emphasis is on the construction of institutions rather than cooperation with civil society and helping to foster democratic or cosmopolitan politics. The courageous strategy of Paddy Ashdown might have saved multiculturalism in the immediate aftermath of Dayton. Unfortunately, it simply came too late.

The big question is whether the practical experience of humanitarian law-enforcement and state-building, as well as the weakness of economic reconstruction efforts, can influence the philosophy and organization of international interventions in the future, particularly those involving the European Union, or whether international interventions have become discredited. Was the experience of the Bosnian War a brief moment between the Cold War and the War on Terror when a humanitarian international approach seemed possible? Or has the intervention left a lasting legacy that is already shaping at least the European Union's approach towards security?

4

The Politics of New Wars

During the war in Bosnia–Herzegovina, Sarajevo was divided territorially between a Serb-controlled part and a Bosnian (mainly Muslim) part. But wartime Sarajevo could also be described in terms of a non-territorial divide. There was a group of people who could be described as the globalists – UN peace-keepers, humanitarian agencies, journalists, and Sarajevans who spoke English and were employed as assistants, interpreters and drivers. Protected by armoured cars, flak jackets and blue cards, they were able to move freely in and out of the city and across the territorial divide. At the same time, there were also the local territorially tied inhabitants of the city. On one (the Bosnian) side, they were under siege for the duration of the war, living off humanitarian aid or the black market (if they were lucky enough to have Deutschmarks), prey to sniper fire and occasional shelling. On the other (Serb) side, material conditions were somewhat better, although the climate of fear was worse. On both sides, they were vulnerable to the press gang and the various militias and mafia-types who roamed the streets and claimed legitimacy in terms of the national struggle.

The political goals of the new wars are about the claim to power on the basis of seemingly traditional identities – nation, tribe, religion. Yet the upsurge in the politics of particularistic identities cannot be understood in traditional terms. It has to be explained in the context of a growing cultural dissonance between those who participate in transnational networks, which communicate through e-mail, faxes, telephone and air travel, and those who are excluded from global processes and are tied to localities, even though their lives may be profoundly shaped by those same processes.

It would be a mistake to assume that this cultural divide can be expressed in simple political terms, that those who support particularistic identity politics are reacting against the processes of globalization, while those who favour a more tolerant, multicultural universalistic approach are part of the new global class. On the contrary, among the globalists are to be found diaspora nationalists and fundamentalists, 'realists' and neoliberals who believe that compromise with nationalism offers the best hope for stability, as well as transnational criminal groups who profit from the new wars. And while there are many among the territorially tied who are likely to cling to traditional identities, there are also courageous individuals and citizens' groups who refuse particularisms and exclusiveness.

The point is rather that the processes known as globalization are breaking up the cultural and socio-economic divisions that defined the patterns of politics which characterized the modern period. The new type of warfare has to be understood in terms of this global dislocation. New forms of power struggle may take the guise of traditional nationalism, tribalism or religious fundamentalism, but they are, nevertheless, contemporary phenomena arising from contemporary causes and displaying new characteristics. Moreover, they are paralleled by a growing global consciousness and sense of global responsibility among an array of governmental and non-governmental institutions as well as individuals.

In this chapter, I describe some of the key characteristics of the process known as globalization and how they give rise to new forms of identity politics. In the last section, I shall try to outline the emerging political cleavage between the politics of particularistic identity and the politics of cosmopolitan or humanist values.

The Characteristics of Globalization

In his book *Nations and Nationalism*, Ernest Gellner analyses the association between nationalism and industrialization.[1] He describes the emergence of vertically organized secular national cultures based on vernacular languages which enabled people to cope with the demands of modernity – everyday encounters with industry and government. As varied rural occupations were replaced with factory production, and as the state intruded into more and more aspects of daily life, people needed to be able to communicate both verbally and in writing in a common administrative language, and they needed to acquire certain standardized skills. Earlier societies were characterized by horizontal high cultures, e.g. Latin, Persian, Sanskrit, etc., which were based on religion and were not necessarily linked to the state. These were combined with a great variety of vertical low folk cultures. Whereas earlier high cultures were reproduced in religious institutions and low cultures were passed on through oral traditions, the new vertical national cultures were generated by a new class of intellectuals – writers, journalists, schoolteachers – which emerged along with the establishment of printing, the publication of secular literature such as newspapers and novels, and the expansion of primary education.

The process of globalization, it can be argued, has begun to break up these vertically organized cultures. What appear to be emerging are new horizontal cultures arising out of the new transnational networks, based on one or other of the emerging transnational languages: English, of course, often associated with the culture of mass consumerism linked to globally known names such as Coca-Cola or McDonald's or Starbucks, but also Arabic, fostered by new satellite TV channels like Al Jazeera or Al Arabiya, as well as the spread of social media, Chinese, Spanish or Hindu. These are combined with a medley of national, local and regional cultures as a result of a new assertion of local particularities.

The term globalization conceals a complex process which actually involves both globalization and localization, integration and fragmentation, homogenization and differentiation, etc. On the one hand, the process creates inclusive transnational networks of people. On the other hand, it excludes and atomizes large numbers of people – indeed, the vast majority. On the one hand, people's lives are profoundly shaped by events taking place far away from where they live over which they have no control. On the other hand, there are new possibilities for enhancing the role of local and regional politics through being linked in to global processes.

As a process, globalization has a long history. Indeed, some argue that there is nothing new about the present phase of globalization; from its inception, capitalism was always a global phenomenon.[2] What is new, however, in the last two decades, is the astonishing revolution in information and communications technology. I would argue that these technological changes impart a qualitative deepening to the process of globalization which is, as yet, by no means determined. The current contours of the process are shaped by the post-war institutional framework and, in particular, the deregulatory policies pursued by governments during the 1980s and 1990s. Its future will depend on the evolution of political and social values, actions and forms of organization. Here, I outline some key trends relevant to an understanding of that evolution.

In the economic sphere, globalization is associated with a set of changes variously described as post-Fordism, flexible specialization, or the New Economy. These changes generally refer to a transformation in what is known as the techno-economic paradigm, the prevailing way in which the supply of products and services is organized to meet the prevailing pattern of demand.[3] The relevant features of these changes are the dramatic decline in the importance of territorially based mass production, the globalization of finance and technology and the increased specialization and diversity of markets. Improved information means that physical production is less important as a share of the overall economy, both because of the increased importance of services and because an increasing proportion of the value of individual products consists of know-how – design, marketing, legal and financial advice. Likewise, the standardization of products, which is linked to territorially based economies of scale, can be supplanted by greater differentiation according to local or specialist demand. Hence, national levels of economic organization have declined in importance along with the relative decline of territorially based production. On the other hand, global levels of economic organization have greatly expanded because of the global character of finance and technology, while local levels of economic organization have also become more significant because of the increasing differentiation of markets.

Globalization also involves the transnationalization and regionalization of governance. There has been, since the war, an explosive growth in international organizations, regimes and regulatory agencies. More and more activities of government are regulated through international agreement or integrated into transnational institutions; more and more departments and ministries are engaged in formal and informal forms of cooperation with their equivalents in other countries; more and more policy decisions are coopted upwards to often unaccountable international forums. At the same time, recent decades have witnessed a reassertion of local and regional politics, especially, but not only, for development purposes. This reassertion has taken a variety of forms, ranging from science- and business-led initiatives, as in the case of 'technopoles' such as Silicon Valley, California or Cambridge, England; to a rediscovery of municipal traditions, as in Northern Italy; and peace- or Green-led initiatives such as nuclear-free zones or waste-recycling projects; as well as new or renewed forms of local clientelism and patronage.[4]

Parallel to the changing nature of governance has been a striking growth in informal non-governmental transnational networks.[5] These include NGOs – both those which undertake functions formerly undertaken by government, e.g. humanitarian assistance, and those which campaign on global issues, e.g. human rights, ecology, peace, etc. These NGOs are most active at local and transnational levels, partly because these are the sites of the problems with which they are concerned and partly because access to national politics is blocked by nationally organized political parties. Thus, organizations such as Greenpeace or Amnesty International are known all over the world; their effectiveness comes from operating at several different levels – local and global as well as national – and in many different places at the same time. In addition, other kinds of transnational networks have flourished: links between a variety of cultural and sporting activities; transnational religious and ethnic groups; transnational crime. Tertiary education is increasingly globalized both because of student and faculty exchanges, and because of the privileged use of the Internet.

These economic and political changes also involve far-reaching changes in organizational forms. Most societies are characterized by what Bukharin called a 'monism of architecture'.[6] In the modern era, nation-states, enterprises and military organizations had very similar vertical forms of hierarchical organization – the influence of modern war, particularly the experience of World War II on organizational forms, was pervasive. Robert Reich, in his book *The Work of Nations*, describes how enterprises have been transformed from national vertical organizations, where power is concentrated in the hands of owners at the top of a pyramid-shaped chain of command, into global phenomena whose organizations most resemble a spider's web, with power in the hands of those who possess technical or financial know-how and who are spread around the points of the web:

> Their dignified headquarters, expansive factories, warehouses, laboratories, and fleets of trucks and corporate jets are leased. Their production workers, janitors, and bookkeepers are under temporary contract; their key researchers, design engineers and marketeers are sharing in the profits. And their distinguished executives, rather than possessing great power and authority over this domain, have little direct control over much of anything. Instead of imposing their will over a corporate empire, they guide ideas through the new webs of enterprise.[7]

Something similar is happening to governmental and non-governmental organizations. Government departments, at all levels, are developing horizontal transnational links; government activity is increasingly contracted out through various forms of privatization and semi-privatization arrangements. The decentralized and horizontal forms of organization typical of NGOs or new social movements are often contrasted to the traditional, vertical forms of organization typical of political parties.[8] Yet political leaders, like corporate executives, have become, at most, facilitators and opinion-shapers and, at least, images or symbols – public representations of interconnected webs of activity over which they have little control.

Globalization has profoundly affected social structures. In advanced industrial countries, the traditional working classes have either declined or are declining along with the drop in territorially based mass production. Because of improvements in productivity and because production work is less skilled, manufacturing production employs fewer and lower-paid workers, especially women and immigrants, or else it is relocated to low-wage countries.

What has grown in number has been those people whom Alain Touraine calls information workers[9] and Robert Reich calls symbolic analysts, those people who possess and use know-how, who, to quote Reich, identify, solve and broker problems through 'manipulations of symbols – data, words, oral and visual representations'.[10] These are the people who work in technology or finance, in expanded higher education, or in the growing myriad of transnational organizations. The majority of people fit neither of these two categories. They either work in services, as waiters and waitresses, salespersons, taxi-drivers, cashiers, etc., or they join the increasing ranks of unemployed made redundant by the productivity increases associated with globalization. This emerging social structure is reflected in growing income disparities both between those in work and those not in work and among those in work depending on skill.

Income disparities are also associated with geographical disparities, both within and across continents, countries and regions. There is the growing disparity between those areas, mainly the advanced industrial regions, that can capitalize on their technological capabilities and the rest. Some areas may thrive, at least temporarily, through attracting volume production, i.e. Southeast Asia, Southern Europe and, potentially, Central Europe. The remainder are caught up in the global economy as traditional sources of livelihood are eroded, but can participate neither in production nor in consumption. Maps drawn by global enterprises of the segmentation of their markets generally leave out the larger part of the world. But even within countries, continents or, indeed, cities, these widening geographical disparities can be found – and this is true of both the advanced industrial world and the rest. Everywhere, boundaries are being drawn between protected and prosperous global enclaves and the anarchic, chaotic, poverty-stricken areas beyond.

The trends outlined above are simultaneously haphazard and constructed. There is no inevitability, for example, about the growth of social, economic and geographical disparities; in part, they are the consequence of disorganization or of organization evolving out of past inertia. What can, however, be accepted as a given is the historic shift away from vertical cultures characteristic of the era of the nation-state which gave rise to a sense of national identity and a sense of security. The abstract symbols, such as money and law, which form the basis of social relations in societies no longer dominated by face-to-face interactions, were a constitutive part of these national cultures.[11] It is now commonplace to talk about a 'crisis of identity' – a sense of alienation and disorientation that accompanies the decomposition of cultural communities.

It is also possible, however, to point to certain emerging forms of cultural classification. On the one hand, there are those who see themselves as part of a global community of like-minded people, mainly well-educated information workers or symbolic analysts, who spend a lot of time on aeroplanes, tele-conferencing, etc., and who may work for a global corporation, an NGO, or some other international organization, or who may be part of a network of scholars or sports clubs or musicians and artists, etc. On the other hand, there are those who are excluded and who may or may not see themselves as part of a local or particularistic (religious or national) community.

As yet, the emerging global groupings are not politicized, or, at least, are hardly politicized. That is to say, they do not form the basis of political communities on which new forms of power could be based. One reason is the individualism and anomie that characterizes the current period: the sense that political action is futile given the enormity of current problems, the difficulty of controlling or influencing the web-like structure of power, the cultural fragmentation of both horizontal networks and particularistic loyalties. Both what Reich calls the laissez-faire cosmopolitan, who has 'seceded' from the nation-state and who pursues his or her individualistic consumerist interests, and the restless young criminals, the new adventurers, to be found in all the excluded zones, reflect this political vacuum.

Nevertheless, there are seeds of politicization in both groupings. Cosmopolitan politicization can be located, both within the new transnational NGOs or social movements and within international institutions, as well as among individuals, around a commitment to human values (universal social and political rights, ecological responsibility, peace and democracy, etc.) and to the notion of transnational civil society – the idea that self-organized groups, operating across borders, can solve problems and lobby political institutions. The Arab Spring and the globally linked-up protests against the banks offer the potential for cosmopolitan politicization. At the same time, the new politics of particularistic identities can also be interpreted as a response to these global processes, as a form of political mobilization in the face of the growing impotence of the modern state.

Identity Politics

I use the term 'identity politics' to mean movements which mobilize around ethnic, racial or religious identity for the purpose of claiming state power.[12] And I use the term 'identity' narrowly to mean a form of labelling. Whether we are talking about tribal conflict in Africa, religious conflict in the Middle East or South Asia, or nationalist conflict in Europe, the common feature is the way in which labels are used as a basis for political claims. Such conflicts are often described as ethnic conflicts. The term 'ethnos' has a racial connotation even though a number of writers insist that 'ethnie' refers to a cultural community rather than a blood-based community. Although it is clear that there is no racial basis to ethnic claims, the point is that these labels tend to be treated as something one is born with and cannot change; they are ascribed and cannot be acquired through conversion or assimilation. You are German if your grandmother was German, even if you cannot speak the language and have never been to Germany; but you are not German if your parents were Turkish, even if you live and work in Germany. A Catholic born in West Belfast is doomed to remain a Catholic even if he or she converts to Protestantism. A Croat cannot become a Serb by adopting the Orthodox religion and writing in a Cyrillic script. To the extent that these labels are considered birthrights, conflicts based on identity politics can also be termed ethnic conflicts. In many cases, these identities are both religious and nationalist.[13] To claim the political identity of a Muslim in Bosnia, a Catholic in Northern Ireland, or a Hindu in India is, at one and the same time, to claim a national identity. There are, of course, forms of identity politics where labels are not birthrights but can be voluntarily or forcibly imposed. And indeed, in areas of endemic conflict, identity politics often becomes more extreme and morphs into fundamentalism, that is to say, rigid adherence to doctrine. Certain sects of militant Islam, for example, aim to create pure Islamic states through the conversion of non-Muslims as opposed to exclusion.[14]

The term 'politics' refers to the claim to political power. In many parts of the world there are religious revivals, or renewed interest in the survival of local cultures and languages, and this, in part, is a response to the stresses of globalization. Political campaigns to protect or promote religion or culture may often lead to demands for power in order to ensure that policies are adopted. Nevertheless, this is not what is meant by identity politics. Such political campaigns are demands for cultural and religious rights. These are quite different from the demand for political rights based on identity, that is to say, the right to power on the basis of identity as opposed to the demand for power on the basis of a political programme. Identity politics is a form of communitarianism that is distinct from and may conflict with individual political rights.

Another way of expressing this difference is by contrasting the politics of identity with the politics of ideas. The politics of ideas is about forward-looking projects. Thus, religious struggles in Western Europe in the seventeenth century were about freeing the individual from the oppressive hold of the established Church. Early nationalist struggles in nineteenth-century Europe or in colonial Africa were about democracy and state-building. They were conceived as ways of welding together diverse groups of people under the rubric of nation for the purpose of modernization. More recently, politics has been dominated by abstract secular ideas such as socialism or environmentalism which offer a vision for the future. This type of politics tends to be integrative, embracing all those who support the idea, even though, as recent experience has demonstrated, the universalistic character of such ideas can serve as a justification for totalitarian and authoritarian practices.

In contrast, identity politics tends to be fragmentative, backward-looking and exclusive. Political groupings based on exclusive identity tend to be movements of nostalgia, based on the reconstruction of an heroic past, the memory of injustices, real or imagined, and of famous battles, won or lost. They acquire meaning through insecurity, through rekindled fear of historic enemies, or through a sense of being threatened by those with different labels. Labels can always be divided and subdivided. There is no such thing as cultural purity or homogeneity. Every exclusive identity-based polity necessarily generates a minority. At best, identity politics involves psychological discrimination against those labelled differently. At worst, it leads to population expulsion and genocide.

The new identity politics arises out of the disintegration or erosion of modern state structures, especially centralized, authoritarian states. The collapse of communist states after 1989, the loss of legitimacy of post-colonial states in Africa or South Asia, or even the decline of welfare states in more advanced industrial countries provide the environment in which the new forms of identity politics are nurtured.

The new identity politics has two main sources, both of which are linked to globalization. On the one hand, it can be viewed as a reaction to the growing impotence and declining legitimacy of the established political classes. From this perspective, it is a politics fostered from above which plays to and inculcates popular prejudices. It is a form of political mobilization, a survival tactic, for politicians active in national politics either at the level of the state or at the level of nationally defined regions, as in the case of the republics of the former Yugoslavia or the former Soviet Union or in places such as Kashmir or Eritrea before independence. On the other hand, it emerges out of the insecurity associated with the process of globalization and, in particular, the advent of what can be described as the parallel economy – new forms of legal and illegal ways of making a living that have sprung up among the excluded parts of society – and constitutes a way of legitimizing these new shadowy forms of activity. Particularly in Eastern Europe, the events of 1989 compressed the impact of globalization both in undermining the nation-state and in releasing new forms of economic activity into a short 'transitional' space of time, so that this form of nationalism from below merged with nationalism from above in an explosive combination.[15]

In Eastern Europe, the use of nationalism as a form of political mobilization pre-dated 1989. Particularly in the former communist multinational states, national consciousness was deliberately cultivated in a context in which ideological differences had been disallowed and when societies had, in theory, been socially homogenized and 'socially cleansed'.[16] Nationality, or certain officially recognized nationalities, became the main legitimate umbrella for pursuing various forms of political, economic and cultural interests. This was particularly important in the former Yugoslavia and Soviet Union, where national difference was 'constitutionally enshrined'.[17]

These tendencies were reinforced by the functioning of economies of shortage. In theory, planned economies are supposed to eliminate competition. Such planning does of course eliminate competition for markets. But it gives rise to another form of competition – competition for resources. In theory, the plan is drawn up by rational planners and transmitted downwards through a vertical chain of command. In practice, it is 'built up' through a myriad of bureaucratic pressures and subsequently 'broken down'. In effect, the plan operates as an expression of bureaucratic compromise, and, because of the 'soft budget' constraint, individual enterprises always spend more than is anticipated. The consequence is a vicious circle in which shortage intensifies the competition for resources and the tendency among ministries and enterprises for hoarding and autarchy, which further intensifies shortage. In this context, nationality becomes a tool which can be used to further the competition for resources.[18]

Already in the early 1970s there were writers who were warning of a nationalist explosion in the former Soviet Union as a result of the way in which nationality policy was used to prop up the decaying socialist project.[19] In a classic article, published in 1974, Teresa Rakowska-Harmstone used the term the 'new nationalism' to describe 'a new phenomenon which is present even among people who, at the time of the revolution, had only an inchoate sense of a common culture'.[20] Soviet policy created a hierarchy of nationalities based on an elaborate administrative structure in which the status of nationalities was linked to the status of territorially based administrative units – republics, autonomous regions and autonomous provinces. Within these administrative arrangements the indigenous language and culture of the so-called titular nationality was promoted, and members of the titular nationality were given priority in local administration and education.[21] The system gave rise to what Zaslavsky has described as an 'explosive division of labour' in which an indigenous administrative and intellectual elite presided over an imported Russian urban working class and an indigenous rural population.[22] The local elite used the development of national consciousness to promote administrative autonomy, especially in the economic sphere.

As I argued in the previous chapter, a similar process took place in the former Yugoslavia, especially after the 1974 constitution entrenched the nations and republics that made up the federation and restricted the powers of the federal government. What held these multinational states together was the monopoly of the Communist Party. In the aftermath of 1989, when the socialist project was discredited and the monopoly of the party was finally broken, and when democratic elections were held for the first time, nationalism erupted into the open. In a situation where there is little to choose between parties, where there has been no history of political debate, where the new politicians are hardly known, nationalism becomes a mechanism for political differentiation. In societies where people assume that they are expected to vote in certain ways, where they are not habituated to political choice and may be wary of taking it for granted, voting along national lines became the most obvious option.

Nationalism represents both a continuity with the past and a way of denying or 'forgetting' a complicity with the past. It represents a continuity partly because of the ways in which it was nurtured in the preceding era, not only in multinational states, and partly because its form is very similar to the preceding Cold War ideologies. Communism, in particular, thrived on an us–them, good–bad war mentality and elevated the notion of an homogeneous collective community. At the same time, it is a way of denying the past because communist regimes overtly condemned nationalism. As in the case of rabid attachment to the market, nationalism is a form of negation of what went before. Communism can be treated as an 'outsider' or 'foreigner', particularly in countries occupied by Soviet troops, thus exculpating those who accepted, tolerated or collaborated with the regime. National identity is somehow pure and untainted in comparison with other professional or ideological identities that were determined by the previous context.

Similar tendencies can be observed in other places. Already by the 1970s and 1980s, the fragility of post-colonial administrative structures was becoming apparent. States in Africa and Asia were having to cope with the disillusion of post-independence hopes, the failure of the development project to overcome poverty and inequality, the insecurity of rapid urbanization and the break-up of traditional rural communities, as well as the impact of structural adjustment and policies of stabilization, liberalization and deregularization. Moreover, as in the case of the former Yugoslavia, the loss of an international identity based on membership of the non-aligned movement in the aftermath of the Cold War had domestic repercussions as well. Both ruling politicians and aspiring opposition leaders began to play upon particularistic identities in different ways – to justify authoritarian policies, to create scapegoats, to mobilize support around fear and insecurity. In many post-colonial states, the ruling parties saw themselves as left parties occupying the space for emancipatory movements. As in post-communist states, the absence of a legitimate emancipatory movement opened politics up to claims based on tribe or clan, or religious or linguistic group.

In the pre-colonial period, most societies had only a loose sense of ethnic identity. The Europeans, with their passion for classification, with censuses and identity papers, imposed more rigid ethnic categories, which then evolved along with the growth of communication, roads and railways, and the emergence, in some countries, of a vernacular press. In some cases, the categories were quite artificial: the Hutu–Tutsi distinction in Rwanda and Burundi was a rough, largely social distinction before the Belgian administration introduced identity cards; likewise, the Ngala, the tribe former President Mobutu of Zaire (now the Democratic Republic of Congo) claimed to come from, was largely a Belgian invention. In the post-independence period, most ruling parties espoused a secular national identity that embraced the often numerous ethnic groups within the artificially defined territory of the new nations. As post-independence hopes faded, many politicians began to appeal to particularistic tendencies. In general, the weaker the administrative structures, the earlier this took place. In some countries, such as Sudan, Nigeria or Zaire, what have been called 'predatory' regimes developed in which access to power and personal wealth depended on religion or tribe.[23] In India, where democracy was sustained for almost all of the post-independence period, the Congress Party's use of Hindu rituals and symbols in the 1970s paved the way for new forms of political mobilization based on identity, particularly religion.[24]

Many of these states were strongly interventionist. As foreign assistance began to be replaced by commercial borrowing in the 1970s, as foreign debt mounted and 'structural adjustment' programmes were introduced, state revenues declined and, as in the former communist countries, political competition for control over resources intensified. The end of the Cold War meant the reduction of foreign assistance to countries such as Zaire or Somalia which had been considered strategically important. At the same time, pressure for democratization led to increasingly desperate bids to remain in power, often through fomenting ethnic tension and other forms of identity politics. In the Middle East, the growth of Islamic movements was associated with the disillusion with secular nationalist post-colonial regimes.

Even in advanced industrial countries, the erosion of legitimacy associated with the declining autonomy of the nation-state and the corrosion of traditional, often industrially based sources of social cohesion became much more transparent in the aftermath of 1989. A specifically Western identity defined in relation to the Soviet threat was undermined because it was more difficult to defend democracy with reference to its absence elsewhere. Indeed the rhetoric of the 'War on Terror' can be viewed as a way of reinventing that distinctive Western identity. Of equal significance is the growing consensus of major political parties as the space for substantive political difference on economic and social issues narrows in the context of globalization and a prevailing ideology that emphasizes budgetary discipline and control of inflation. Nationalism or seeds of nationalism, such as asylum laws or anti-immigrationism, are exploited as party political forms of differentiation. In recent years, extreme right-wing parties have managed to capture significant shares of the vote in places such as France, the Netherlands, Belgium and elsewhere. In the United States, the Republican Party has deliberately built up its constituency among fundamentalist Christian churches and the more recent Tea Party movement. In Australia, the Conservative Party captured power on an explicit anti-asylum platform. Particularly in the aftermath of 9/11, xenophobic ideas have capitalized on a growing sense of insecurity.

Western countries do not of course share the experience of collectivist authoritarianism, although regions such as Northern Ireland, where particularist politics are strong, tend to be those where democracy has been weak. An active civil society tends to counterbalance the distrust of politicians, the alienation from political institutions, the sense of apathy and futility that provide a potential basis for populist tendencies. Nevertheless, the 'secession' of the new cosmopolitan classes and the fragmentation and dependence of those excluded from the benefits of globalization are characteristic of advanced industrial countries as well.

The other main source of the new identity politics is the insecurity associated with globalization, particularly rapid urbanization and the parallel economy. To a large extent, this can be attributed to the neo-liberal policies pursued in the 1980s and the 1990s – macro-economic stabilization, deregulation and privatization – which effectively represented a speeding up of the process of globalization. These policies increased the level of unemployment, resource depletion and disparities in income, and led to rapid urbanization, and increased migration both from countryside to town and across borders. These changes, in turn, provided an environment for growing criminalization and the creation of networks of corruption, black marketeers, arms and drug traffickers, etc. In societies where the state controlled large parts of the economy and where self-organized market institutions do not exist, policies of 'structural adjustment' or 'transition' effectively mean the absence of any kind of regulation. The market does not, by and large, mean new autonomous productive enterprises; it means corruption, speculation and crime. New groups of shady 'businessmen', often linked in to the decaying institutional apparatuses through various forms of bribery and 'insider' dealing, are engaged in a kind of primitive accumulation – a grab for land and capital. They use the language of identity politics to build alliances and to legitimize their activities. Often these networks are linked to wars, e.g. in Afghanistan, Pakistan and large parts of Africa, and to the disintegration of the military-industrial complex in the aftermath of the Cold War. Often, they are transnational, linking up to international circuits of illegal goods sometimes through diaspora connections.

In addition, religious institutions or humanitarian organizations linked to nationalist or religious parties often provide the only social safety net available to newly arrived immigrants from the countryside or from other countries. Likewise, religious schools and community organizations have been growing in the context of economic policies, which involve cuts in social spending, including education.

A typical phenomenon consists of the new bands of young men, the new adventurers, who make a living through violence or through threats of violence, who obtain surplus weapons through the black market or through looting military stores, and who either base their power on particularistic networks or seek respectability through particularistic claims. These networks can include hostage-takers in the Transcaucasus, who take prisoners in order to exchange them for food, weapons, money, other hostages and even dead bodies; mafia-rings in Russia; the new Cossacks who don the Cossack uniform in order to 'protect' Russian diaspora groups in the near abroad; nationalist militia groups of unemployed youths in Western Ukraine or Western Herzegovina. All these groups feed, like vultures, on the remnants of the disintegrating state and on the frustrations and resentments of the poor and unemployed. A similar breed of restless political adventurer is to be found in conflict areas in Africa and South Asia.[25]

The new identity politics combines these two sources of particularism in varying degrees. Former administrative or intellectual elites ally with a motley collection of adventurers on the margins of society to mobilize the excluded and abandoned, the alienated and insecure, for the purposes of capturing and sustaining power. The greater the sense of insecurity, the greater the polarization of society, the less is the space for alternative integrative political values. In conditions of war, such alliances are cemented by shared complicity in war crimes and a mutual dependence on the continued functioning of the war economy. In Rwanda, the plan for mass genocide has been explained as the way in which the extremist Hutus could retain their grip on power in the context of economic crisis and international pressure for democratization. According to the NGO Africa Rights: 'The extremists' aim was for the entire Hutu populace to participate in the killings. That way, the blood of genocide would stain everybody. There could be no going back.'[26] The intensification of the war in Kashmir, including the involvement of Afghan *Mujahidiin*, created a polarization between Hindu and Muslim identities which has increasingly supplanted syncretic traditions and the common bonds based on Kashmiri identity – the *kashmiriyat*.[27] One of the explanations for the ferocity of nationalist sentiment in the former Yugoslavia is the fact that all the various sources of the new identity politics are concentrated there: the former Yugoslavia had the most Westernized, indeed cosmopolitan, elite of any East European country, thus exacerbating the resentments of those excluded; it experienced nationalistic bureaucratic competition typical of the centralized state in decline; and, because it was exposed to the transition to the market earlier than other East European countries, its parallel economy was more developed. Even so, a vicious war was required to create the hatred on which exclusive identities could be reconstructed.

The new form of identity politics is often treated as a throwback to the past, a return to pre-modern identities temporarily displaced or suppressed by modernizing ideologies. It is of course the case that the new politics draws on memory and history and that certain societies where cultural traditions are more entrenched are more susceptible to the new politics. But, as I have argued, what really matters is the recent past and, in particular, the impact of globalization on the political survival of states. Moreover, the new politics has entirely new contemporary attributes.

First of all, it is horizontal as well as vertical, transnational as well as national. In nearly all the new nationalisms, the diasporas play a much more important role than formerly because of the speed of communication. There were always expatriate nationalist groups plotting their country's liberation in cafés in Paris or London. But such groups have become much larger and more significant because of the scale of emigration, the ease of travel and the spread of electronic communication. There are two types of diaspora. On the one hand, there are minorities living in the near abroad, fearful of their vulnerability to local nationalisms and often more extreme than those living on home territory. These include Serbians living in

Croatia and Bosnia–Herzegovina, Russian minorities in all the new ex-Soviet republics, the Hungarian minority in Vojvodina, Romania, Ukraine and Slovakia, Tutsis living in Zaire or Uganda. On the other hand, there are disaffected groups living far away, often in the new melting-pot nations, who find solace in fantasies about their origins which are often far removed from reality. The idea of a Sikh homeland, Khalistan, the notion of uniting Macedonia and Bulgaria, the call for an independent Ruthenia – all originated from diaspora communities in Canada. Irish-American support for the Irish Republican Army (IRA), violent conflict between the Greek and Macedonian communities in Australia and the pressure from Croatian groups in Germany for recognition of Croatia are all further examples of diaspora influence.

Among Kosovo Albanians, the diaspora played a critical role, especially in Germany and Switzerland. Many of those who had taken part in protests and student demonstrations in the early 1980s left the country. During the 1990s, a 3 per cent income tax was collected from half a million Kosovar Albanians who lived and worked abroad. Moreover, an Albanian-language television service was run from Switzerland and could be received by those Kosovar Albanians who had satellite dishes. After 1997, the increasingly influential role of the KLA (the Kosovo Liberation Army) was made possible because many in the diaspora switched support from the non-violent nationalist movement to the KLA.

Diaspora groups provide ideas, money, arms and know-how, often with disproportionate effects. Among the individuals who make up the new nationalist compacts are romantic expatriates, foreign mercenaries, dealers and investors, Canadian pizza-parlour owners, etc. Radha Kumar has described the support given by Indians living in the United States to Hindu fundamentalists: 'Separated from their countries of origin, often living as aliens in a foreign land, simultaneously feeling stripped of their culture and guilty for having escaped the troubles "back home", expatriates turn to diaspora nationalism without understanding the violence that their actions might inadvertently trigger.'[28] The same kinds of transnational networks are to be found among religious groupings. Islamic connections are well known, but such links also apply to other religious groupings. I visited the office of the so-called foreign minister of South Ossetia, a breakaway region of Georgia, and he had a picture of the Bosnian Serb leader Karadžić on his wall. He explained that he had been given it by the delegation from Republika Srpska when he attended a meeting of Eastern Orthodox Christians.

Second, the capacity for political mobilization is greatly extended both as a result of the improved education and the expansion of educated classes and as a consequence of new technologies. Many explanations for the growth of political Islam focus on the emergence of newly literate urban classes, who are often excluded from power, the increase in Islamic schools and the expansion of newspaper readership.[29] Growing literacy in the vernacular languages, together with the spread of tabloid-type communitarian newspapers, as well as radio and television in vernacular languages that reach people who have never had a reading habit, as well as SMS messaging, access to websites and forums through the Internet, or the circulation of videos, create new 'imagined communities'. These new forms of electronic communication provide rapid and effective ways of disseminating a particularistic message. Specifically, the electronic media has an authority that newspapers cannot match; in parts of Africa, the radio is 'magic'. The circulation of cassettes with sermons by militant Islamic preachers, the use of 'hate' radio to incite people to genocide in Rwanda, the websites that celebrate atrocities, the control of television by nationalist leaders in Eastern Europe – all provide mechanisms for speeding up the pace of political mobilization.

Cosmopolitanism versus Particularism

A.D. Smith, in his book *Nations and Nationalism in a Global Era*, takes issue with the view that nation-states are an anachronism.[30] He argues that the new global classes still need to feel a sense of community and identity based on what he calls ethnies to overcome the alienation of their technical scientific universalizing discourse. And he criticizes what he calls the modernist fallacy that nation-states are artificial and temporary polities, staging-posts in the evolution towards global society. He sees the new nationalism as evidence of the persistence of ethnies, and he offers a positive perspective on cultural separatism, which he sees as a way of grounding nation-states more firmly around a dominant ethnie while, at the same time, enabling them to embrace civic ideals.

It may well be that the new particularistic identities are here to stay, that they are the expression of a new post-modern cultural relativism. But it is difficult to argue that they offer a basis for humanistic civic values precisely because they are unable to present a forward-looking project relevant to the new global context. The main implication of globalization is that territorial sovereignty is no longer viable. The effort to reclaim power within a particular spatial domain will merely further undermine the ability to influence events. This does not mean that the new form of particularistic identity politics will go away. Rather, it is a recipe for new closed-in chaotic statelets with permanently contested borders dependent on continuing violence for survival.

The particularists cannot do without those people who are labelled differently. Globalization, as its name implies, is global. Everywhere, in varying proportions, those who benefit from globalization have to share territory with those excluded from its benefits but who are nevertheless deeply affected by it. Both losers and gainers need each other. No patch of territory, however small or large, can any longer insulate itself from the outside world.

Of course, it is possible to envisage, and it is already happening especially in the Middle East, a new assertion of regional and local politics, a claim for greater democratic accountability at regional and local levels. But if such claims are to succeed, they would have to be situated in a global context; they would have to involve greater access and openness towards global levels of governance, and they would have to be based on greater democratic accountability for all inhabitants of the territory in question, not just for those with a particular label. This type of politics would thus need to be embedded in what might be described as a cosmopolitan political consciousness.

By cosmopolitanism, I do not mean a denial of identity. Rather, I mean a celebration of the diversity of global identities, acceptance and, indeed, enthusiasm for multiple overlapping identities, and, at the same time, a commitment to the equality of all human beings and to respect for human dignity. The term originates in the Kantian notion of cosmopolitan right that is combined with recognition of separate sovereignties; thus it brings together both universalism and diversity. Kwame Anthony Appiah talks about the 'cosmopolitan patriot' or the 'rooted cosmopolitan, attached to a home of one's own, with its own cultural particularities, but taking pleasure from the presence of other different people'. He distinguishes cosmopolitanism from humanism 'because cosmopolitanism is not just the feeling that everybody matters. For the cosmopolitan also celebrates the fact that there are *different* local human ways of being; humanism, by contrast, is consistent with the desire for global homogeneity.'[31]

Two possible sources of a cosmopolitan political consciousness can be identified. One, which could be described as cosmopolitanism from above, is to be found in the growing myriad of international organizations, a few of which, most notably the EU, are developing supra-national powers. These institutions develop their own logics and internal structures. They enable activities to be carried out rather than undertaking them through their own resources. They function through complex partnerships, cooperation agreements, negotiation, and mediation with other organizations, states, and private or semi-private groups. They are restricted both by lack of resources and, relatedly, by the inter-governmental arrangements which make it extremely difficult for them to act, except on the basis of time-consuming and often unsatisfactory compromises. In many of these institutions there are committed idealistic officials. They have an interest in seeking alternative sources of legitimacy to their frustrating national masters.

The other source is what could be described as cosmopolitanism from below, the new social movements as well as what came to be called NGOs in the 1990s. This new form of activism has developed since the early 1980s primarily in response to new global problems, but it has burst forth in the wake of the financial crisis and the crisis of authoritarianism in the Middle East in the politics of public squares and tent cities and Facebook. The forerunners of these new movements were the social forums that emerged in the early 2000s. The eleven million people who demonstrated all over the world on 15 February 2003 against the war in Iraq testified to their growing organization. Of course, not everyone who participates in these activities is a cosmopolitan. Many are anti-globalization, yearning for a return to the nation-state, who sometimes make common cause with groups associated with identity politics, nationalists or Islamists in the Middle East, for example.

At present, cosmopolitanism and particularism coexist side by side in the same geographical space. Cosmopolitanism tends to be more widespread in the West and less widespread in the East and South. Nevertheless, throughout the world, in remote villages and towns, both sorts of people are to be found. The new particularistic conflicts throw up courageous groups of people who try to oppose war and exclusivism – both local people, often women, and those who volunteer to come from abroad to provide humanitarian assistance, to help mediate, etc. Local groups gather strength in so far as they can gain access to or support and protection from transnational networks.

It is in wars that the space for cosmopolitanism is narrowed. Particularisms need each other to sustain their exclusive identities; hence the paradoxical combination of conflict and cooperation. It is cosmopolitanism that undermines the appeal of particularism and it is the representatives of humane civic values that are often targeted in wars. Indeed, war itself can be understood as a form of political mobilization, constructing an environment of insecurity, in which particularist groups thrive. Areas of conflict become 'black holes' – havens for fanatics and criminals, breeding the new terrorism. More and more no-go areas come into being, such as Somalia or Afghanistan and now Iraq, where isolated humanitarian agencies gingerly negotiate and bribe their way through to help those in need. Some argue that such situations are the harbingers of the future for much of the world.[32] Nothing is more polarizing than violence and more likely to induce a retreat from utopian inclusive projects. 'Sarajevo is Europe's future. This is the end of history', Sarajevo's disenchanted cosmopolitans used to say. But politics is never determined. Whether another future can be envisaged is, in the end, a matter of choice.

5

The Globalized War Economy

The term 'war economy' used to refer to a system which is centralized, totalizing and autarchic, as was the case in the total wars of the twentieth century. Administration is centralized to increase the efficiency of the war and to maximize revenue to pay for the war. As many people as possible are mobilized to participate in the war effort either as soldiers or in the production of arms and necessities. By and large, the war effort is self-sufficient, although in World War II Britain and the Soviet Union received lend-lease assistance from the United States. The main aim of the war effort is to maximize the use of force so as to engage and defeat the enemy in battle.

The new type of war economy is almost totally the opposite. The new wars are 'globalized' wars. They involve the fragmentation and decentralization of the state. Participation is low relative to the population both because of lack of pay and because of lack of legitimacy on the part of the warring parties. There is very little domestic production, so the war effort is heavily dependent on local predation and external support. Battles are rare, most violence is directed against civilians, and cooperation between warring factions is common.

Those who conceive of war in traditional Clausewitzean terms, based on definable geo-political goals, fail to understand the underlying vested interests, both political and economic, in the continuation of war. They tend to assume that political solutions can be found without any need to address the underlying economic logic. At the same time, however, those who recognize the irrelevance of traditional perceptions of war, and observe the complexity of the political, social and economic relationships expressed in these wars, tend to conclude that this type of violence can be equated with anarchy. In these circumstances, the most that can be done is to treat the symptoms through, for example, humanitarian assistance.

In this chapter, I argue that it is possible to analyse the typical political economy of new wars so as to draw conclusions about possible alternative approaches. Indeed, the implication of such an analysis is that many of the well-meaning efforts of various international actors, based on inherited assumptions about the character of war, may turn out to be counterproductive. Conflict resolution from above may merely enhance the legitimacy of the warring parties and allow time for replenishment; humanitarian assistance may contribute to the functioning of the war economy; peacekeeping troops may lose legitimacy either by standing aside when terrible crimes are committed or by siding with groups who commit terrible crimes.

In the first section, I describe the various fighting units typical of contemporary wars and how they have emerged out of the disintegration of the state's formal security capacities. Then, I analyse patterns of violence and the character of military strategy and the way these have evolved out of the conflicts that developed during and after World War II as a way of reacting against or coping with modern conventional war – guerrilla warfare, counter-insurgency and the 'low-intensity' conflicts of the 1980s. Next, I consider how the fighting units acquire resources with which to fight the new wars and the interaction between the new pattern of violence and the social relations that are generated in the context of war. In the final section, I describe how the new wars, or rather the social conditions of the new wars, tend to spread.

The Privatization of Military Forces

Terms like 'failed', 'failing', 'fragile', 'weak' or 'collapsing' are increasingly used to describe countries with weak or non-existent central authority – the classic examples are Somalia and Afghanistan. Some scholars argue that many African states never enjoyed state sovereignty in the modern sense – that is, 'unquestioned physical control over the defined territory, but also an administrative presence throughout the country and the allegiance of the population to the idea of the state'.[1] One of the key characteristics of failing states is the loss of control over and fragmentation of the instruments of physical coercion. A disintegrative cycle sets in, which is almost the exact opposite of the integrative cycle through which modern states were established. The failure to sustain physical control over the territory and to command popular allegiance reduces the ability to collect taxes and greatly weakens the revenue base of the state. In addition, corruption and personalistic rule represent an added drain on state revenue. Often, the government can no longer afford reliable forms of tax collection; private agencies are sometimes employed who keep part of the takings, much as happened in Europe in the eighteenth century. Tax evasion is widespread both because of the loss of state legitimacy and because of the emergence of new forces who claim 'protection money'. This leads to outside pressure to cut government spending, which further reduces the capacity to maintain control and encourages the fragmentation of military units. Moreover, outside assistance is predicated on economic and political reforms which many of these states are constitutionally incapable of implementing. A downward spiral of loss of revenue and legitimacy, growing disorder, and military fragmentation creates the context in which the new wars take place. Effectively, the 'failure' of the state is accompanied by a growing privatization of violence.

Typically, the new wars are characterized by a multiplicity of types of fighting units, both public and private, state and non-state, or some kind of mixture. For the purpose of simplicity, I identify five main types: regular armed forces or remnants thereof; paramilitary groups; self-defence units; foreign mercenaries; and, finally, regular foreign troops, generally under international auspices.

Regular armed forces are in decay, particularly in areas of conflict. Cuts in military spending, declining prestige, shortages of equipment, spare parts, fuel and ammunition, and inadequate training all contribute to a profound loss of morale. In many African and post-Soviet states, soldiers no longer receive training or regular pay. They may have to seek out their own sources of funding, which contributes to indiscipline and breakdown of the military hierarchy. Often this leads to fragmentation, situations in which local army commanders act as local warlords, as in Tadjikistan. Or soldiers may engage in criminal behaviour as, for example, in Zaire (now the Democratic Republic of Congo), where unpaid soldiers were encouraged to loot or pillage. In other words, regular armed forces lose their character as the legitimate bearers of arms and become increasingly difficult to distinguish from private paramilitary groups. This is compounded in situations where the security forces were already fragmented as a result of deliberate policy; often there were border guards, a presidential guard and a gendarmerie, not to mention various types of internal security forces. By the end, President Mobutu of what was then Zaire could rely only on his personal guard to protect him. Saddam Hussein engaged in a similar proliferation of security agencies, and, as with Mobutu, it was only the motley group known as Firqat Fedayeen Saddam, Saddam's Martyrs, that offered sporadic resistance to the initial American invasion. Indeed in much of the Middle East, dictators rely on brutal internal security forces rather than regular armies; in both Tunisia and Egypt, the army was pivotal in the fall of dictators in 2011, while Muammar Gadafi was increasingly dependent on mercenaries recruited from Sub-Saharan Africa.

The most common fighting units are paramilitary groups, that is to say, autonomous groups of armed men generally centred on an individual leader. Often these groups are established by governments in order to distance themselves from the more extreme manifestations of violence. This was probably the case for Arkan's Tigers in Bosnia, or so Arkan himself insisted. Likewise, the pre-1994 Rwandan government recruited unemployed young men to a newly formed militia linked to the ruling party; they were given training by the Rwandan army and granted a small salary.[2] In a similar vein, the South African government secretly supplied arms and training to the Inkatha Freedom Party (IFP), which had been promoting the violent activities of groups of Zulu workers during the transition to democracy. Often, paramilitary groups are associated with particular extremist parties or political factions. In Georgia, after independence, each political party, except the

Greens, had its own militia; after his recall to power, Eduard Shevardnadze tried to re-establish a monopoly over the means of violence by welding together these militias into a regular army. It was this ragbag of armed bands that was defeated by a combination of the Abkhazian National Guard and Russian military units in Abkhazia. One of the most notorious paramilitary groups in Kosovo was known as 'Frenki's Boys'. According to intelligence sources, Franko Simatović was the link between Milošević and freelance paramilitary groups.

The paramilitary groups are often composed of redundant soldiers, or even whole units of redundant or defecting soldiers like the brigades in Iraq and more recently Syria. They also include common criminals, as in the former Yugoslavia, Iraq, Libya and now Syria, where many were deliberately released from prison for the purpose. And they may attract volunteers, often unemployed young men in search of a living, a cause or an adventure. They rarely wear uniforms, which makes them difficult to distinguish from non-combatants, although they often sport distinctive clothing or signs. Symbols of global material culture often serve as important quasi-uniforms; for example, Ray-Ban sunglasses, Adidas shoes, jogging suits and caps. Reportedly, Frenki's Boys had their headquarters at the back of a dress shop in Djakovica. They wore cowboy hats over ski masks, and painted Indian stripes on their faces. Their trademark was the sign of the Serbian Chetniks and a silhouette of a destroyed city with the words 'City Breakers' in English.[3]

The use of child soldiers is not uncommon in Africa; there have also been reports of fourteen-year-old boys operating in Serbian units. In Charles Taylor's National Patriotic Front of Liberia, for example, which invaded Sierra Leone on Christmas Eve 1989, some 30 per cent of the soldiers were said to be under the age of seventeen; Taylor even created a 'Boys' Own Unit'. He supported an invasion of Sierra Leone by a rather small number of rebels, after which the Sierra Leone government recruited large numbers of citizens into its army, including boys some of whom were as young as eight years old: 'Many of the boys recruited into the government army were street-children from Freetown, involved in petty theft before their recruitment. Now they were given an AK47 and a chance to engage in theft on a larger scale.'[4] RENAMO (Resistência

Nacional Mocambiçana – the movement founded by Portuguese Special Forces after the independence of Mozambique and supported by South Africa) also recruited children, some of whom were forced to return to their own villages and attack their families. Child soldiers were also used by the LTTE (Liberation Tigers of Tamil Eelam) in Sri Lanka.

Self-defence units are composed of volunteers who try to defend their localities. These would include local brigades in Bosnia–Herzegovina who tried to defend all the citizens of their locality, for example in Tuzla; self-defence units of both Hutus and Tutsis who tried to stop the massacres in 1994; the self-defence units in South Africa set up by the African National Congress (ANC) to defend localities from Inkatha; or the brigades of the Free Syrian Army. Such units are very difficult to sustain mainly because of inadequate resources. Where they are not defeated, they often end up cooperating with other armed groups and getting sucked into the conflict.

Foreign mercenaries include both individuals on contract to particular fighting units and mercenary bands. Among the former are former Russian officers working on contract with the new post-Soviet armies, and British and French soldiers made redundant by the post-Cold War cuts, who used to train, advise and even command armed groups during the wars in Bosnia and Croatia and still do so in various African countries. A growing phenomenon is private security companies, often recruited from retired soldiers from Britain or the United States, who are hired both by governments and by multinational companies and are often interconnected. During the 1990s, a notorious example was the South African mercenary company Executive Outcomes and its partner, the British company Sandline International. Sandline International became famous as a result of the scandal concerning arms sales to Sierra Leone in early 1998. Executive Outcomes has been credited with considerable military success in defending diamond mines in Sierra Leone and Angola. In February 1997 the government of Papua New Guinea hired Sandline International to launch a military assault against the secessionist Bougainville Revolutionary Army (BRA) and to reopen the Bougainville copper mine; Sandline International subcontracted the work to Executive Outcomes.[5] American private security companies like Blackwater, now Xe company, have become a characteristic feature of American interventions, especially in Iraq and Afghanistan. Particularly well-known names include MPRI (Military Professional Resources Inc.), which trained the Croatian army towards the end of the war in Bosnia and has now become part of L-3 Communications, and DymCorps, which tends to undertake policing duties, recently bought by Veritas Capital.

Foreign fighters may be motivated not only by money. Even before the Iraq war the *Mujahidiin*, veterans from the Afghan war, were generally to be found in all conflicts involving Islam, funded by the Islamic states, most notably Iran and Saudi Arabia. Since the 'War on Terror', so-called jihadists have joined the fight against the West in Iraq, Afghanistan, Somalia and Yemen as well as in terrorist incidents in different parts of the world.

The final category is regular foreign troops, usually operating under the umbrella of international organizations, mainly the UN but also NATO in Bosnia, Kosovo and Afghanistan, ECOMOG (Economic Community of West African States Ceasefire Monitoring Group) in Liberia, the African Union (AU) in Darfur, the EU in the DRC, Aceh, Chad and the Balkans, and the CIS (Commonwealth of Independent States) or OSCE, which have both provided umbrellas for different Russian peacekeeping operations. In general, these troops are not directly involved in the war, although their presence is very significant and I will discuss their role in chapter 6. In some cases, these troops have become involved in fighting, as in the case of ECOMOG in Liberia and Sierra Leone or Russian peacekeepers in Tadjikistan, and, in such instances, they have taken on some of the characteristics of the other fighting units. In the war in DRC, several neighbouring countries (Uganda, Angola, Rwanda, Burundi) sent troops to participate on different sides. And, of course, as I discuss in chapter 7, the United States and Britain and some other countries have troops in Iraq and Afghanistan.

With the exception of the final category, the small-scale character of the fighting units has much in common with those involved in guerrilla warfare. But they lack the hierarchy, order and vertical command systems that have been typical of guerrilla forces and that were borrowed from modern warfare as well as the structure of Leninist or Maoist political parties.

These various groups operate both autonomously and in coop-eration. What appear to be armies are actually horizontal coali-tions of breakaway units from the regular armed forces, local militia or self-defence units, criminal gangs, groups of fanatics, and hangers-on, who have negotiated partnerships, common projects, divisions of labour or spoils. Robert Reich's concept of the 'spider's web' to characterize the new global corporate structure, which I referred to in the previous chapter (see p. 76), is probably also applicable to the new warfare.

Because of cost, logistics and inadequate infrastructure and skills, these 'armies' rarely use heavy weapons, although where they are used they may well make a considerable difference. The Serbian monopoly of heavy artillery was important in Bosnia, as was the intervention of Russian units with aircraft and artillery in Abkhazia. One of the reasons given for the success of Executive Outcomes has been their ability 'to carry out sophisticated operations such as flying helicopter gunships and light ground-attack fixed-wing aircraft'.[6]

For the most part, light weapons are used – rifles, machine guns, hand grenades, landmines and, at the upper end of the scale, low-calibre artillery and short-range rockets. Although these weapons are often described as 'low-tech', they are the product of a long and sophisticated technological evolution. Compared with the weapons used in World War II, they are much lighter, easier to use and transport, more accurate and more difficult to detect. In contrast to heavy weapons, they can be used to great effect by unskilled soldiers, including children. Modern communications are also very important to enable the fighting groups to cooperate, especially radios and mobile telephones. US forces in Somalia were unable to eaves-drop the commercially bought cellular phones used by Somali militiamen. In the last decade, new technologies and tactics have developed, such as IEDs (improvised explosive devices) or suicide bombers.

The end of the Cold War and of related conflicts such as those in Afghanistan or South Africa greatly increased the availability of surplus weapons. In some cases, wars are fought with weapons raided from Cold War stockpiles; this was largely the case in Bosnia–Herzegovina. In other cases, redundant sol-diers sell their weapons on the black market, or small-scale producers (as in Pakistan) copy their designs. In addition, arms enterprises which have lost state markets seek new sources of demand. Certain conflicts, for example in Kashmir, took on a new character as a result of the influx of arms, in this case a spill-over from the conflict in Afghanistan. An important factor in the escalation of the conflict in Kosovo was the sudden availability of arms after the Albanian state collapsed in the summer of 1997; arms caches were opened and hundreds of thousands of Kalashnikovs were available for sale at a few dollars each and could easily be brought across the border into Kosovo. The new wars could be viewed as a form of military waste-disposal – a way of using up unwanted surplus arms generated by the Cold War, the biggest military build-up in history.

Patterns of Violence

The techniques of these fighting units owe much to the types of warfare that developed during and after World War II as a reaction to modern war. Revolutionary warfare, as articulated by Mao Tse-tung and Che Guevara, developed tactics that were designed to find a way around large-scale concentrations of conventional forces and that were almost counter to conventional strategic theory.

The central objective of revolutionary warfare is the control of territory through gaining support of the local population rather than through capturing territory from enemy forces. The zones under revolutionary control are usually in remote parts of the country which cannot easily be reached by the central administration. They provide bases from which the military forces can engage in tactics which sap the morale and efficiency of enemy forces. Revolutionary warfare has some similarities with manoeuvre theory. It involves decentralized dispersed military activity, with a great emphasis on surprise and mobility. But a key feature of revolutionary warfare is the avoidance of head-on collisions which guerrilla units are likely to lose because of inferior numbers and equipment. Strategic retreats are frequent. According to Mao Tse-tung: 'The ability to run away is precisely one of the characteristics of guerrillas. Running away is the chief means of getting out of passivity and regaining the initiative.'[7] Great stress is placed by all revolutionary writers on winning 'hearts and minds', not just in the territory under revolutionary control but in enemy territory as well, so that the guerrilla can operate, according to Mao's well-known dictum, 'like a fish in the sea', although, of course, terroristic methods were also used.

Counter-insurgency, which has been an almost universal failure,[8] was designed to counter this type of warfare using conventional military forces. Although it has been reformulated as a result of experiences in Iraq and Afghanistan, as I elaborate in chapter 7, historically, the main strategy was to destroy the environment in which the revolutionaries operate, to poison the sea for the fish. Techniques like forcible resettlement developed by the French in Algeria and the British in Malaya, or area destruction through scattering mines or herbicides or napalm developed by the Americans in Vietnam, have also been used by, for example, the Indonesians in East Timor or the Turkish government against the Kurds.

The new warfare borrows from both revolutionary warfare and classic counter-insurgency. It borrows from revolutionary warfare the strategy of controlling territory through political means rather than through capturing territory from enemy forces. This is somewhat easier than it was for revolutionary forces, since in most cases the central authority is very weak and the main contenders for the control of territory are not governments with conventional modern forces but rather similar types of fighting units, even if they bear the name of regular armies. Nevertheless, as in the case of revolutionary warfare, the various factions continue to avoid battle mainly in order to conserve men and equipment. Strategic retreats are typical and ground is conceded to what appears to be the stronger party. Often, the various factions cooperate in dividing up territory between them.

An important difference between revolutionaries and the new warriors, however, is the method of political control. For the revolutionaries, ideology was very important; even though fear was a significant element, popular support and allegiance to the revolutionary idea was the central aim. Hence, the revolutionaries tried to build model societies in the areas under their control. In contrast, the new warriors establish political control through allegiance to a label rather than an idea. In the brave new democratized world, where political mobilization is based on labels and where elections and referenda are often forms of census-taking, this means that the majority of people living in the territory under control must admit to the right label. Anyone else has to be eliminated. Indeed, even in non-democratized areas, fear of opposition, dissidence or insurgency reinforces this demand for homogeneity of population based on identity.

This is why the main method of territorial control is not popular support, as in the case of revolutionary warfare, but population displacement – getting rid of all possible opponents. To achieve this, the new warfare borrows from counter-insurgency techniques for poisoning the sea – techniques which were refined by guerrilla movements created or promoted by Western governments with experience of counter-insurgency to topple left-wing governments in the 'low-intensity' conflicts of the 1980s, such as RENAMO in Mozambique, the *Mujahidiin* in Afghanistan, or the Contras in Nicaragua. Indeed, this approach was a reaction to the failure of counter-insurgency in Vietnam and Southern Africa and the implicit realization that a conventional modern war is no longer a viable option.

Instead of a favourable environment for the guerrilla, the new warfare aims to create an unfavourable environment for all those people it cannot control. Control of one's own side depends not on positive benefits, since in the impoverished, disorderly conditions of the new warfare there is not much that can be offered. Rather, it depends on continuing fear and insecurity and on the perpetuation of hatred of the other. Hence the importance of extreme and conspicuous atrocity and of involving as many people as possible in these crimes so as to establish a shared complicity, to sanction violence against a hated 'other' and to deepen divisions.

The techniques of population displacement include:

1   Systematic murder of those with different labels, as in Rwanda. The killing of Tutsis in 1994 was directed by government officials and the army. According to Human Rights Watch: 'In such places as the commune of Nyakizu in Southern Rwanda, local officials and other killers came to "work" every morning. After they had put in a full day's "work" killing Tutsi, they went home "singing" at quitting time ... The "workers" returned each day until the job had been finished – that is, until all the Tutsi had been killed.'[9]

2   Ethnic cleansing, that is to say, forcible population expulsion, as in Bosnia–Herzegovina (see chapter 3) or the Transcaucasus or Darfur. In Abkhazia, another example, the Abkhaz inhabitants accounted for only 17 per cent of the population. In order to control the territory, the secessionist forces had to expel most of the remaining population, mainly Georgian. Even after the expulsion of the Georgians, the Abkhaz remain a minority. A typical tactic is to instil fear through grisly and well-publicized executions or atrocities.

3   Rendering an area uninhabitable. This can be done physically, through scattering anti-personnel landmines or through the use of shells and rockets against civilian targets, especially homes, hospitals or crowded places such as markets or water sources. It can be done economically through forced famines or sieges. By depriving the people of their livelihood, they either die of hunger, as in Southern Sudan, or they are forced to migrate. And it can be done psychologically by instilling unbearable memories of what was once home, by desecrating whatever has social meaning. One method is the destruction of history and culture by removing the physical landmarks that define the social environment for particular groups of people. The destruction of religious buildings and historic monuments is supposed to erase all traces of cultural claim to a particular area. In Banja Luka, at the height of the war, the Serbs destroyed all seventeen mosques and all but one of the Catholic churches. In particular, they flattened two very beautiful sixteenth-century mosques; they were demolished on a Friday, and on Monday the ground was razed and turfed over. The wanton destruction of the ancient Buddhist statues in Afghanistan by the Taliban was presumably supposed to achieve something similar. Another method is defilement through systematic rape and sexual abuse, which is characteristic of several wars, or by other public and very visible acts of brutality. Psychological methods have the advantage of differentiating between people with different labels.

These techniques violate international law, whether we are talking about international humanitarian law, human rights law, or the Genocide Convention. Essentially, what were considered to be undesirable and illegitimate side-effects of old war have become central to the mode of fighting in the new wars. It is sometimes said that the new wars are a reversion to primitivism. But primitive wars were highly ritualistic and hedged in by social constraints. These wars are rational in the sense that they apply rational thinking to the aims of war and refuse normative constraints.

The pattern of violence in the new type of warfare is confirmed by the statistics of the new wars. The tendency to avoid battle and to direct most violence against civilians is evidenced by the dramatic increase in the ratio of civilian to military casualties. The exact numbers are hotly disputed as I discuss in the afterword to this book. But there is general agreement about the decline in the share of battle-related deaths to overall deaths so that nowadays the number of both military and civilians killed in direct fire between the warring parties is tiny compared with those killed from what is sometimes known as one-sided violence against civilians and other war-related deaths.[10] Likewise, the number of regular soldiers killed in wars is very small in comparison with the total numbers of casualties.

The importance of population displacement is evidenced by the figures on refugees and displaced persons. According to UNHCR, the global refugee population rose from 2.4 million people in 1975 to 10.5 million people in 1985 and 14.4 million people in 1995, and subsequently declined to 9.6 million in 2004, primarily as a consequence of increased repatriation, and rose again to 15.4 million in 2010.[11] This figure includes only refugees who cross international boundaries. According to the IDMC (Internal Displacement Monitoring Centre) in Geneva, the number of internally displaced people increased from 17 million in 1998 to 27.5 million in 2010.[12] It should be noted, of course, that these numbers are cumulative unless displaced people are repatriated. Also methods of estimating numbers of internally displaced persons have greatly improved so the earlier figures may be underestimated. Nevertheless there does seem to be a trend towards increasing displacement per conflict. Using the American Refugee Council data, Myron Weiner calculated that the number of refugees and internally displaced persons per conflict increased from 327,000 in 1969 to

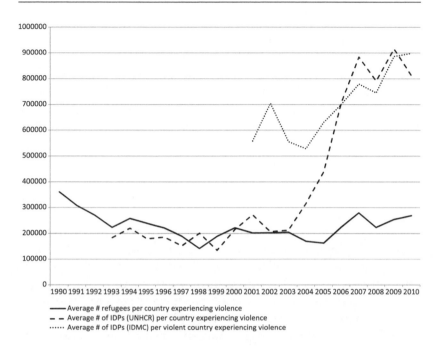

Figure 5.1 *Numbers of refugees and internally displaced persons in countries experiencing violence 1990–2010*

1,316,000 in 1992.[13] (1992 was, of course, a peak year for conflict.) Using the Uppsala Conflict database and figures from UNHCR and the IDMC, an upward trend in refugees and internally displaced persons can be observed per conflict. Figure 5.1 shows the rise in annual numbers of refugees and internally displaced persons in countries experiencing not only armed conflict but what the UCDP describes as sub-state conflict and one-sided violence.

Financing the War Effort

The new wars take place in a context which could be represented as an extreme version of globalization. Territorially based production more or less collapses either as a result of liberalization and the withdrawal of state support; or through physical destruction (pillage, shelling, etc.); or because markets are cut off as a result of the disintegration of states, fighting, or deliberate blockades imposed by outside powers, or, more likely, by fighting units on the ground; or because spare parts, raw materials and fuel are impossible to acquire. In some cases, a few valuable commodities continue to be produced – e.g. diamonds in Angola and Sierra Leone, lapis lazuli and emeralds in Afghanistan, oil in Angola or Chechnya or Iraq, drugs in Colombia, Afghanistan and Tadjikistan – and they provide a source of income for whoever can offer 'protection'. Unemployment is very high and, as long as governments continue to spend, inflation is rampant. In extreme cases, the currency collapses to be replaced by barter, the use of valuable commodities as currency or the circulation of foreign currencies, e.g., dollars or euros.

Given the erosion of the tax base both because of the collapse of production and because of the difficulties of collection, governments, like privatized military groups, need to seek alternative sources of funding in order to sustain their violent activities. Given the collapse of productive activity, the main sources of funding are either what Mark Duffield calls 'asset transfer',[14] i.e. the redistribution of existing assets so as to favour the fighting units, or external assistance. The simplest forms of asset transfer are looting, robbery, extortion, pillage and hostage-taking. This is widespread in all contemporary wars. Rich people are killed and their gold and valuables stolen; property is transferred in the aftermath of ethnic cleansing; cattle and livestock are raided by militiamen;[15] shops and factories are looted when towns are taken. Hostages are captured and exchanged for food, weapons or other hostages, prisoners of war or dead bodies.

A second form of asset transfer is market pressure. A typical characteristic of the new wars is the numerous checkpoints which control the supply of food and necessities. Sieges and blockades, the division of territory between different paramilitary groups, allow the fighting units to control market prices. Thus a typical pattern, observed in Sudan, former Yugoslavia and other places, is that urban dwellers or even farmers will be forced to sell their assets – cars, fridges, televisions or cows – at ridiculously low prices in exchange for highly priced necessities simply in order to survive.

More sophisticated income-generating activities include 'war taxes' or 'protection' money from the production of primary commodities and various forms of illegal trading. The production and sale of drugs is a key source of income in Afghanistan, Colombia, Peru and Tadjikistan. It was estimated in the 1990s that income from drugs accounted for 70 per cent of the opposition revenue in Tadjikistan, while the income of the Colombian guerrillas was said to amount to some $US800 million a year, which compares with government defence expenditure of $US1.4 billion.[16] Chechen warlords sold oil from backyard oil wells to Russian commanders, who in turn sold their oil provided by the Russian Ministry of Defence on Moscow markets thereby financing soldiers' wages. Revenue from oil and natural gas fuelled the fighting in Angola, parts of Colombia, and Aceh in Indonesia while smuggling in oil products helps to sustain Nagorno-Karabakh.[17] Sanctions-busting and trading in drugs, arms or laundered money are all examples of revenue-raising criminal activities in which the various military groups are engaged.

However, given the collapse of domestic production, external assistance is crucial, since arms, ammunition and food, not to mention Mercedes cars or Ray-Ban sunglasses, have to be imported. External assistance can take the following forms:

1   Remittances from abroad to individual families, for example, Sudanese or Palestinian workers in the oil-rich countries of the Middle East, Bosnian and Croatian workers in Germany or Austria. These remittances can be converted into military resources through the various forms of asset transfer described above.
2   Direct assistance from the diaspora living abroad. This includes material assistance, arms and money, for example from Irish Americans to the IRA, from Armenians all over the world to Nagorno-Karabakh, from Canadian Croatians to the ruling Croatian party, and so on.
3   Assistance from foreign governments. During the Cold War period, both regular forces and guerrillas relied on their superpower patrons. This source of assistance has largely dried up, although the United States still provides support to a number of governments. Neighbouring states often fund particular factions, to assist minorities or because of the presence of large numbers of refugees or because of involvement in various types of (illegal) trading arrangements. Thus Serbia and Croatia have provided support to

their client statelets in Bosnia–Herzegovina; Armenia aids Nagorno-Karabakh; Russia has backed a variety of secessionist movements on its borders, whether as a way of re-establishing control over post-Soviet space, or because of mafia or military vested interests, is a matter for speculation; Rwanda encouraged the opposition in DRC as a way of preventing Hutu militiamen from operating from refugee camps there; and Uganda supported the Rwandan Patriotic Front which took over after the massacres of 1994 and continues to abet the SPLA in Southern Sudan (and, in return, the Sudanese government supports the Lord's Resistance Army in Uganda). Other foreign governments that offer a source of finance include former colonial powers concerned about 'stability', for example France and Belgium in Central Africa, or Islamic states.

4   Humanitarian assistance. There are various ways in which both governments and warring factions divert humanitarian assistance for their own use. Indeed, donors regard a 5 per cent diversion of humanitarian aid or even more as acceptable in view of the needs of the most vulnerable parts of the population. The most common method is 'customs duties'. The Bosnian Croats demanded 27 per cent for humanitarian assistance transported through so-called Herzeg–Bosne, which, at the height of the war, was the only way to reach certain areas in Central Bosnia. But there are also other ways, including robbery and ambush. By insisting on the use of an overvalued official exchange rate, both the Sudanese and Ethiopian governments were able to profit from the provision of humanitarian aid.

Essentially, the fragmentation and informalization of war is paralleled by the informalization of the economy. In place of the national formal economy, with its emphasis on industrial production and state regulation, a new type of globalized informal economy is established in which external flows, especially humanitarian assistance and remittances from abroad, are integrated into a local and regional economy based on asset transfer and extra-legal trading. Figure 5.2 illustrates the typical resource flows of a new war. It is assumed that there is no production and no taxation. Instead, external support to ordinary people, in the form of remittances and humanitarian

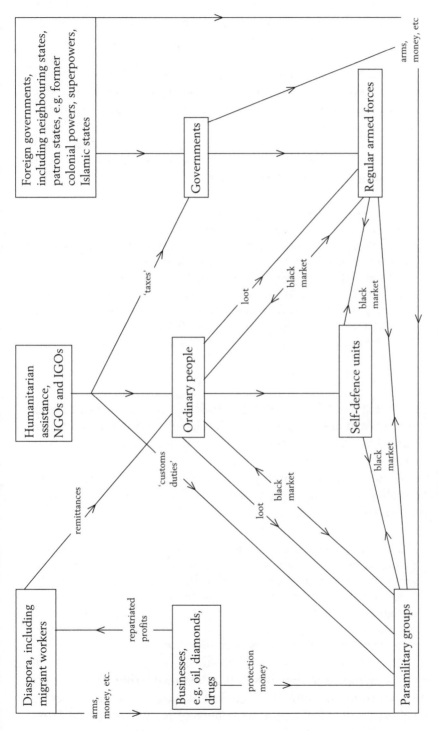

Figure 5.2 *Resource flows in new wars*

assistance, is recycled via various forms of asset transfer and black-market trading into military resources. Direct assistance from foreign governments, protection money from producers of commodities, and assistance from the diaspora enhance the capacity of the various fighting units to extract further resources from ordinary people and thus sustain their military efforts.

Mark Duffield describes how this functioned in the Sudanese case, where an illegal dollar trade involving Sudan, Zaire and Uganda was operated, making use of relief convoys both for transport and to control prices:

> In the case of Sudan, the parallel economy consists of a number of interconnecting levels or systems. Local asset transfer is linked to national level extra-legal mercantile activity. In turn, this articulates with higher-level political and state relations together with regional and international parallel networks which trade in commodities and hard currency. It is this level that provides the initial site for the integration of international aid and relief assistance with the parallel economy. As assets flow upwards and outwards, culminating in capital flight, international assistance flows downwards through the same or related systems of power.[18]

Just as it is possible to find examples of military cooperation between fighting units so as to divide up territory or to foster mutual hatred among the respective populations, so it is possible to find examples of economic cooperation. David Keen describes what is known as the 'sell-game' in Sierra Leone, through which government forces sell arms and ammunition to the rebels:

> [Government forces] withdraw from a town, leaving arms and ammunition for the rebels behind them. The rebels pick up the arms and extract the loot, mostly in the form of cash, from the townspeople and then they themselves retreat. At this point, the government forces reoccupy the town and engage in their own looting, usually of property (which the rebels find hard to dispose of) as well as engaging in illegal mining.[19]

John Simpson describes how Peruvian government soldiers set free captured Shining Path guerrillas 'apparently in order to perpetuate insecurity in areas where officers can benefit from illegal trading, in this case principally the trade in cocaine.'[20] There are similar examples in the Bosnian War, which I have described in chapter 3.

Some writers argue that economic motivation explains the new type of warfare and this has generated a debate among scholars about greed versus grievance.[21] David Keen suggests that a 'war where one avoids battles but picks on unarmed civilians and perhaps eventually acquires a Mercedes may make more sense ... [than] risking death in the name of the nation-state with little or no prospect of significant financial gain.'[22] But economic motivation alone is insufficient to explain the scale, brutality and sheer viciousness of new wars.[23] No doubt some join the fighting as a way of legitimizing criminal activities, providing a political justification for what they do and socially sanctioning otherwise illegal methods of financial gain. No doubt there are others – rational power-seekers, extreme fanatics or victims intent on revenge – who engage in criminal activities to sustain their political military goals. Yet others are press-ganged into the fighting, propelled by fear and hunger.

The point is rather that the modern distinctions between the political and the economic, the public and the private, the military and the civil are breaking down. Political control is required to embed the new coercive forms of economic exchange, which in turn are required to provide a viable financial basis for the new gangsters/powerholders in the context of state disintegration and economic marginalization. A new retrograde set of social relationships is being established in which economics and violence are deeply intertwined within the shared framework of identity politics.

The Spread of Violence

The new type of warfare is a predatory social condition.[24] While it may be possible to contain particular groups or individuals, it is very difficult to contain the social condition either in space or in time. Neighbouring countries are the most immediately affected. The cost of the war in terms of lost trade, especially where sanctions or communications blockades are introduced or where borders are closed, either deliberately or because of fighting; the burden of refugees, since generally it is the neighbouring states who accept the largest numbers; the spread of illegal circuits of trade; and the spillover of identity politics – all these factors reproduce the conditions that nurture the forms of violence.

The NGO Saferworld has enumerated the cost of conflict to neighbouring countries in several cases. One example is the war in Mozambique, which was an important trade route for landlocked countries such as Zambia, Zimbabwe, Malawi, Botswana and Swaziland. Malawi lost all its trade with Mozambique, and the additional costs of transport during the height of the war were estimated at 11 per cent of annual export earnings; likewise, trade with Zimbabwe fell dramatically and the cost of rerouting goods through South Africa was estimated at $US825 million at 1988 prices.[25] In the Balkans, the decline in GDP following the wars in Croatia and Bosnia–Herzegovina, as a result of the loss of trade following the closure of borders and sanctions and the increased cost of transportation, was more or less inversely proportionate to distance from the epicentre of violence. The decline in GDP in Bosnia–Herzegovina was most dramatic, falling from $US2,719 per head before the war broke out to just $US250 per head when the war ended. Surrounding Bosnia–Herzegovina is an inner ring of countries – Serbia/Montenegro, Croatia and Macedonia – whose GDPs fell to 49 per cent, 65 per cent and 55 per cent of their 1989 levels, respectively. By 1996, Serbia/Montenegro and Macedonia had just managed to arrest the decline, while Croatia was able to achieve a very small growth rate. Surrounding these three countries is an outer ring of further affected countries – Albania, Bulgaria, Romania and Slovenia – whose GDPs fell to 81 per cent, 88 per cent, 73 per cent and 90 per cent of their 1989 levels, respectively. Finally, the outermost ring – Hungary, Greece and Turkey – all also reported economic losses as a consequence of the war.[26]

As well as direct economic costs, the neighbouring countries bear the main burden of refugees. Most refugees are based in neighbouring countries. According to UNHCR figures, out of the 14.5 million refugees recorded for 1995, the majority (6.7 million and 5.0 million, respectively) were based in Africa and Asia. Countries hosting more than 500,000 refugees included Guinea (from Liberia and Sierra Leone), Sudan (mainly from Ethiopia, Eritrea and Chad), Tanzania (mainly from Rwanda and Burundi), Zaire (which, as of 1995, had received 1.7 million refugees, of whom 1.2 million came from Rwanda and the remainder mainly from Angola, Burundi and Sudan), Iran (from Afghanistan and Iraq), Pakistan (also from Afghanistan and Iraq), Germany (mainly from the former Yugoslavia) and the United States. In Europe, after Germany, the biggest recipients of refugees have been Croatia and Serbia/Montenegro. In 2004, the pattern had changed somewhat. Out of the 9.6 million refugees, some 60 per cent were based in Africa, the Middle East and Central Asia. The biggest recipients of refugees were Iran and Pakistan (from Afghanistan), Germany and Tanzania. As of 2010 nearly 80 per cent of the 9.9 million refugees of concern to UNHCR were based in Africa and Asia (including the Middle East). Countries hosting more than 500,000 refugees were Iran, Pakistan and Syria, reflecting the dominance of refugees from Afghanistan and Iraq.[27]

Not only are these huge concentrations of refugees an immense economic burden on countries that are already poor, but they represent a permanent source of tension between the refugees and the host populations – for economic reasons, since they are competing for resources; for political reasons, since they constitute a permanent pressure on host governments to take action in order that they can return; and for security reasons, because the camps are often used as bases for various radical factions. The most long-standing example of both economic and political burdens is the Palestinian refugees squashed into the West Bank and Gaza or based in Jordan and the Lebanon. As in the case of the Palestinian refugees, up to a million or so Azeri refugees from Nagorno-Karabakh in Azerbaijan, or the Georgian IDPs (internally displaced persons) from Abkhazia in Georgia or the refugees and IDPs in the former Yugoslav republics all constitute a permanent source of political pressure for radical action. In Zaire (now DRC), the Hutu refugee camps served as a base for Hutu militiamen and contributed to the mobilization of Zairian Tutsis against the Mobutu regime.

Illegal circuits of trade are another conduit for the spread of the new type of war economy. Trade routes necessarily cross borders. The instability in Albania in the mid-1990s was mainly the consequence of the growth of mafia groups well connected to the ruling circles involved in sanctions-busting to

Serbia/Montenegro and gun-running to Bosnia–Herzegovina. The pyramid schemes that collapsed so dramatically were used to finance these activities – a classic case of asset transfer. The huge transfer of arms by the United States to Afghan guerrilla groups in the 1980s (much of which was largely diverted) transformed itself into networks of arms and drug trade covering Afghanistan, Pakistan, Kashmir and Tadjikistan.[28] Mark Duffield shows how the illegal dollar trade linked to the war in Sudan involved 'Zairois with gold wanting imported goods, food and fuel; Sudanese with dollars wanting food, clothing and coffee; and Ugandans with imported goods wanting gold and dollars for Kampala's parallel markets.'[29]

Finally, the politics of identity, itself, has a tendency to spread. All identity-based groups, whether defined in terms of language, religion or some other form of differentiation, spill over borders; after all, it is precisely the heterogeneity of identities that offers the opportunity for various forms of exclusivism. Majorities in one country are minorities in another: Tutsis in Rwanda, Burundi and DRC; Russians in most post-Soviet states, especially so-called Cossacks on the borders of Russia; Islamic groups in Central Asia – these are among the many vectors through which identity politics passes.

It is possible to identify spreading regional clusters characterized by this predatory social condition of the new war economies. Myron Weiner calls them 'bad neighbourhoods'. The clearest examples are the Balkan region surrounding Bosnia–Herzegovina; the Caucasus stretching south from Chechnya as far as Western Turkey and Northern Iran; the Horn of Africa, including Ethiopia, Eritrea, Somalia and Sudan; Central Africa, especially Rwanda, Burundi and the Democratic Republic of Congo; and Central Asia, from Tadjikistan to India. The countries hosting Palestinian refugees might be treated as another cluster; since Israel made peace with the neighbouring states, the conflict is no longer expressed in terms of inter-state war and has begun to exhibit many of the characteristics of the new types of conflict.

Conclusion

The new wars have political goals. The aim is political mobilization on the basis of identity. The military strategy for achieving this aim is population displacement and destabilization so as to get rid of those whose identity is different and to foment hatred and fear. Nevertheless, this divisive and exclusive form of politics cannot be disentangled from its economic basis. The various political/military factions plunder the assets of ordinary people as well as the remnants of the state, and cream off external assistance destined for the victims, in a way that is only possible in conditions of war or near war. In other words, war provides a legitimation for various criminal forms of private aggrandizement while at the same time these are necessary sources of revenue in order to sustain the war. The warring parties need more or less permanent conflict both to reproduce their positions of power and for access to resources.

While this predatory set of social relationships is most prevalent in the war zones, it also characterizes the surrounding regions. Because participation in the war is relatively low (in Bosnia, only 6.5 per cent of the population took part directly in the prosecution of the war), the differences between zones of war and apparent zones of peace are not nearly as marked as in earlier periods. Just as it is difficult to distinguish between the political and the economic, public and private, military and civil, so it is increasingly difficult to distinguish between war and peace. The new war economy could be represented as a continuum, starting with the combination of criminality and racism to be found in the inner cities of Europe and North America and reaching its most acute manifestation in the areas where the scale of violence is greatest.

If violence and predation are to be found in what are considered zones of peace, so it is possible to find islands of civility in nearly all the war zones. They are known about far less than violence and criminality, because it is these and not normality that is generally reported. But there are regions where local state apparatuses continue to function, where taxes are raised, services are provided and some production is maintained. There are groups who defend humanistic values and refuse the politics of particularism. The town of Tuzla in Bosnia–Herzegovina represents one celebrated example. The self-defence units created in Southern Rwanda are another example. In isolation, these islands of civility are difficult to preserve, squeezed by the polarization of violence, but the very fragmentary and decentralized character of the new type of warfare makes such examples possible.

Precisely because the new wars are a social condition that arises as the formal political economy withers, they are very difficult to end. Diplomatic negotiations from above fail to take into account the underlying social relations; they treat the various factions as though they were proto-states. Temporary ceasefires or truces may merely legitimize new agreements or partnerships that, for the moment, suit the various factions.

Peacekeeping troops sent in to monitor ceasefires which reflect the status quo may help to maintain a division of territory and to prevent the return of refugees. Economic reconstruction channelled through existing 'political authorities' may merely provide new sources of revenue as local assets dry up. As long as the power relations remain the same, sooner or later the violence will start again.

Fear, hatred and predation are not recipes for long-term viable polities; indeed, this type of war economy is perennially on the edge of exhaustion. This does not mean, however, that they will disappear of their own accord. There has to be some alternative. In the next chapter, I will consider the possibilities for such an alternative; in particular, how islands of civility might offer a counterlogic to the new warfare.

6

Towards a Cosmopolitan Approach

After the end of the Cold War, there was a lot of optimism about the possibilities for solving global problems, particularly wars. In the *Agenda for Peace*, the UN Secretary-General Boutros Boutros-Ghali talked about the 'second chance' for the UN now its activities were no longer blocked by the Cold War. The term 'international community', implying a cohesive group of governments acting through international organizations, entered into everyday usage. Conflicts in a number of countries seemed close to resolution – Cambodia, Namibia, Angola, South Africa, Nicaragua, Afghanistan. And in those conflicts that were not resolved, the idea, enunciated by the French minister and former director of Médecins Sans Frontières Bernard Kouchner, of a right/duty to intervene for humanitarian purposes, seemed to be gaining widespread acceptance.

The number of UN peacekeeping operations increased dramatically in the 1990s, as did the range of tasks they were asked to perform, including the delivery of humanitarian aid, the protection of people in safe havens, disarmament and demobilization, creating a secure environment for elections and reporting violations of international humanitarian law, in addition to the traditional tasks of monitoring and maintaining ceasefires. Mandates were also strengthened; in both Somalia and Bosnia, peacekeeping troops were authorized to act under Chapter VII of the UN Charter, which allows the use of force.

Moreover, the UN was not the only umbrella for multilateral peacekeeping operations; regional organizations such as NATO, the EU, the CIS, the AU or the Economic Community of West African States (ECOWAS) were also responsible for organizing peacekeeping missions. In 2001, the International Commission on Sovereignty and Intervention chaired by Gareth Evans and Mahomed Sahnoun came up with the concept of 'Responsibility to Protect', which was formally adopted by the United Nations General Assembly in 2005 and has been increasingly incorporated into UN doctrines.[1]

Yet despite the hopes and good intentions, the experience so far of what has come to be known as humanitarian intervention has been frustrating, to say the least. At best, people have been fed and fragile ceasefires have been agreed, although it is not clear whether this can be attributed to the presence of peacekeeping troops. At worst, the UN has been shamed and humiliated, as, for example, when it failed to prevent genocide in Rwanda, when the so-called safe haven of Srebrenica was overrun by Bosnian Serbs, or when the hunt for the Somali warlord Aideed ended in a mixture of farce and tragedy. Moreover, the term humanitarian intervention has been used to justify wars, as in Kosovo, and now Iraq and Afghanistan, giving rise to scepticism about the whole concept; hence the phrase 'military humanism' coined by Noam Chomsky.[2] Even the recent intervention in Libya, hailed by some as the first example of 'Responsibility to Protect', raises questions about the way the term is being used.

There have been many explanations for the failures – the short-termism of politicians, the role of the media, which raises public consciousness at particular times and particular places, the lack of coordination of governments and international agencies, inadequate resources – and all of these have some merit. But the most important explanation is misperception, the persistence of inherited ways of thinking about organized violence, the inability to understand the character and logic of the new warfare. One response to the new wars has been to treat them as Clausewitzean wars in which the warring parties are states or, if not states, groups with a claim to statehood. Many of the terms used, such as 'intervention', 'peacekeeping', 'peace enforcement', 'sovereignty', 'civil war', are drawn from conceptions of the nation-state and of modern war that are not only difficult to apply in the current context, but may actually pose an obstacle to appropriate action. The other response is fatalistic. Because the wars cannot be understood in traditional terms, they are thought to represent a reversion to primitivism or anarchy, and the most that can be done, therefore, is to ameliorate the symptoms. In other words, wars are treated as natural disasters; hence the use of terms such as 'complex emergencies', which are emptied of political meaning. Indeed the very term 'humanitarian' is supposed to have a non-political meaning. It has come to be associated with the provision of humanitarian relief assistance in wars, or help to non-combatants or the wounded, rather than with respect for human rights which was implied in the classic usage of the term 'humanitarian intervention'.[3]

The analysis in the previous chapters implies a different approach towards trying to solve these conflicts. What is needed is a much more political response to the new wars. A strategy of capturing 'hearts and minds' needs to be counterposed to the strategy of sowing 'fear and hate'. A politics of inclusion needs to be counterposed against the politics of exclusion. Respect for international principles and legal norms needs to be counterposed against the criminality of the warlords. In short, what is needed is a new form of cosmopolitan political mobilization, which embraces both the so-called international community and local populations, and which is capable of countering the submission to various types of particularism. A sceptic might argue that a form of cosmopolitan politics is already on the international agenda; certainly, respect for human rights, abhorrence of genocide and ethnic cleansing are increasingly part of the accepted rhetoric of political leaders. But political mobilization involves more than this; it has to override other considerations – geo-politics or short-term domestic concerns; it has to constitute the primary guide to policy and action which has not been the case up to now.

In this chapter, I develop this argument, first with some general considerations about the construction of legitimacy and the terminology of humanitarian intervention; second, I will explore what a cosmopolitan approach might mean in political, military and economic terms.

The Reconstruction of Legitimacy

The key to the control of violence is the reconstruction of legitimacy. I agree with Hannah Arendt when she says that power rests on legitimacy and not on violence. By legitimacy, I mean both consent and even support for political institutions, as well as the notion that these institutions acquire their authority on the basis of operating within an agreed set of rules – the rule of law. Arendt claims that:

> No government exclusively based on the means of violence has ever existed ... Single men without others to support them never have enough power to use violence successfully. Hence, in domestic affairs, violence functions as the last resort of power against criminals or rebels – that is, against single individuals who, as it were, refuse to be overpowered by the consensus of the majority. And as for actual warfare ... an enormous superiority in the means of violence can become helpless if confronted with an ill-equipped but well-organized opponent who is much more powerful.[4]

The same point is made by Giddens. The internal pacification of modern states was achieved not by violence, but by the extension of the rule of law and, concomitantly, the administrative reach of the state, including the extension of surveillance. The monopoly of legitimate organized violence implied the control of violence and much less reliance on the use of physical coercion, except, of course, in the international arena. Pre-modern states were much more violent in domestic affairs than the modern state, but also much less powerful. In so far as external violence contributed to internal pacification, it was an indirect contribution, arising from the increased legitimacy of the state associated with the defence of territory from external enemies and the augmentation of administrative capacities.

In the new wars, the monopoly of legitimate violence has broken down. And what is crucial is not the privatization of violence, as such, but the breakdown of legitimacy. As I have argued in the previous chapter, the goals of the new warfare are particularistic. The strategy is political control on the basis of exclusion – in particular, population displacement – and the tactics for achieving this goal are terror and destabilization. For this reason, it is virtually impossible for any of the warring parties to re-establish legitimacy. Violence may be controlled sporadically through uneasy truces and ceasefires, but in situations in which the moral, administrative and practical constraints against private violence have broken down, they rarely last long. At the same time, however, isolated citizens' groups or political parties who try to re-establish legitimacy on the basis of inclusive politics are relatively powerless in conditions of continuing violence.

'Cosmopolitanism', used in a Kantian sense, implies the existence of a human community with certain shared rights and obligations. In 'Perpetual Peace', Kant envisaged a world federation of democratic states in which cosmopolitan right is confined to the right of 'hospitality' – strangers and foreigners should be welcomed and treated with respect.[5] I use the term more extensively to refer both to a positive political vision, embracing tolerance, multiculturalism, civility and democracy, and to a more legalistic respect for certain overriding universal principles which should guide political communities at various levels, including the global level. In other words, cosmopolitanism combines respect for universal human principles with a commitment to non-sectarianism and even more strongly a celebration of cultural diversity, an appreciation and a pride in the different ways of being human.

The underlying human principles are already contained in various treaties and conventions that comprise the body of international law.[6] In chapter 2, I referred to the various rules of engagement and laws of war which deal with the abuses of armed power. Laws and customs of war which date back to early modern times were codified in the nineteenth and twentieth centuries; particularly important were the Geneva Conventions sponsored by the ICRC and the Hague Conferences of 1899 and 1907. The Nuremberg trials after World War II marked the first enforcement of 'war crimes' or, even more significantly, 'crimes against humanity'. To what was known as international humanitarian law, human rights norms were added in the post-war period. The difference between humanitarian and human rights law has to do largely with whether violation of the law takes place in war or peacetime. The former is confined to abuses of power in wartime situations. The assumption tends to be that war is usually modern inter-state war and that such abuses are inflicted by a foreign power – in other words, aggression. The latter is equally concerned with abuses of power in peacetime, in particular those inflicted by a government against its citizens – in other words, repression.[7]

The violations of international norms with which both bodies of law are concerned are, in fact, those which form the core of the new mode of warfare. As I have argued, in the new wars the classic distinctions between internal and external, war and peace, aggression and repression are breaking down. A war crime is at one and the same time a massive violation of human rights. A number of writers have suggested that humanitarian law should be combined with human rights law to form 'humane' or 'cosmopolitan' law.[8] More recently Rudi Teitel has coined the term 'Humanity's Law'. Elements of a cosmopolitan regime do already exist.[9] NGOs and the media draw attention to violations of human rights or to war crimes, and to some extent governments and international institutions respond through methods ranging from persuasion and pressure to, as yet tentative, enforcement. Particularly important in the latter respect has been the establishment of international tribunals with respect to violations of international humanitarian law for Rwanda and former Yugoslavia, and the creation of an International Criminal Court (ICC) to deal with 'core crimes' – war crimes, crimes against humanity and genocide. War crimes tribunals were established in 1993 and 1994, and the ICC in 1998.

These tentative steps towards a cosmopolitan regime, however, conflict with many of the more traditional geo-political approaches adopted by the so-called international community which continue to emphasize the importance of state sovereignty as the basis of international relations. This is especially true since 9/11 and the promulgation of the 'War on Terror'. The prevalence of geo-politics is reflected in the terminology used to describe the response of the international community to post-Cold War conflicts. The literature is replete with discussions about intervention and non-intervention.[10] Intervention is taken to mean an infringement of sovereignty and, in its strong version, a military infringement. The prohibitions against intervention, expressed in particular in Article 2(1) of the UN Charter, which refers to the 'principle of sovereign equality', is considered important as a way of restricting the use of force, respecting pluralism and acting 'as a brake on the crusading, territorial and imperial ambitions of states'.[11]

But what does intervention and non-intervention mean nowadays? The new types of war are both global and local. There is already extensive international involvement, both private through diaspora connections, NGOs, etc., and public through patron states or international agencies providing aid or loans or other kinds of assistance. Indeed, as I argued in the previous chapter, the various parties to the conflict are totally dependent on outside support. Likewise, these are wars usually characterized by the erosion or disintegration of state power. In such a situation, what does it mean to talk about infringements of sovereignty?

An illustration of the artificiality of these terms was the debate about whether the war in Bosnia was an international or a civil war. Those who argued that this was an international war favoured intervention to support the Bosnian state. They argued that the Bosnian state had been internationally recognized and that the war was the result of an act of aggression by Serbia. Hence, intervention was justified under Chapter VII of the UN Charter, since Serbian aggression was a 'threat to international peace and security'. Those who argued that this was a civil war were against intervention. They claimed that this was a nationalist war between Serbs, Croats and Bosnians to control the remnants of the Yugoslav state – intervention would have been a violation of sovereignty. Both positions missed the point. This was a war of ethnic cleansing and genocide. What did it matter whether the crime was committed by Serbs from Belgrade or by Serbs from Bosnia? What did it matter, in practical terms, whether Yugoslavia or Bosnia was the internationally recognized state? Something had to be done to protect the victims and to uphold respect for international humanitarian norms. In effect, the debate about whether the conflict was an international or a civil war treated it as an old war between the fighting sides, in which violence against civilians is merely a side-effect of the war.

Moreover, because outside involvement in various forms is already so extensive in this type of conflict, there is no such thing as non-intervention. The failure to protect the victims is a kind of tacit intervention on the side of those who are inflicting humanitarian or human rights abuses.

It is sometimes argued that intervention refers only to military intervention. Military means are often contrasted with political means as a way of solving conflicts. Behind this distinction is an assumption that these wars are comparable to modern wars. Military intervention implies military support for one side in the conflict. A political approach, on the other hand, implies negotiation between the sides. Hence, the debate about whether the war in Bosnia was an international or a civil war was sometimes presented as a debate about military versus political means. Again, this debate missed the point. The question was not whether to use military or political means, but what kind of politics would guide the use of military force. Both the argument for intervention on the side of the Bosnian state and the argument for negotiation which might lead to the use of troops in a peacekeeping role presuppose a traditional geo-political view of the conflict in which both sides were proto-states and in which a political solution would emerge either as a result of the victory of one side or as a result of a compromise. The solution had to do with the division of territory.

An alternative cosmopolitan approach starts from the assumption that no solution is workable based on the political goals of the warring parties and that legitimacy can only be restored on the basis of an alternative politics which operates within cosmopolitan principles. Once the values of inclusion, tolerance and mutual respect are established, the territorial solutions will easily follow. What this means in practical terms is the subject of the rest of this chapter.

From Top-down Diplomacy to Cosmopolitan Politics

The international community has been relatively successful in bringing at least a temporary end to conflicts through negotiated solutions between the warring parties. However, there are several drawbacks to this approach.

First, the talks usually involve those who are responsible for the violence. Thus they raise the profile of the warring parties and confer a sort of public legitimacy on individuals who may be criminals. During the Bosnian war, many people remarked on the paradox that international negotiators were seen on television shaking hands with Karadžić and Mladić, both of whom had earlier been named by the International Tribunal and by leading Western politicians as war criminals. The same contradiction applied to the involvement of the Khmer Rouge in the Paris talks which led to the agreements to end the war in Cambodia, to the high-profile talks between Mohammed Aideed and Ali Mahdi about the division of Mogadishu shortly after the arrival of US troops in Somalia in December 1992, or to the current emphasis on talks with the Taliban in Afghanistan.

Second, because of the particularistic nature of the political goals of the warring parties, it is extremely difficult to find a workable solution. One option is territorial partition – a kind of identity-based apartheid. The other option is power-sharing on the basis of identity. The record of such agreements is dismal. Partitions do not provide a basis for stability; refugees, displaced persons or newly created minorities constitute a long-term source of tension, as the history of partitions in Cyprus, India and Pakistan, Ireland or Palestine testifies.[12] Nor do power-sharing agreements fare any better. The constitutions of both Cyprus and Lebanon offer examples of unworkable compromises which exacerbated ethnic and/or religious competition and mutual suspicion. Today, the Washington Agreement between Croats and Muslims, the Dayton Agreement, the Oslo Agreement between Israel and the Palestinians, the Taif Agreement in Lebanon are all displaying the strains of trying to combine incompatible forms of exclusivism.

A third drawback is that such agreements tend to be based on exaggerated assumptions about the power of the warring parties to implement agreements. Since the power of the warring parties depends largely on fear and/or self-interest and not on consent, they need an insecure environment to sustain themselves both politically and economically. Politically, identity is based on fear and hatred of the other; economically, revenues depend on outside assistance for the war effort and on various forms of asset transfer based on loot and extortion or on price distortions resulting from restrictions on freedom of movement. In peacetime, these sources of sustenance are eroded.

It is often argued that, despite these drawbacks, there is no alternative. These are the only people who can end the violence. It is true that those responsible for the violence have to end it, but it does not follow that these are the people who can make peace. Negotiations with warlords may sometimes be necessary, but they need to take place in a context where alternative non-exclusive political constituencies can be fostered. The aim is to establish conditions for an alternative political mobilization. This means that the mediators have to be very clear about international principles and standards and refuse compromises that violate those principles, otherwise the credibility of the institutions will suffer and any kind of implementation could be very difficult. The point of the talks is to control violence so that space can be created for the emergence or re-emergence of civil society. The more 'normal' the situation, the greater the possibilities for developing political alternatives. There is, as it were, another potential source of power that has to be represented at the talks, involved or consulted in any compromise and, generally, made more visible. Precisely because these are not total wars, participation is low, loyalties change, sources of revenue dry up; it is always possible to identify local advocates of cosmopolitanism, people and places that refuse to accept the politics of war – islands of civility.

In chapter 3, I described the example of Tuzla in Bosnia–Herzegovina (see p. 56). Northwest Somaliland represents another example where local elders have succeeded in establishing relative peace through a process of negotiation. In Armenia and Azerbaijan, the local branches of the Helsinki Citizens' Assembly succeeded in negotiating with local authorities on each side of the border, Kazakh and Echevan, and establishing a peace corridor; the corridor provided a place where hostages and prisoners of war were released and where dialogue between women's groups, young people and even security forces was organized. In Sierra Leone, the women's movement played a critical role in pressing for democracy and paving the way for peace.[13] In Afghanistan, a Civic Platform for National Interest and Human Security has been established, comprising a combination of religious and tribal leaders, women and youth groups, teachers, doctors and others who define themselves as concerned about the public interest.[14]

In South Africa, there were many cases of locally negotiated peace accords during the violence between Inkatha and the ANC. Davin Bremmer has described how the Wilgespruit Fel-

lowship Centre was able to establish a zone of peace in the
Meadowlands Hostel in Soweto, which had been a flashpoint
of violence between the IFP and the ANC.[15] In the Mpuma-
langa community in KwaZulu-Natal, two local leaders representing the two main political factions joined with other
residents to form the Peace and Hope Foundation Trust, which
provided mediation and other conflict resolution services at a
local level, such as a 'rumour control system'.[16] In the Philip-
pines, a peace zones strategy was adopted after a town in the
north, Hungduan, convinced guerrillas to withdraw from the
town and then acted to prevent the military from moving in;
the peace zones strategy is said to have been an important
factor in ending the war.[17]

Many other examples from Northern Ireland, Central
America, Vojvodina or West Africa can be enumerated. In
nearly all these cases, women's groups play an important role.
They are rarely reported because they are not news. They may
involve local negotiations and conflict resolution between local
factions or pressure on the warring parties to keep out of the
area. They are often difficult to sustain because of the pressures of the war economy – influxes of refugees seeking safety,
unemployment, and propaganda, especially television, radio
and video cassettes controlled by the warring parties. But they
need to be taken seriously and given credibility by outside
support.

These groups represent a potential solution. To the extent
that they are capable of mobilizing support, they weaken the
power of the warring parties. To the extent that the areas they
control can be extended, so the zones of war are diminished.
They also represent a repository of knowledge and information
about the local situation; they can advise and guide a cosmopolitan strategy.

In many places, there is a growing emphasis by governments
and international organizations on the role of local NGOs and
grass-roots initiatives, and they provide funding and other
forms of support. In some cases, support for NGOs is seen as
a substitute for action. They are supposed to undertake the
tasks that the international community is unable to fulfil. But
what is not understood is that, in a context of war, the survival
of such groups is always precarious. Civil society needs a state.
If the local state does not provide the conditions in which

alternative politics can develop, there has to be support from international organizations. However courageous those engaged in NGOs are, they cannot operate without law and order. The peace movement in Bosnia–Herzegovina was destroyed when the Serbs began to shoot demonstrators. What happened in Rwanda is a classic illustration of what happens to local advocates of cosmopolitanism without outside support. According to Alex de Waal:

> Rwanda had an exemplary 'human rights community'. Seven indigenous human rights NGOs collaborated closely with their foreign friends and patrons, providing unrivalled documentation of the ongoing massacres and assassinations ... They predicted massive atrocities unless named perpetrators were called to account. But there was no 'primary movement' that could underpin the activists' agenda, no political establishment ready to listen to their critique and act on it, and no international organizations ready to take measures and risks necessary to protect them ... On April 6 1994, the Hutu extremists called the bluff of the human rights community and launched their final solution. As well as eradicating all Tutsis, they embarked upon the systematic assassination of all critics. The UN ran away, while the US government thought up nice excuses for inaction.[18]

Just as the warring factions depend on outside support, so there needs to be a conscious strategy of building on local cosmopolitan initiatives. What form support takes, whether or not it involves sending troops, depends on each situation and what the local groups consider necessary. But there is still a reluctance to engage in a serious dialogue on a par with the dialogue with the warring parties, to see these groups as partners in a shared cosmopolitan project and to work out jointly a mutual strategy for developing a peace constituency. There is a tendency on the part of Western political leaders to dismiss such initiatives as worthy but insignificant; 'citizens can't make peace', said David Owen when negotiator in the former Yugoslavia. This attitude can perhaps be explained by the horizontal character of top-level communication, the fact that leaders generally talk only to leaders. It also has to do with the colonial mentality that seems to grip representatives of international institutions when on missions in faraway countries – there are widespread complaints, whether in Somalia, Bosnia or the Transcaucasus, about the seemingly systematic failure to consult local experts or NGOs.

A Somali driver in Mogadishu commented on the negotiations between Mohammed Aideed and Ali Mahdi in the following terms:

> Everyone agrees that these men have caused so much unnecessary suffering in this country. We understand that the US Embassy had to deal with these men. But did the embrace have to be so fast so public? They are all war criminals in my view. What the outside world should be doing is giving them the message that, yes, other leaders should be allowed to emerge. Why didn't the US embassy also invite religious leaders, elders, women, professionals, when Aideed and Ali Mahdi met, to let these men know that these are the people they have stolen power from? It is a great pity they did not think of it. It sent all the wrong signals.[19]

In fact, this had been the strategy of Mohamed Sahnoun, who was appointed UN Special Representative to Somalia in April 1992 and resigned in October because of frustration over UN policy. Sahnoun's role has become 'mythologized', to use Alex de Waal's word, in Somalia. He explicitly pursued what he called a 'civil society' strategy, including elders, women and neutral clans in a variety of talks: 'His strategy was not so much one of marginalizing the warlords as of including the non-warlords in political discussions.'[20]

The failure to take seriously alternative sources of power displays a myopia about the character of power and the relationship between power and violence. An effective response to the new wars has to be based on an alliance between international organizations and local advocates of cosmopolitanism in order to reconstruct legitimacy. A strategy of winning 'hearts and minds' needs to identify with individuals and groups respected for their integrity. They have to be supported, and their advice, proposals and recommendations need to be taken seriously. There is no standard formula for a cosmopolitan response; the point is rather that, in each local situation, there has to be a process involving these individuals and groups through which a strategy is developed. The various components of international involvement – the use of troops, the role of negotiation, funds for reconstruction – need to be worked out jointly.

It is often argued that it is difficult to identify local cosmo-politans. Are they just marginal groups of intellectuals? Are there moderate religious and nationalist groups who count as cosmopolitan? There has to be, of course, widespread consulta-tion. But through such a consultation it is possible to situate those who are concerned about the future of the whole society and not just sectarian interest. Women's groups usually play a key role in a more inclusive approach. Even if the cosmopoli-tans are a small minority, they are often the best source of ideas and proposals.

This argument also has implications for the way in which political pressure from the international community is exerted on political and military leaders to reach agreement or to consent to peacekeeping forces. Typical methods include the threat of air strikes or economic sanctions, which have the consequence of identifying the leaders with the population instead of isolating them, treating them as representative of 'sides', as legitimate leaders of states or proto-states. Such methods can easily be counterproductive, alienating the local population and narrowing the possibilities of pressure below. There may be circumstances in which these methods are an appropriate strategy and others where more targeted approaches may be more effective – arraigning the leaders as war criminals so that they cannot travel, exempting cultural communication so as to support civil society, for example. The point is that local cosmopolitans can provide the best advice on what is the best approach; they need to be consulted and treated as partners.

From Peacekeeping and/or Peace-enforcement to Cosmopolitan Law-enforcement

In the literature about peacekeeping, a rigid division tends to be drawn between peacekeeping and peace-enforcement.[21] Both terms are based on traditional assumptions about the character of war. Peacekeeping is based on the assumption that an agreement has been reached between the two sides in a war; the task of the peacekeeper is to supervise and monitor implementation of the agreement. The principles of peacekeeping as developed in the post-war period are consent, impartiality and the non-use of force. Peace-enforcement, on the other hand, which is authorized under Chapter VII of the UN Charter, is basically war-fighting; it means intervening in a war on one side. The distinction is considered important because war-fighting is assumed to involve the use of maximum force, since Clausewitzean wars tend to extremes. General Rose's preoccupation during the war in Bosnia–Herzegovina with 'crossing the Mogadishu line' is about maintaining this distinction and not sliding from peacekeeping to peace-enforcement.

The analysis of new wars suggests that what is needed is not peacekeeping but enforcement of cosmopolitan norms, i.e. enforcement of international humanitarian and human rights law. Precisely because these wars are directed mainly against civilians, they do not have the same extremist logic as modern wars. Therefore, it ought to be possible to devise strategies for the protection of civilians and the capture of war criminals. The political aim is to provide secure areas in which alternative forms of inclusive politics can emerge. Many of the tactics that have been developed in recent wars are relevant – for example, the use of safety zones, humanitarian corridors, or no-fly zones – but their implementation up to now has been hampered by inflexible mandates and/or rigid adherence to what are viewed as the principles of peacekeeping. A number of authors have proposed new definitions for what is needed that fall between the perception of peacekeeping and peace-enforcement – such as 'second generation peacekeeping', 'robust peacekeeping', or the official British term 'wider peacekeeping' (which the British insist is still peacekeeping and not an in-between term) – but all of them tend to remain within the traditional framework of thinking about wars.[22]

Cosmopolitan law-enforcement is somewhere between soldiering and policing. Some of the tasks that international troops may be asked to perform fall within traditional ambits, for example, separating belligerents, maintaining ceasefires or controlling airspace. Others are essentially new tasks, e.g. the protection of safety zones or relief corridors. And yet others are close to traditional policing tasks – ensuring freedom of movement, guaranteeing the safety of individuals, especially returned refugees or displaced persons, and the capture of war criminals. Policing has been the great lacuna of peacekeeping. Back in the 1960s, when peacekeeping forces were sent to Cyprus, they were unable to prevent communal conflict because policing was not part of their mandate. Military forces have been notoriously unwilling to undertake police tasks, but, at the same time, it has proved difficult to recruit policemen because they are needed in their own societies. However one judges their record, the British forces in Northern Ireland did undertake policing tasks. Given the unlikelihood of another old war, military forces will eventually have to be reoriented to combine military and policing tasks.

Such tasks require enforcement and therefore necessarily involve the use of force, but in terms of the principles governing their application, the tasks of cosmopolitan law-enforcement are closer to peacekeeping. It is worth spelling out those principles and showing how they would need to be reformulated.

Consent

In the scenarios that were developed when preparing the official British peacekeeping manual, it was concluded that 'forcible pacification' is impracticable:

> Without the broader co-operation and consent of the majority of the local population and the leadership of the principal ruling authorities, be they parties to the dispute or government agencies, success is simply not a reasonable or realistic expectation. The risks entailed and force levels required of an approach that dispensed with a broad consensual framework is simply not a reasonable or realistic expectation. Put simply, consent (in its broadest form) is necessary for any prospect of success.[23]

According to this argument, consent is required at both the operational and the tactical level. At an operational level, consent is required before the mission is established. At a tactical level, commanders need to negotiate local consent.

The argument that 'forcible pacification' is impossible is clearly correct. The implication of the argument in this book is that international military forces have to be seen to be legitimate – that is to say, they have to operate on the basis of some sort of consent and even support, and to be acting within an agreed set of rules. Otherwise, there is a risk that they will become just another party to the conflict, as seems to have happened to some extent to the ECOMOG peacekeeping force in Liberia, where lack of pay, equipment and training meant that soldiers became engaged in the black market and/or theft of humanitarian supplies, and where the troops veered from neutrality to support for particular factions.[24]

However, unqualified consent is impossible; otherwise there would be no need for peacekeeping forces. If, for example, protection of humanitarian convoys is based on consent, then this can be negotiated as easily and perhaps more effectively by unarmed UN agencies or NGOs. The need for troops is based on the fact that not everyone consents and that those who prevent the convoys may have to be dealt with forcefully. For similar reasons, it may be impossible to obtain consent from *both* the local population and the warring parties. If an agreement has to be negotiated with a war criminal, then the credibility of the operation in the eyes of the local population may be damaged.

In general, international troops can expect considerable initial goodwill. In former Yugoslavia, the standing of the UN was very high; many local people had served in UN contingents. But the failure to react forcefully against those who interrupted aid convoys, to protect effectively safe havens, to capture war criminals or even to maintain the no-fly zone greatly undermined the legitimacy of the entire organization. The same was true in Somalia, where many local people hoped that the American troops who arrived in large numbers would disarm the warring parties. There was great disappointment when the Americans announced they would not disarm the factions and opened negotiations with the warlords. As a former Somali banker put it:

> You mean they have come all this way, with all this equipment and all these weapons just to move food from Baidoa to Berdara? (Laughter) Sooner rather than later, the fighting that continues in many parts of the country will displace people and create hunger and havoc in a few months. Then what? You can be sure there will not be more troops: Somalia, they will say, had its chance.[25]

What *is* important is widespread consent from the victims, the local population, whether or not formal consent has been obtained from the parties at an operational level. If consent at the operational level can be obtained, without sacrificing the goals of the mission, it is clearly an advantage. Retaining and building on the consent of the local population at a tactical level may well mean acting without the consent of one or other of the parties.

Impartiality

Impartiality tends to be interpreted as not taking sides. The ICRC makes a useful distinction between impartiality and neutrality. The principle of impartiality, it states, means that it 'makes no discrimination as to nationality, race, religious beliefs, class, or political opinions. It endeavours to relieve the suffering of individuals, being guided solely by their needs, and to give priority to the most urgent cases of distress.' The principle of neutrality means that, in 'order to continue to enjoy the confidence of all, the Red Cross may not take sides in hostilities or engage at any time in controversies of a political, racial, religious or ideological character'.[26]

In practice, impartiality and neutrality have been confused. The distinction is important for cosmopolitan law-enforcement. The law has to be enforced impartially, that is to say, without any discrimination on the basis of race, religion, etc. Since it is almost inevitable that one side violates the law more frequently than another, it is impossible to act according to both impartiality and neutrality. Neutrality may be important for an organization such as the Red Cross which depends on consent for its activities, although the insistence on neutrality has frequently raised questions, particularly during World War II. It could also be important for the traditional concept of peacekeeping or for a purely humanitarian conception of the role of peacekeepers, i.e. the delivery of food. But if the task of the troops is to protect people and to stop violations of human rights, then insistence on neutrality is, at best, confusing and, at worst, undermines legitimacy.

In the aftermath of the bombing of the United Nations headquarters in Iraq in the summer of 2003, many NGOs and humanitarian agencies have been calling for a return to the Red

Cross principles and a renewed separation of the military and those who undertake humanitarian tasks so as to preserve humanitarian space. The problem is that, in the new wars, humanitarian space has been squeezed. It is no longer possible to separate military and humanitarian activities. Rather, the military have to operate differently so as to protect humanitarian space. In Iraq, US forces were war-fighting forces and the international agencies were identified with the United States. There was no force capable of or responsible for cosmopolitan law-enforcement.

According to Mackinlay: 'A UN soldier has the same approach as a policeman enforcing the law. He will uphold it regardless of which party is challenging him. But legitimacy must be intact at all levels.' However, Mackinlay seems to think that, if the UN soldier enforces the rules impartially, it is possible to retain the respect of both sides.[27] The same point is made by Dobbie, one of the authors of the British peacekeeping manual, when he compares the role of the peacekeeper to the role of the referee at a football match. But these wars are not football matches; the various parties do not accept the rules. On the contrary, the nature of these wars is rule-breaking. The point is rather to persuade ordinary people of the advantages of rules so as to isolate and marginalize those who break them.

Use of Force

Traditional peacekeeping insisted on the non-use of force. The British peacekeeping manual uses the term 'minimum necessary force', defined in the manual as 'the measured application of violence or coercion, sufficient only to achieve a specific end, demonstrably reasonable, proportionate and appropriate; and confined in effect to the specific and legitimate target intended.'[28]

The British contrast this position with what is known as the Weinberger–Powell doctrine of overwhelming force. The UN intervention in Somalia is often cited as an example of the perils of using force. It was largely an American intervention authorized under Chapter VII of the UN Charter. After an attack by his forces on Pakistani peacekeepers, the Americans began a manhunt for Mohammed Aideed. Bombardments in Southern Mogadishu resulted in many deaths and the manhunt

for Aideed failed. (Owing to the refusal of the Americans to
share intelligence information with the UN, a careful raid on
what was supposed to be Aideed's hideout failed because it
turned out to be a UN office.) The nadir for the Americans
was reached when Aideed succeeded in shooting down two US
helicopters, killing eighteen soldiers, whose mutilated bodies
were publicly paraded in front of television cameras, and
wounding seventy-five others.

The problem, as various commentators have pointed out,
was not the use of force as such, but the assumption of overwhelming force and the failure to take into account the local
political situation and the need to act in such a way as to lend
support to legitimacy and credibility. Ioan Lewis and James
Mayall describe the American reaction to the initial killing of
Pakistani peacekeepers:

> Instead of holding an independent legal enquiry and seeking to
> marginalize Aideed politically, Admiral Howe's forces reacted
> with injudicious force causing considerable Somali casualties
> – not necessarily all supporters of Aideed ... Admiral Howe,
> behaving as if he were the Sheriff of Mogadishu, proclaimed
> Aideed an outlaw, offering a reward of $20,000 for his capture.[29]

Much the same dilemma is faced by American forces in Iraq
and Afghanistan.

Modern armies are uneasy about using minimum force
because they are organized along Clausewitzean lines and have
been trained to confront other similarly organized armies. As
was shown in the case of Somalia, when confronted with the
challenge of new wars, they find it extremely difficult to identify a middle way between the application of massive firepower
and doing nothing. Unlike war-fighting, in which the aim is to
minimize casualties on your own side whatever the cost in
casualties on the other side, and peacekeeping, which does not
use force, cosmopolitan law-enforcement has to minimize casualties on all sides. The significance of Nuremberg was that
individuals and not collectivities were held responsible for war
crimes. It is the arrest of individuals who may have committed
war crimes or violations of human rights that is required for
cosmopolitan law-enforcement, not the defeat of sides.

Cosmopolitan law-enforcement may mean risking the lives
of peacekeepers in order to save the lives of victims. This is

perhaps the most difficult presupposition to change. International personnel are always a privileged class in the new wars. The lives of UN or national personnel are valued over the lives of local people, despite the UN claim to be founded on the principles of humanity. The argument about humanitarian intervention revolves around whether it is acceptable to sacrifice national lives for the sake of people far away. The preference of Western powers, especially the United States, for air strikes, despite the physical and psychological damage caused even with highly accurate munitions, arises from this privileging of nationals or Westerners. This type of national or statist thinking has not yet come to terms with the concept of a common human community.

In effect, the proposal for cosmopolitan law-enforcement is an ambitious proposal to create a new kind of soldier-cum-policeman which will require considerable rethinking about tactics, equipment and, above all, command and training.[30] The kind of equipment required is generally cheaper than that which national armed forces order for imagined Clausewitzean wars in the future. Transportation, especially air and sealift, is very important, as are efficient communications. Much of this equipment can be bought or rented from civilian sources, although military equipment tends to be more easily available and flexible.

More importantly, the new cosmopolitan forces will have to be professionalized and civilianized. They have to develop a culture of cosmopolitan law-enforcement and see themselves as different from the traditional military whose aim was to defeat an enemy. This is why civilian command is so important. They have to know and respect the laws of war and follow a strict code of conduct. Reports of corruption or violations of human rights have to be properly investigated.[31] Above all, the motivations of these new forces have to be incorporated into a wider concept of cosmopolitan right. Whereas the soldier, as the legitimate bearer of arms, had to be prepared to die for his or her country, the international soldier/police officer risks his or her life for humanity.

The Examples of Kosovo and Libya

The wars over Kosovo and Libya illustrate the problem of using war-fighting techniques for humanitarian ends. The intervention over Kosovo in 1999 was hailed as the first war for human rights. The British prime minister, Tony Blair, used the occasion of NATO's fiftieth anniversary, which took place during the air strikes, to enunciate a new 'Doctrine of International Community'. 'We are all internationalists now whether we like it or not', he told an audience in Chicago. 'We cannot refuse to participate in global markets if we want to prosper. We cannot ignore new political ideas in other countries if we want to innovate. We cannot turn our backs on conflicts and the violation of human rights in other countries if we still want to be secure.'[32]

Just over a decade later, the NATO intervention in the Libyan revolution was hailed as the first legally mandated Responsibility to Protect operation. United Nations Security Council Resolution 1973, adopted on 17 March 2011, was a huge achievement just in time to prevent Gadafi forces from overrunning the Eastern town of Benghazi which pro-democracy protestors had liberated. For the first time, the goal of Responsibility to Protect moved beyond a Euro-American preserve. It was pushed by the Arab League and both Russia and China abstained. The resolution called on member states and regional organizations to 'take all necessary measures ... to protect civilians and civilian populated areas under threat of attack in the Libyan Arab Jamahiriya, including Benghazi, while excluding a foreign occupation force of any form on any part of Libyan territory'.[33] Moreover, resolution 1973 was preceded by Resolution 1970, which referred Libya to the ICC and imposed sanctions.

But the actual record of both wars is much more ambiguous. In both cases the proclaimed goal represented an innovation and an important precedent in international behaviour. However, the methods were much more in keeping with a traditional conception of war and had little connection with the proclaimed goal. In both cases, NATO relied on air strikes. In the case of the Kosovo war, some 36,000 sorties were flown, of which 12,000 were strike sorties. Some 20,000 'smart' bombs and 5,000 conventional bombs were dropped. But it appears that not much damage was done to the Yugoslav military machine. For fifty years, the Yugoslav army had been trained to withstand a superior enemy. A vast underground network had been built, including stores, airports and barracks. Tactics had been developed which involved constructing decoys, hiding tanks and artillery, conserving air defences and avoiding troop concentrations. NATO did not succeed, in the initial stages, in knocking out the Yugoslav air-defence system: this is why NATO aircraft continued to fly at 15,000 feet. Nor did they succeed in doing much damage to Serb forces on the ground. NATO claims that the air strikes did constrain Serb forces and prevented them from bringing equipment into the open, but, nevertheless, the air strikes evidently did not prevent operations against Kosovar Albanian civilians. There was more success in hitting civilian targets – roads, bridges, power stations, oil depots and factories. Because of the insistence that aircraft fly above 15,000 feet, pilots could not see what was happening on the ground and were dependent on intelligence from numerous, often badly coordinated, sources.

Consequently, repeated mistakes were made, as became embarrassingly clear for the duration of the air strikes. Low points included the bombing of the Chinese Embassy and of refugees inside Kosovo. Some 1,400 people were killed in so-called collateral damage. Environmentalists are only now assessing the consequences of damage to industrial facilities. Historic sites were destroyed, in Novi Sad for example. A TV transmitter was blown up, killing journalists inside. And targets were hit in Montenegro, whose government had refused to participate in the war in Kosovo.

Far from halting the exodus of Kosovar Albanians, the Serb forces accelerated the process under the cover of the bombing. In the period up to 24 March 1999, when the bombing began, KLA activities were used as an excuse for ethnic cleansing, mainly by regular Yugoslav forces and Serb police – some 400,000 people left the country. After 24 March, some 10,000 people were killed in the cleansing operation, including children, and more than a million were forced to leave the country. When NATO forces entered in June, only 600,000 people were left in Kosovo and, of these, 400,000 were internally displaced.[34]

Moreover, the process of reverse ethnic cleansing began soon after the entry of NATO troops, and some 160,000 Serbs left the country. Today, the Serbs that remain live in protected enclaves, and the tension between Serbs and Albanians remains very high, as evidenced by the divided city of Mitrovica and the riots in March 2004.

It can be argued that the political consequences of this type of bombing were also counterproductive. Despite what NATO spokesmen claimed, that there is a big difference between killing by mistake and killing deliberately, this difference was not obvious to the victims of the bombing. Who determines whether the killing of civilians counts as a 'massacre' or as 'collateral damage'? Likewise, the insistence of Western leaders that the bombing was directed against the regime and not against Serbs was not at all evident to those who experienced its effects. The air strikes mobilized Serbian national sentiment, allowing Milošević to crack down on NGOs and independent media during the war and thus minimize domestic constraints against his activities in Kosovo and permitting the sense of victimhood to overshadow any sense of responsibility for the wars. Together with the influx of refugees, the air strikes polarized opinion in both Macedonia and Montenegro, accentuating domestic tensions and the risk of the further spread of violence. They also polarized international opinion: for many in the East and South, the claim that this was a war for human rights was viewed as a cover for the pursuit of Western imperial interests in the Balkans.

In the end, Milošević capitulated and the refugees returned to Kosovo. A United Nations transitional administration was installed. On the one hand, it seems possible after over a decade that a solution might be found and that Serbs may eventually recognize the independence of Kosovo. On the other hand, the trauma of ethnic cleansing on all sides can never be reversed and tensions between the two communities as well as widespread human rights violations persist.

In the case of intervention in Libya in 2011, NATO and partner aircraft conducted some 24,200 sorties including over 9,000 strike sorties. NATO claims to have destroyed some 5,900 military targets including over 400 military and command control centres. The initial targets were air defences and heavy weaponry in the vicinity of rebel strongholds, but gradually the range of targets was extended to include command centres and military convoys in the open desert. Essentially, NATO entered the war on the side of the rebels. Indeed British and French special forces were on the ground in civilian clothes advising and training the rebels. Because NATO controlled the air space and because of improvements in precision over the last decade, NATO was much more successful at minimizing civilian casualties from air strikes than during the Kosovo war. But this is still not the same as protecting civilians. The air strikes were, of course, aimed at destroying Gadafi's capacity to attack peaceful protests. But the aim of the operation shifted from the protection of civilians to support for the rebels, so evidently civilians were bound to get caught up in the crossfire. At the time of writing there are no casualty figures for the war; estimates vary from 2,000 to 100,000. But because this was a war, many civilians died as a result of the fighting. In the end Gadafi was overthrown but the fighting has empowered armed militias and the long-term prospects for democracy are still difficult to assess.

Both these interventions were wars rather than humanitarian interventions. There is an argument in both cases for supporting those wars because, in the case of Kosovo, refugees were able to return and, in the case of Libya, a brutal dictator was overthrown. But wars always involve human tragedies and have long-term consequences for the way power is exercised in the aftermath.

Was there any alternative? A cosmopolitan approach is aimed directly at protecting people. It is more like policing than war-fighting and involves techniques like safe havens, humanitarian corridors, international monitors, no-fly zones and arrests of war criminals. The aim is to establish a secure environment where people can act freely without fear and where inclusive forms of politics can be nurtured. There were alternative possibilities in both cases but such an approach is always difficult and has rarely been tried.

From Humanitarian Assistance to Reconstruction

Mark Duffield writes about a two-tier system of economic assistance in the 1990s. On the one hand, official assistance is predicated on structural adjustment programmes or transition strategies which contribute to the decline of the formal economy. On the other hand, a safety net to cope with the consequences has been developed, largely based on contracting out the provision of assistance to NGOs.[35] A similar point is made by Alvaro de Soto and Graciana del Castillo in their discussion of the lack of coordination between the IMF and the World Bank, on the one hand, and the UN, on the other. The consequences and the cost in political and humanitarian terms of the policies of the former agencies are simply not taken into account. They describe the problems of implementing a peace programme in El Salvador against the backdrop of an IMF stabilization programme. In order to keep within the IMF spending limits, El Salvador was unable to afford to build a national civil police force and to embark on an arms-for-land programme to reintegrate guerrillas as required by the peace agreement: 'The adjustment program and the stabilization plan, on the one hand, and the peace process, on the other, were born and reared as if they were children of different families. They lived under different roofs. They had little in common other than belonging roughly to the same generation.'[36]

During the last two decades, there has been a big increase in humanitarian assistance; in 2000 it amounted to over 10 per cent of official development assistance, and by 2009 it had reached 13 per cent. The establishment of the UN Department of Humanitarian Affairs in 1991 and of the European Community Humanitarian Office (ECHO) in 1992 was an expression of the growing importance of humanitarian assistance. In chapter 5, I described the way in which the provision of humanitarian assistance is built into the functioning of the war economy. In fact, humanitarian assistance also contributes to the failures of the formal economy. It substitutes for local production. In Somalia, the policy of flooding the country with food in late 1992 in order to ensure that some aid reached those who really needed it led to a dramatic fall in prices, so that it was no longer economical for farmers to produce food.[37] In Tuzla, a centre of salt-mining, several tons of salt were being thrown away every day because it was dangerous to halt mining, yet UNHCR was importing salt from the Netherlands for humanitarian purposes. Providing humanitarian assistance in camps often means that poor farmers abandon their own means of livelihoods.[38] Humanitarian programmes also tend to bypass local specialists and create new hierarchies, in which those who work for international agencies receive salaries and other perks, while well-qualified local people, such as doctors and teachers, live off humanitarian aid.

Humanitarian assistance is essential; otherwise, people would starve. But it needs to be much more carefully targeted, taking the advice of local experts who really know the local situation. And it needs to be accompanied by assistance for reconstruction. By reconstruction, I mean the rebuilding of a formal political economy, based on accepted rules, and the reversal of the negative social and economic relationships I described in chapter 5. The word 'reconstruction' has other connotations drawn from earlier wars. It is usually assumed to be a programme of economic assistance, on the 1947 Marshall Plan model, that is put into effect once an overall political settlement has been reached. Aid agencies often insist that no reconstruction assistance can be provided before a political settlement is reached and, indeed, that the lure of reconstruction assistance represents an incentive to reach a political settlement. But I have argued that a lasting settlement can only be reached in a situation based on alternative politics, the politics of civility – which is very difficult so long as these negative social and economic relations persist. Instead, reconstruction should be viewed as a strategy to achieve peace rather than a strategy to be implemented after peace has been established.

The situation in what might be called near war economies is not so very different from situations of war. Whether we are referring to places where ceasefires have recently been agreed or to 'bad neighbourhoods' where the negative relationships of war have spread, the symptoms are much the same – unemployment, breakdown of basic infrastructure, pervasive criminality – and these are the symptoms that contribute to the outbreak or renewal of war. In other words, reconstruction is both a pre-war and a post-war strategy, aimed at prevention and at cure.

Reconstruction has to mean, first and foremost, the rebuilding of political authorities, even if only at the local level, and the reconstruction of civil society in the sense both of law and order and of providing the conditions in which alternative political groupings can mobilize. It does not mean reconstruction of what went before. Necessarily, it must entail the restructuring of political and economic arrangements so as not to repeat the conditions that gave rise to war. The adaptation of appropriate forms of governance and the introduction of regulated market relationships take time, and have to be part of a long-term process through which different groups in society can participate.

It is often argued that reconstruction has to encompass transition, in the sense that there is clearly a need to reform the institutions that preceded the war. Unfortunately, the term transition has come to be associated with a standard formula for democratization and transition to the market, which includes the formal aspects of democracy, for example elections, as well as economic liberalization and privatization. In the absence of meaningful political institutions through which genuine debate and participation can take place, and in situations where the rule of law is weak and where trust and confidence are lacking, this standard formula can exacerbate the underlying problems, providing incentives for exclusivist politics or for criminalization of formerly state-owned enterprises. Reconstruction has to involve reform, but not necessarily along the lines of the standard transition formula.

Reconstruction should be focused on zones of civility so that they can act as models encouraging similar initiatives in other places. Where legitimate local authorities do not exist, local trusteeships or protectorates could be proposed. The experience of international administrations has led to scepticism about the idea of local trusteeships. Such administrations lack local knowledge and sufficient capacity, especially for policing and justice mechanisms. The rhetoric of self-help and the notion of a culture of dependence are used as arguments against trusteeships or protectorates, but it is very difficult for people to help themselves when they are at the mercy of gangsters.

The primary requisite is the restoration of law and order in order to create a situation in which normal life can resume and refugees and displaced persons can be repatriated. This task includes disarmament, demobilization, protection of the area, capture of war criminals, policing and/or establishing and training local police forces, and the restoration of the judiciary.

Despite greatly increased efforts at achieving disarmament and demobilization, the record is mixed.[39] It is very difficult for UN forces to achieve more than partial disarmament, and techniques such as weapons 'buy-back' programmes have tended to result in the handing back of sub-standard weapons, while the high-quality weapons remain hidden. Moreover, there are now so many sources for acquisition, at least of small arms, because of both the high number of producers and the availability of surplus weapons, that the task is never-ending. Creating a secure environment may well turn out to be more important than disarmament. Effective policing and the capture of war criminals are essential conditions for security, whether they are undertaken by international forces, together with civilian affairs officers, or by local police forces under international supervision, or whether local authorities can take responsibility, perhaps with some outside support, as is the case in better-established zones of civility.

As well as disarmament and policing, law and order needs an independent and trustworthy judiciary and an active civil society, i.e. the creation of a relatively free public space. For this reason, investment in education and a free media are essential to stop the relentless particularistic propaganda and to end not just physical intimidation but also psychological intimidation. These conditions are much more important than the formal procedures of democracy. Outsiders often insist on elections as a way of providing a timetable and terminal point for their involvement. But without the preconditions of security, public space, reconciliation and open dialogue, elections may end up legitimizing the warring parties, as was the case, for example, in Bosnia after Dayton, and indeed provoking more violence, as in Iraq and Afghanistan.

To create a self-sustaining zone of civility, so that law and order, education and media can be paid for, soldiers find jobs and education, and taxes are paid, the local economy has to be restored. As well as disarmament, demobilization is also difficult, and not only because of the insecure environment. Indeed, the biggest weakness of DDR (disarmament, demobilization and reintegration) programmes has been reintegration. Many soldiers would like to give up banditry and find settled jobs or, in the case of children and young people, an education. But reintegration programmes have not been very successful because of unemployment and labour shortages and inadequate educational facilities.

The priorities are basic services and local production. Infrastructure – water, power, transport, post and telecommunications – needs to be restored at both local and regional levels. As well as being necessary on grounds of need, infrastructure is vital for the restoration of normal trade links and can be a subject of negotiation even when there is no agreement in other areas. Even at the height of wars, it is sometimes possible to reach agreement on these kinds of concrete issue, especially where there is a mutual interest. Gas supplies to Sarajevo were maintained more or less throughout the war, for example. The other area is support for local production of basic necessities so as to reduce the need for humanitarian assistance, especially food, clothing, building materials, and so on. Along with public services, this is a good way to generate local employment.

In so far as reconstruction is a strategy for peace, it has to provide economic security and hope for the future so as to remove the atmosphere of fear in which people live, and to offer, to young people especially, an alternative livelihood to the army or the mafia. What needs to be done is specific to each situation, but certain principles can be specified.

First, all assistance projects should be based on the principles of openness and integration. It is all too easy, in the interests of restoring services, to accept divisions and partitions established through war and, thereby, legitimize the status quo instead of helping to change it. In Mostar, for example, the EU administration was supposed to reintegrate the town, which was divided into Croat and Muslim halves. Although in a few limited cases, for example water supply, the EU managed to negotiate common projects, for the most part it has turned out to be easier to introduce separate projects in each half of the town, thereby explicitly following a strategy of separate development. Because there was no secure environment and because the EU feared taking sides, everything had to be negotiated between the nationalist leaders. Openness and integration means that anyone should be able to benefit from the projects and that projects are explicitly directed towards bringing people together, through, for example, employing refugees, displaced persons or demobilized soldiers, or involving an element of sharing. Openness and integration need to be fostered not only at a local level, but also at national and regional levels.

Second, assistance needs to be decentralized and to encourage local initiatives. By spreading recipients, more people are involved in the programme, there are greater possibilities to experiment and there is less risk of aid being creamed off or

being distorted by political compromises. Where demobilization has taken place, it has been local community-based programmes, often organized by the veterans themselves, that
seem to have been the most successful – for example, the
Uganda Veterans' Board or the National Demobilization Commission in Somaliland, which developed a programme of
demobilization and reintegration together with the veterans'
organization SOYAAL. Some veterans explained:

> The boys on the 'technicals' (pick-up vehicles mounted with
> machine guns or anti-tank guns) are themselves tired. They see
> no benefit, only death. They climb the technicals out of need.
> Some of those in secure jobs now include some who were the
> worst gangsters. They prefer the $200 that comes with a settled
> job to the millions they get as bandits.[40]

A relatively successful programme in Sierra Leone is the 'arms
for development programme', where local communities disarm
themselves with the help of police and, when they are declared
'weapons free', they receive a reward of a development project
of their choosing.[41]

Third, it is very important to make use of local specialists
and to encourage a wide-ranging local debate about how aid
should be provided. This is important in order to increase
efficiency by using people who have knowledge and experience
of the area, to increase transparency, to reduce corruption and
to build up civic engagement. One of the worst consequences
of international assistance has been the displacement of skilled
people as a result of foreign contracts and a distorted pay scale.
Highly skilled doctors, engineers, teachers or lawyers often
take jobs as drivers and interpreters because the salaries are so
much higher. Bosnia, Kosovo and Afghanistan all provide
examples of this pattern of skill displacement.

Even in areas that seem the most intractable, there are some
possibilities for funding assistance based on these principles.
The strategy of expanding zones of civility to offset the spread
of 'bad neighbourhoods' needs to be able to extend itself
directly into the bad neighbourhoods. Poor, uncivil areas
become caught in a vicious circle in which assistance is refused
because of the behaviour of the local 'authorities'; unemployment and criminality flourish, thereby helping to sustain the

position of the particularist warlords. It is all the more important to identify ways to support certain bottom-up projects
that cross war divides in order to begin to open up spaces in
these areas.

Reconstruction can be thought of as a new approach to
development, an alternative to both structural adjustment/
transition and humanitarianism. As is the case of cosmopolitan
law-enforcement, it is bound to be costly in the short term, to
require greater resources than rich countries have so far been
willing to commit to peacekeeping and overseas assistance. It
would mean abandoning some of the neo-liberal assumptions
about levels of public expenditure that have dominated international economic orthodoxy in recent years. Reconstruction
means that politics, economics and security issues have to be
integrated into a new type of humanistic global policy which
should be capable of enhancing the legitimacy of international
institutions and mobilizing popular support.

7

The New Wars in Iraq and Afghanistan

'In the images of falling statues', said President Bush on 1 May 2003, as he announced the end of hostilities in Iraq, on the deck of USS *Abraham Lincoln*, 'we have witnessed the arrival of a new era.'[1] Like his Defense Secretary, Donald Rumsfeld, President Bush claimed to have discovered a new form of warfare, making use of information technology so that war can be rapid, precise, and low in casualties. In the immediate aftermath of the invasion, military commentators were jubilant. Bush himself described the invasion as 'one of the swiftest advances in history'.[2] Max Boot, writing in *Foreign Affairs*, described the war as 'dazzling'. 'That the United States and its allies won anyway – and won so quickly – must rank as one of the signal achievements of military history.'[3]

The wars in Afghanistan and Iraq, which followed the terrible events of 9/11 and were the expression of the so-called War on Terror, were, indeed, new types of war but of the kind described in this book. It is true that all kinds of new technologies, ranging from sophisticated satellite-based systems to cellular phones and the Internet not to mention drones and other robotics, were used. But if we are to understand the wars in ways that are useful to policy makers, then their novel character should not be defined in terms of technology. What is new about these wars needs to be analysed in terms of the disintegration of states and the changes in social relations under the impact of globalization rather than in terms of technology along the lines developed in previous chapters.

Bush and Rumsfeld's conception of a new war, it can be argued, was more like an updated version of old war, making use of new technology. The failure by the United States to understand the reality on the ground in both Afghanistan and Iraq and the tendency to impose its own view of what war should be like has been immensely dangerous. It has fomented real new wars and it carries the risk of being self-perpetuating. In a way, these wars could be treated as a test case of the central argument developed in this book – the danger of not adjusting our conceptions of war to the new global context.

In what follows, I first describe why the American view of the wars they were fighting is better described as updated 'old war', then analyse the reality on the ground as a 'new war': the context of failing states; the warring parties and their goals, tactics and methods of finance; and the extent to which the United States and its allies tried to adapt. In the final section, I describe the possibilities for alternative strategies to reduce the risks posed both to the Afghan and Iraqi populations and to the wider international community.

Technology-intensive Old War

During the last decades of the twentieth century, successive American administrations developed the notion that the United States could use advanced technology to fight long-distance wars in such a way as to retain American military predominance and thus reassure American citizens that the US government can defend them, and preserve American security, without risking, or risking very few, American casualties and without requiring additional taxation.

The origins of this idea can be traced back to the Cold War framework. During the Cold War, deterrence could be understood as imaginary war.[4] Throughout the period of the Cold War, both sides behaved as though they were at war, with military build-ups, technological competition, espionage and counter-espionage, war games and exercises. This activity helped to remind people of World War II and, on the American side, to sustain a belief in the American mission to defend the world against evil through the use of superior technology. Technological developments responded to what planners imagined the Soviet Union might acquire – the so-called worst-case scenario. This introverted planning, as I have argued elsewhere, meant that American and Soviet technological change was better explained as though they were both arming against a phantom German military machine that continued to evolve in the planners' imaginations, rather than against each other.[5]

The advent of information technologies generated a debate about the future direction of military strategy in the 1970s and 1980s. The so-called military reform school argued that the platforms of the World War II era were now as vulnerable as soldiers were in World War I because of the use of precision-guided munitions (PGMs) and that the advantage had shifted to the defence. High attrition rates in the Vietnam and Middle East wars as a result of the use of hand-held missiles seemed to confirm that argument. The advocates of traditional American strategy argued that the offensive manoeuvres of World War II were even more important, since the use of area destruction munitions could swamp defensive forces and missiles, and unmanned aerial vehicles (now known as UAVs) could replace vulnerable manned aircraft. The consequence was the AirLand Battle strategy of the 1980s, with its centrepiece, 'deep strike', to be carried out by the then new Tomahawk cruise missiles, at that time armed with nuclear warheads.

After the end of the Cold War, US military spending declined by one-third, but this affected mainly personnel. Military research and development (R&D) declined by much less than military spending as a whole, and this allowed for the development of both follow-ons to traditional Cold War platforms and the new technologies associated with what became known as the Revolution in Military Affairs (RMA). Effectively RMA was the successor to AirLand Battle, but with even more emphasis on technology. For RMA enthusiasts, the advent of information technology is as important as was the discovery of the stirrup or the internal combustion engine in revolutionizing warfare. RMA is spectacle war; it is war carried out at long distance using computers and new communications technologies.[6] An important aspect of the new technologies is the improvement in virtual war-gaming, which further underscores the imaginary nature of contemporary conceptions of war. Increasingly, the Defense Department has recruited Holly-wood producers to help invent future worst-case scenarios, giving rise to what James Der Derian describes as MIME-NET, the military-industrial-entertainment network.[7] One of the most quoted remarks of the Iraq War was that of General William Wallace, commander of the army's V Corps and in charge of all US Army units in Iraq, that 'the enemy we're fighting is a bit different from the one we war-gamed against.'[8]

For the Bush administration, the term 'defence transforma-tion' came to supplant RMA as the new jargon. As one enthu-siast for defence transformation has put it:

> However jerky the transmission belt, the qualities of the modern American economy – its adventurousness, spontaneity and willingness to share information – eventually reach the American military. Just as the teenager who grew up tinkering with automobile engines helped to make the motorized armies of WWII work, so do the sergeants accustomed to playing video games, surfing web pages, and creating spread sheets make the information-age military of to-day effective.[9]

Donald Rumsfeld claimed that defence transformation 'is about more than building new high-tech weapons – although that is certainly part of it. It is also about new ways of thinking and new ways of fighting.'[10]

He talked about 'overmatching' power as opposed to 'over-whelming' power:

> In the 21st century, mass may no longer be the best measure of power in a conflict. After all, when Baghdad fell, there were just over 100,000 American forces on the ground. General Franks overwhelmed the enemy not with the typical three to one advantage in mass but by overmatching the enemy with advanced capabilities in innovative and unexpected ways.[11]

Yet it is hard to escape the conclusion that information tech-nology is being grafted on to traditional assumptions about the ways in which military forces should be used and to traditional institutional defence structures. The methods have not changed much since World War II.[12] Despite the changed names every decade – AirLand Battle, Revolution in Military Affairs, and

Defence Transformation – they involve a combination of aerial bombardment at long distance and rapid offensive manoeuvres. The very use of video gaming feeds in the assumptions of the gamers who have been schooled in the Cold War framework.

In the case of the invasion of Afghanistan, there was no time to plan a ground-based conventional attack. Instead the CIA was tasked with coordinating the anti-Taliban forces known as the Northern Alliance, largely based in the North and the North East. The CIA provided them with money, weapons and supplies, much as they had done during the earlier war against the Soviet occupation. Special Forces took part on the ground, fighting alongside Afghans, sometimes on horseback and, using their GPS positions, were able to call in US air strikes with devastating effects.

In the invasion of Iraq, much was made of the American information advantage. Coalition forces were able to process information received both from satellite pictures and from reports from the ground so that, at any one moment, the wireless Internet system could show the deployment of troops with enemy forces in red and friendly forces in blue. Known as Force XXI Battle Command, Brigade and Below, it was installed on nearly every vehicle. This allowed red forces to be directly destroyed from the air. Max Boot points out that, at the beginning of World War II, Germany managed to defeat France, the Netherlands and Belgium in forty-four days at a cost of 'only' 27,000 casualties (quotes are his); in comparison, the Americans and the British took twenty-six days to invade Iraq, a country three-quarters the size of France, at a cost of 161 dead (many of them by friendly fire – or 'blue on blue', as the jargon put it).

Both wars were portrayed as powerful moral crusades. There was always an idealist strain in American Cold War thinking. Bush's 'Axis of Evil' echoes Ronald Reagan's 'Evil Empire'. The argument is that America is a cause, not a nation, with a mission to convert the rest of the world to the American dream and to rid the world of enemies. The wars were represented in terms of the 'War on Terror' – a global conflict as far-reaching and ambitious as was the Cold War, designed to establish a new world order. 'We will not leave the safety of America and the peace of the planet at the mercy of a few mad terrorists and tyrants', said Bush, speaking at the West Point graduation ceremony on 1 June 2002. 'We will lift this dark threat from our country and the world.'[13] And, in his victory speech on USS *Abraham Lincoln*, he described the 'liberation of Iraq' as a 'crucial advance in the campaign against terror.'[14]

But in both cases there was rather little resistance – more in Afghanistan than in Iraq. There was some fighting in Northern Afghanistan; there was a horrific episode in which hundreds of Taliban prisoners, who had surrendered to the Northern Alliance, were bombed and executed at the Dasht-i-Leili prison. In fact the Taliban withdrew from Kabul and later surrendered the remaining provinces it controlled in the South. The US and its allies also tried and failed to capture Osama Bin Laden in the caves of Tora Bora. In the case of Iraq, the Iraqi Army and the Republican Guard simply melted away. The Americans dropped leaflets in Arabic telling soldiers to take off their uniforms and go home, and most of them obeyed instructions. There was, as one commentator put it, an 'unpleasant short-lived episode of violent irregular combat' in the third week of March, when Firqat Fedayeen Saddam (Saddam's Martyrs), and other small units established to defend the regime, tried to resist.[15]

But, by and large, the Americans entered both Afghanistan and Iraq with the consent of the people. The situation appeared calm initially in both countries. This was not because the coalition forces were in control. Rather in Afghanistan it was because they were welcomed by the people of Afghanistan who hoped that the invasion would bring an end to religious oppression and decades of violence. And in Iraq, it was because people were ready to give the coalition forces the benefit of the doubt, describing what had happened as 'liberation/occupation'. In fact, the only areas the coalition forces actually occupied were Kabul in the case of Afghanistan and their own protected bases in the case of Iraq.

Failing States

Toppling regimes is not the same as building democracy. Afghanistan and Iraq are very different countries. Afghanistan is one and a half times the size of Iraq and largely rural. It is one of the poorest countries in the world. The life expectancy of an average Afghan is 43 years; less than a third of the population, and only 12 per cent of women, can read and write. By contrast Iraq is largely urban with a sophisticated, highly educated middle class and, before the wars and sanctions, a world-class health system. Indeed Iraq is one of the oldest civilizations in the world; arithmetic was invented there and the House of Wisdom, which I visited in 2004, is the oldest think tank in the world, founded in the ninth century.

But what Afghanistan and Iraq had in common at the time of the invasions was that they were both on the verge of state collapse. Afghanistan had always had a weak state dependent on revenue from outside powers, and the national government never exercised much control outside Kabul. Decades of war, involving physical destruction and large-scale population displacement, had greatly weakened both traditional governance structures and the capacity of the state. Indeed the war against Soviet occupation from 1979 to 1989 could be viewed as part of the evolution towards new wars. The Soviet Union had conducted a classic counter-insurgency strategy involving 'air bombardments, the widespread use of land mines, search-and-destroy sweeps and the depopulation of most of the country'.[16] The *Mujahidiin*, financed by Saudi Arabia and the United States via the Pakistani intelligence service ISI, were the forerunners of today's warring parties – indeed many are the same people – developing an enterprise of resistance that replicated some of the worst aspects of counter-insurgency strategies and which, at the same time, became a way of life and a source of revenue. As Thomas Barfield has put it:

> Unfortunately, the successful resistance strategy by making the country ungovernable for the Soviet occupier also ended up making Afghanistan ungovernable for the Afghans themselves. While the Afghans had recovered from many earlier periods of state collapse, the body politic was now inflicted with an autoimmune disorder in which the antibodies of the resistance threatened to destroy any state structure, regardless of who controlled it or its ideology.[17]

The Soviet Union withdrew in 1989 and the communist government remained in power until 1992 when Soviet aid dried up. A period of infighting among the different *Mujahidiin* commanders led to the rise of the Taliban – a more strictly religious faction of the *Mujahidiin*, whose recruits were drawn mainly from young men, especially refugees, trained in the Pakistani madrassahs. In fact, the Taliban never entirely controlled the country and although they imposed an oppressive misogynist order, they contributed little to state-building or development, which is why they were so easy to topple.

In the case of Iraq, both President Bush, advised by the exiled opposition, and Saddam Hussein had a common interest in portraying the Iraqi regime as a classic totalitarian system, controlling every aspect of society and removable only by force.[18] In fact, at the time of the invasion, the regime exhibited characteristics that are typical of the last phases of totalitarianism – a system that is breaking up under the impact of globalization, unable to sustain its closed autarchic tightly controlled character. After two major wars and the imposition of economic sanctions, tax revenue had declined dramatically, as had the provision of services. The last years of Saddam's rule saw the rise of tribalism, with Saddam Hussein making deals with tribal leaders to maintain power, the spread of criminality both because of sanctions and because of the failures of the command economy, as well as the emergence of sectarian politics, both ethnic and religious, as Ba'athist ideology lost its appeal. In other words, on the eve of the invasion, Iraq was showing all the signs of incipient state failure – lack of legal revenue sources, decline of state services, loss of legitimacy, erosion and proliferation of military and security agencies, and the rise of sectarian identity politics and of criminality. The invasion simply condensed that process into a short three-week period.

The invasions of both countries effectively destroyed not just the regime but what was left of the state as well. In Afghanistan, the small civil service and security forces were undermined by infiltration of the militias that had assisted the Americans in toppling the regime, as well as by the fact that the huge international effort diverted skills and knowledge so that poorly paid government employees were ready to take much lower but better-paid positions in international agencies or NGOs, often just as drivers or interpreters.[19] In Iraq the newly established Coalition Provisional Authority further undermined the state by two decrees – one dismissing all former members of the Ba'ath Party, effectively denuding government service of all skilled people since membership of the Ba'ath Party was a necessary condition for promotion, and the other dismantling the army, thereby removing the one unifying security service and humiliating and impoverishing those very people who had taken off the uniforms and allowed the Americans to intervene (and who still had access to weapons).

Conventional military force cannot rebuild states. At the time of the invasions, the general view in the United States, expressed forcefully both by Colin Powell, the Secretary of State, and his successor, Condoleezza Rice, was that the job of the military was war-fighting and that soldiers should not be used for what Powell dismissively called 'constabulary duties'.[20] 'The President must remember', wrote Rice in *Foreign Affairs*, 'that the military is a special instrument. It is lethal and is meant to be. It is not a civilian peace force. And it is most certainly not designed to build a civilian society.'[21] The result was a security vacuum. While the Americans in Afghanistan continued to hunt for Al Qaeda leaders through a separate command, Operation Enduring Freedom, the internationally authorized NATO force, ISAF (International Security Assistance Force), which might have acted as a 'peace force', was initially confined to Kabul. In Iraq, the Americans did nothing to prevent the widespread looting that followed the invasion (except to protect the oil ministry and oil installations), allowing in particular the loss of irreplaceable ancient objects and manuscripts from museums that are part of the world's civilizational heritage. 'Stuff happens' was Donald Rumsfeld's famously laconic response.

Nor was there a serious civilian effort to reconstruct the state. Much more was done in Afghanistan than Iraq. The United Nations led a nation-building process, based on the Bonn Agreement that had brought together all the different Afghan factions and power brokers, except the Taliban. Even so, the process was hampered by the continued American reliance on the Northern Alliance, which brought the former commanders (or warlords) and their militias into the government, and also by the lack of security outside Kabul. In the North, for example, the restoration of former commanders led to ethnic discrimination against the Pashtun population, from whom the Taliban had largely been recruited. And in Kandahar, the Americans insisted on installing the former *Mujahidiin* commander Gul Agha Sherzai as Governor. Under pressure from US Special Forces, who posted rewards for the capture of Taliban leaders, Sherzai's militias were responsible for the killing and torture of former Taliban, despite efforts to surrender.

In Iraq, inexperienced Republican staffers sat in the protected green zone – a large area of Baghdad where the Coalition Provisional Authority (CPA) was based. Grass and palm trees, fountains and pools, palaces and rose gardens offered a calm environment for coalition staff, who beavered away trying to introduce 'off the shelf' models of democracy in Iraq. They developed a twelve-step plan for introducing democracy; one official told me in November 2003 that 'we have to finish this quickly because we know best how to do democracy; political pressure will force us to hand over sovereignty to Iraqis who don't know how to do it as well as us.' They were heavily reliant on expatriates like the former Halal butcher from North London I met, who was made policy planner in the newly created Ministry of Defence. When an interim Iraqi government was eventually established as well as a political process leading to elections, it was organized largely by a bevy of foreign and Iraqi exile advisors, who rarely left the green zone. Moreover, influenced by the experience of the former Yugoslavia, the political process was heavily weighted by ethnosectarian considerations so that when, in 2005, elections did take place, electoral choices were defined in sectarian terms – there were separate Kurdish, Shi'ia and Sunni lists.

So both countries, at the time of the invasions, were typical of the situations in which new wars develop – former authoritarian states unable to adapt for whatever reason to opening up to the outside world. Both countries already exhibited aspects of the predatory political economy that is characteristic of new wars as a consequence of the earlier wars. And in both countries, the old war assumption that all that was needed was the defeat of enemies made things worse.

The New Wars

Even so, it took time for the new wars to develop. In Iraq the insurgency began to emerge in the summer of 2003. In Afghanistan the Taliban only began to regroup and to re-infiltrate certain regions in 2005. Violence steadily increased from then onwards. In Iraq, it reached a peak in the years 2006–8, when the insurgency morphed into a sectarian conflict. In Afghanistan, violence continues to increase and, at the time of writing, is at its highest level since the invasion.

What are the characteristics of the violence that qualify these conflicts as 'new wars'?

The Warring Parties

First of all, these wars are fought by networks of state and non-state actors. In both cases, it is possible to enumerate three main categories: the insurgencies; autonomous militias often on the government side; coalition and government forces. The insurgencies are more like social movements than the typical vertically organized guerrilla insurgencies of earlier periods, while the coalition forces also include large numbers of private security contractors and are therefore more like the hybrid networks that characterize new wars than the regular forces of earlier eras. In both countries, ordinary criminals are also active participants in the violence, but it is often difficult to distinguish criminal groups from the other components of the violence including the government side.

In Iraq, the bulk of the insurgency was Iraqi nationalist and Sunni Islamist and arose more or less spontaneously, starting in the summer of 2003. The most important recruits were former military personnel – some 100,000 former Iraqi security service personnel lost their jobs when the army was dismantled. They were based largely in Fallujah, which was home to the Special Forces, Mosul, where senior army officers were largely located, and parts of Baghdad. It was former military personnel who provided professional know-how and were able to access some of the former regime's weapons stores.

The names of these nationalist and Sunni Islamist cells included the Iraqi National Islamic Resistance, 'The 1920s Revolution Brigades' (a reference to the Iraqi rebellion against British rule), the National Front for the Liberation of Iraq, the General Command of the Armed Forces and Liberation in Iraq, the Popular Resistance for the Liberation of Iraq, the Patriotic Front or the Iraqi Resistance Islamic Front, 'JAMI'.[22] There were also some smaller, leftist and secular groups with names such as the Nasserites, the Al Anbar brigades, or the General Secretariat for the Liberation of Democratic Iraq, as well as a few former Ba'athist factions such as the Firqat Fedayeen Saddam, the Snake's Head Movement, and Al-Adawh (the Return).[23]

In Afghanistan, the majority of the insurgents are Taliban. They were initially concentrated in the South and South East but are increasingly spreading throughout the North. Although they remain under the leadership of Mullah Omar based in Quetta in Pakistan, more and more local groups that seem to act relatively autonomously have been incorporated as the resistance has spread. There are also smaller insurgent groups in other areas. The Haqqani network, led by the former *Mujahidiin* commander Jalaluddin Haqqani and his sons Sirajuddin and Badruddin, has been linked to a series of daring attacks like the Serena Hotel bombing in January 2008, the attempted assassination of President Karzai, and most recently the assassination of Burhanuddin Rabbani, the former President and one of the founders of the *Mujahidiin*, who had been tasked to enter negotiations with the Taliban. Gulbuddin Hekmatyar's Hezb-i-Islami has been fighting since the Soviet occupation, and is usually allied to the Taliban, although it has been involved in clashes with the Taliban in the North; it has a political arm which has members in the Afghan parliament.

Al Qaeda is present in both Iraq and Afghanistan, although it was not evident in Iraq before the March 2003 invasion.[24] In Afghanistan, its terrorist camps were destroyed during the invasion and most operatives fled to Pakistan. Nevertheless, the invasions of both Afghanistan and Iraq acted as a magnet for jihadists all over the world and have greatly expanded the field of operations and the opportunities for training and experience. In both cases there are tensions with locally based insurgent groups. Indeed these tensions led to the birth of what was known as the Awakening in Iraq, when the bulk of the insurgency changed sides, which was the beginning of the dramatic decline in violence.

There are tribal militias in both Afghanistan and Iraq. Tribes are often considered traditional structures. But in both countries the tribes have been reinvented in response to colonialism, war and the modern state. Thus in Iraq, tribes are really common-interest groups with some element of clan or kinship. Whereas traditionally, tribes were rural organizations, in Iraq, rural-urban tribal networks developed during the Saddam period both because Saddam Hussein increasingly relied on the tribes for security and because personal ties became more important with the decline of social welfare and the crushing of civil society.[25] Many tribal militia were linked to insurgent groups. For example, the Zobai tribe was closely associated with the Revolutionary Brigades and the Islamic Army of Iraq. In Afghanistan, as well, tribes have been reinvented after massive displacement and as young commanders increasingly replace tribal elders; tribal narratives sustain local networks, which often work together with the Taliban and other insurgent groups, partly from fear and partly from disillusionment with the Afghan government and coalition forces.

In Afghanistan, there are also militias controlled by former commanders, who are now allied to the government and, indeed, are often provincial governors or ministers; people like Abdul Rashid Dostum, the Uzbek warlord who controlled a Northern fiefdom before 2001 and who led the horsemen who liberated Mazar-i-Sharif in 2001 with great brutality. Until 2008, he was Commander-in-Chief of the Afghan army. Other commanders include Nazir Mohammed, who runs the provincial capital, Faizabad, and whose militias are supposed to protect NATO; Ismail Khan, who dominates the western city of Heart; and Gul Agha Sherzai, who was governor of Kandahar, later replaced by Karzai's half brother.

In Iraq, probably the most important armed militias are attached to political parties and became part of the sectarian competition to control the state apparatus. The Peshmerga are attached to the Kurdish parties, who resisted Saddam Hussein in the North. Some militias were created by parties in exile, of which the most important is the Badr Corps attached to ISCI (the Islamic Supreme Council in Iraq) and trained by the Iranian Revolutionary Guard. Of the militias created since 2001 the most important is the Mahdi army of Moqtada al Sadr, known as Jaish al-Mahdi (JAM). Both the Badr Corps and the JAM infiltrated the Ministry of the Interior and the police between 2005 and 2007. One of the former commanders of the Badr Corps, Bayan Jabr, was Minister for the Interior in 2005–6.

The final category is coalition and government forces. The coalition forces employ hundreds of thousands of private security contractors, both local and international, so that they increasingly come to resemble the networks of regular troops and paramilitary groups to be found in many 'new wars', where the latter are much less disciplined and less familiar with the laws of war. In Iraq, for example, it was private contractors who turned out to have been responsible for some of the worst cases of torture in the Abu Ghraib prison. And in Afghanistan, private contractors appear to be involved in a number of protection rackets.

Great efforts have been made in both Iraq and Afghanistan to rebuild the army and police. In both cases, the security forces, especially the police, have been infiltrated by various militias and have been engaged in the violence. In Afghanistan, repeated efforts have been made to recruit local police – the Afghan National Auxiliary Police (2006), the Afghan Public Protection Program (2008) and most recently Petreaus's 'game-changing' initiative the Afghan Local Police – but they all tend to become merely additional armed militia.

Political Goals

What the insurgent groups have in common is their opposition to the American occupation. Like the movements that have emerged in other 'new wars', they can be understood in terms of the conditions thrown up by globalization. There is a range of individual motivations. In Iraq, many joined the insurgency to defend former power positions or because of humiliation meted out by the Americans through dismissal or raids or checkpoints. In Afghanistan, the backbone of the Taliban is poor displaced young people, educated in the madrassahs of Pakistan, which offer board and food for poor families. But they have been joined by others who have suffered at the hands of pro-government forces and/or local commanders, and who, like their Iraqi counterparts, have been humiliated by night raids and checkpoints and/or who use the insurgency as a cover to settle scores, for protection or for criminal activities. In both cases, whatever the individual motivation, the narrative that unites them (or united them in the case of Iraq) is a blend of Salafi Islam and nationalism.

This narrative is also propagated by Al Qaeda, which is more global and anti-political than the locally based insurgent groups. In effect, its goal is the struggle in itself against the West. It was Al Qaeda that fomented the sectarian violence in Iraq, so that the insurgency increasingly morphed into a civil war, by carrying out spectacular attacks on Shi'ite areas and Shi'ite monuments. It was the bombing of the Golden Dome Mosque on 26 February 2006 in Samarra, one of the most important Shi'ia shrines in the world, which is often thought to have marked the beginning of sectarian conflict.

In Afghanistan, the neo-Taliban, as the current insurgency is sometimes described, is often said to be more moderate than during the time of Taliban rule with more emphasis on natio-nalism and a greater readiness to tolerate health and educatio-nal services. Nevertheless, the evidence shows that young recruits become radicalized after they join the Taliban. Florian Broschk describes the videos shown to Taliban supporters in which:

> The Western military presence in Afghanistan is portrayed in terms of historical continuity: the Meccans, medieval crusaders and Mongols as well as the British and Soviet invaders of Afgha-nistan in the last 200 years are all different faces of the same enemy, who also attacks Muslims in Palestine, Iraq and else-where in the world.[26]

Initially, the Iraqi insurgency did not have a sectarian iden-tity, even though a majority of the insurgents are Sunni. But, as the violence intensified, the notion of a struggle against the West, which mirrors the American idea of a 'War on Terror', increasingly acquired a sectarian character, since it is largely Sunni areas that were targeted by coalition forces. Like other new wars, the violence represented a form of political mobili-zation, a way of constructing Sunni or Shi'ite identities, which were less clearly delineated before the war. Indeed, it was rein-forced by the political process as politicians used sectarian identities to gain votes or ministries.

Although the insurgency in Afghanistan is largely Pashtun, and although the post-2001 government is dominated by tra-ditional ruling tribes, the violence has not yet taken on an ethnic or tribal dimension. As the Taliban spread to the North

166The New Wars in Iraq and Afghanistan

166   *The New Wars in Iraq and Afghanistan*

in 2009, it began to recruit Uzbek and Tajik militias and, already in 2006, Mullah Omar, in his eve of Eid message, had warned against 'sectarian hatred'. Afghanistan has so many ethnic and tribal affiliations that, even though ethnic and tribal rivalries are mobilized for political purposes like winning elections, and even though they feed into the violence, it has been difficult to incorporate these differences into the broader political narrative. As one commentator has put it, the Taliban 'should more properly be seen as a nationalist Islamist insurgency that feeds on and manipulates tribal imbalances and rivalries to its own ends'.[27]

For coalition forces and their local allies, both conflicts have been framed in old war terms – the narrative of the War on Terror is understood as defeating the insurgencies and Al Qaeda in both Iraq and Afghanistan. From time to time, especially in Afghanistan, humanitarian considerations have been expressed, especially within the United Nations mission and the UN-authorized command ISAF as opposed to Operation Enduring Freedom, the US command. But in practice, especially since the two commands were brought together, it is the narrative of the War on Terror that predominates.

Tactics and Methods

The conventional military tactics adopted by coalition forces were a significant contributory factor to the violence. Both during the invasions and after, the United States adopted 'old war' tactics in what were complex twenty-first-century 'new war' conditions. They were aimed at defeating the insurgencies. Both in pursuing Al Qaeda and the Taliban in Afghanistan and in responding to the growing insurgency in Iraq, American military forces largely stayed in their bases and ventured out to attack the enemy. Confronted with the brutal reality of the insurgencies, coalition troops seemed to default to military logic. Like earlier similar types of counter-insurgency in Vietnam, for example, or Algeria, the excessive use of force, widespread detention and torture and abuse as a means of extracting information, and the attempts to destroy the safe havens of the insurgents through the attacks on places such as Fallujah, Samarra, Najaf, or al-Sadr City in Iraq or Kandahar and other Taliban strongholds in Afghanistan follow from this military logic. According to one American soldier in Iraq: '[I] don't think we will put much energy into trying the old saying "win hearts and minds". I don't look at it as one of the metrics of success.'[28]

The events in Fallujah in April 2004 provide an illustration of the overriding nature of military logic in the early years of the war in Iraq. The Marines Expeditionary Force had recently replaced the 82nd Airborne as the force in charge of this restive city. The Marines went to Fallujah with the explicit intention of turning a new page, trying to win over the population while isolating the insurgents who used it as a base from which to launch attacks throughout the country. The Marine commander confidently predicted that his troops would be playing football with the locals in a few weeks' time. What happened, however, was the exact opposite. An attempt to surgically remove the terrorists gradually deteriorated into a siege and an all-out war when four American security contractors were killed and their bodies mutilated in front of television cameras. The use of punitive measures, heavy weapons and indiscriminate fire quickly united the people of Fallujah behind the insurgents and indeed of most of Iraq behind Fallujah. The use of white phosphorus horrified observers and raised the spectre of Vietnam all over again.

Iraqis were pushed to rally behind their worst enemies – regime loyalists who gathered there from all over the country and assorted Arab jihadists. Once they had started taking casualties the Marines' overriding objective turned from winning hearts and minds to a determination to avenge fallen comrades, 'pacify the city' and 'finish the job'. Only intense political pressure allowed the ceasefire to take hold that paved the way for the subsequent security arrangement whereby control of the city was handed over to a former Republican Guard commander. The anti-American sentiment caused by the attack allowed insurgents to return to the city, including the leader of Al Qaeda in Iraq, Abu Musab al-Zarqawi. And in November 2004, US forces attacked again, causing hundreds of thousands of people to leave, much physical destruction and thousands of civilian casualties.

Fallujah confirmed, for many Iraqis, an overriding impression that soon everyone's house would be broken into, civilians fired upon, and young men arbitrarily arrested. It was not possible to be in Iraq in the early years after the invasion without experiencing at first hand the nervy young soldiers at checkpoints. At every checkpoint, ominous signs warned in English and Arabic that troops are 'Authorized to use live fire'. In addition, of course, people were afraid of the presence of coalition forces because they were targets for terrorist attacks and because of their habit of shooting indiscriminately when attacked.

Something similar happened in Afghanistan. In the early years after the invasion, most Taliban militants sought reconciliation. A letter from a group of Taliban leaders requesting immunity from arrest in exchange for abstaining from political life was ignored. Instead, the remaining Taliban were harassed and intimidated both by US Special Forces and by commanders like Sherzai who received financial rewards for killing or capturing Taliban. Arbitrary arrests, night raids and targeted killing all contributed to a profound sense of humiliation. From 2004, the Taliban began to return to the South and the South East. Operation Medusa, undertaken by Canadian ISAF forces, was supposed to clear Kandahar of insurgents: hundreds of Taliban were killed or captured. Like Fallujah, however, the end result was new recruitment and new tactics.

US Special Forces have intensified their kill-or-capture operations in recent years. They make great efforts to minimize civilian casualties but nevertheless mistakes are sometimes made and the offensives are the most important cause of internal displacement at present. As in Iraq, the conventional military approach makes it extremely difficult to gather useful intelligence that might guide a more effective approach. Sitting in their safe compounds, American commanders simply do not know what is going on; they only have satellite information, which may help to pinpoint the whereabouts of specific enemies but not to understand the politics.

A good example of a mistake is the attack in Takhar on 2 September 2010. The attack killed an elderly former Taliban called Zabet Amanullah who had been quietly living in Kabul and had come to Takhar to help his nephew in his election campaign, together with nine other civilians who were all part of a campaign convoy. The Americans were convinced, as a result of signals intelligence, that Zabet Amanullah was the alias for the Taliban shadow governor of the province, even though many ordinary Afghans could have told them that they had got it wrong. As Kate Clark, who investigated the incident, put it:

> Accounts of what happened on September 2, 2010 seem to come from parallel worlds. One is the world of the American military whose knowledge is often driven largely by signals intelligence and reports provided by a very limited number of informants and who generally focus on insurgent behaviour. The other is the normal everyday world of Afghan politics. In the case of the Takhar attack, these worlds did not connect.'[29]

Despite very successful kill-or-capture operations in which literally hundreds of Taliban have been killed, captured or fled, the Taliban have been able to replace commanders and maintain intact their shadow structures. The new younger commanders are more radical, more brutal and less locally rooted. 'For the time being', writes Gopal, 'it appears that the ability of foreign forces to kill or capture commanders is matched by the insurgents' ability to replace them.'[30]

It is the continuing military attacks, the night raids, and the detention of young men, where their dignity is undermined and where they often get recruited to armed groups, that contribute to and/or provide a justification for the intensification of other attacks by the Taliban or by local warlords.

The tactics of the insurgents in both Iraq and Afghanistan are typical of new war tactics. Their main aim is to exert influence over local communities, which they do through fear and intimidation. From 2005, both Iraqi insurgents and other militia groups were engaged in sectarian violence and ethnic cleansing, in ways that were reminiscent of the Yugoslav wars. While the Sunni groups favoured explosives and/or suicide bombers in Shi'ite areas or against Shi'ite monuments, the Shi'ite groups used death squads to kill prominent Sunnis in spectacular ways and take over neighbourhoods expelling the residents. They would seize Sunni properties including houses, villas and stores that had belonged to the Baghdad bourgeoisie since Ottoman times, and rent them to Shi'ite families or loot them. They would extort money from local merchants, festoon the area with Shi'ite flags and infiltrate, coopt or replace the local police. They would take over petrol stations and control the essential sale of petrol, propane and kerosene. And they would levy extensive local 'taxation', in effect setting up a sort of parallel system. Intellectuals and middle classes were particularly targeted; hundreds of academics were killed during the worst of the violence.

In Basra, in the South, violence did not develop until after an Islamist party Al Fadhila had taken power in the provincial elections of 2005. Violence began as revenge attacks against former Ba'athist party members and military officials but graduated into a toxic hybrid mixture of political and criminal activities, including: insurgent attacks against British forces, especially by the Mahdi Army, which forced the British to take cover and protect themselves, reducing their presence on the streets; sectarian cleansing against Sunnis and Christians (in particular, the Christians who were licensed to sell alcohol were targeted); a scramble for resources among various tribal and religious groups including vicious competition to control the oil ministry, oil facilities and the oil workers' trades union so as to siphon off oil revenue; honour killings, killings of prominent intellectuals, and attacks on women who did not wear headscarves; as well as pervasive criminality with rampant kidnapping and hostage-taking for ransom and for political reasons.

In Afghanistan, a typical pattern is that small groups of armed fighters will enter an area from Pakistan and collect *ushr* (tax) or *zakat* (donations). They might issue night letters ordering people not to send their daughters to school or their sons not to join the Afghan army. They may offer their services as mobile courts, which have become very popular in the absence of justice mechanisms. They mobilize the clergy, many of whom have been trained in Pakistan, and they hire criminals to destabilize the area. They kill or expel those who are unsympathetic and they may attack protected buildings like hospitals or mosques so that no one feels safe. Their success is a consequence of the absence or active tolerance of local institutions like the police. They recruit local volunteers and establish local networks, both military and political. The Taliban have established shadow structures with shadow governors for every province in Afghanistan.

After 2006, the Taliban adopted many of the tactics pioneered in Iraq. These include so-called pressure plate improvised explosive devices which detonate when a vehicle goes over them but which do not distinguish between civilian and military targets, targeted killings and suicide bombers (something that had earlier been considered un-Islamic in Afghanistan). Increasingly the insurgents recruit children, trained in madrassahs for the purpose. On 1 May 2011, a twelve-year-old suicide bomber killed three civilians and injured 12 others. On 26 June 2011, insurgents instructed an eight-year-old girl to bring a packet of explosives to a police vehicle; they detonated the explosives remotely, killing the girl.[31] Similar tactics are deployed by warlords who intimidate the local population in order to increase their landholdings, secure electoral support, or control smuggling and other criminal activities.

The main victims of all this violence are civilians. Civilians are killed in collateral damage as a result of American attacks. They are killed in insurgent attacks on coalition targets because they do not have the same protection as soldiers. They are the victims of human rights violations and ethnic cleansing as different groups, on all sides, try to maintain territorial control. One of the most telling aspects of this sorry story that illustrates the value that is put on the lives of American or British soldiers is that no one knows the full extent of civilian casualties. The deaths of soldiers are carefully recorded but civilian deaths are not counted. Iraq Body Count, which is based on media reports, estimates that over 100,000 civilians have been killed in Iraq up to September 2011. Figures estimated by the British medical journal, the *Lancet*, using epidemiological methods of interviewing sample families, are much higher. They suggest some 650,000 excess deaths between March 2003 and the middle of 2006, of which over 600,000 were due to violence.[32] The really intense period of violence when 3,000–4,000 people were killed a month was after the period of the *Lancet* estimate. In January 2008, a British organization, Opinion Research Business, estimated over a million deaths from conflict, based on surveys of individual Iraqi families.[33]

In Afghanistan, systematic collection of civilian fatality data only began in 2007. The United Nations now maintains a database but it is not publicly accessible. According to the UN Mission in Afghanistan, some 8,832 civilians were killed between 2007 and 2010.[34] The number of civilians killed has

increased in every single year, and in the first six months of
2011, some 1,462 people were killed, up from 1,267 in the
same period in 2010. All the increase has been accounted for
by increased attacks by insurgents. The number of civilians
killed by coalition and pro-government forces has slightly declined, reflecting greater efforts to reduce civilian casualties.
Among pro-government forces, the largest single cause of civilian casualties was aerial attacks. Among insurgents, the single
biggest cause of death was IEDs, followed by suicide attacks
and targeted killings.[35]

Displacement numbers are perhaps even more telling. In
Iraq, some four million people were forced to leave their homes;
half went abroad. In Afghanistan, forty per cent of the country's
estimated 28 million population have been displaced at some
time in their lives. Many went abroad; Afghans constitute the
largest refugee population in the world, mostly as a result of
earlier wars and the Taliban regime. But a similar number were
internally displaced and left the countryside to swell the urban
population. Since 2001, over four million refugees returned to
Afghanistan. Yet many are leaving again; at the end of 2010,
UNHCR estimates there were still over three million refugees
outside Afghanistan. Since 2006, the Internal Displacement
Monitoring Centre (IDMC) estimates that some 760,000
people have been internally displaced. The biggest cause has
been Western military offensives. 'While US and ISAF forces
made successful efforts in 2010 to minimise civilian casualties
and loss of life, they have not made the same efforts to reduce
the scale of internal displacement, despite its scale and the
demonstrated impact of forced displacement on support for
international forces.'[36] Other causes of displacement are deliberate expulsion by militias and armed groups; disputes over
land, water access and grazing rights; and some ethnic cleansing
in the case, for example, of minority Shi'ia.

Sources of Finance

The war in Iraq was an oil war. It is usually assumed that this
was a war for oil in the classic 'old war' sense that great powers
compete for control over oil installations and transportation
routes. This was certainly part of the American old war narrative. Vice President Cheney's Energy Task Force, created just

ten days after the Bush administration took office, explicitly argued that it was in the vital interests of the United States to protect its sources of oil in the Middle East at a time of increasingly tight and volatile markets, while Paul Wolfowitz, then Deputy Secretary for Defense, argued: 'The most important difference between North Korea and Iraq is that economically we just had no choice in Iraq. The country swims on a sea of oil.'

But, more importantly, this was an oil war in a new war sense in that oil rents in various ways financed the fighting and indeed access to oil rents became a motivation for fighting. Oil became the key resource in the new war political economy. American officials claimed that the insurgents had 'unlimited money' supplied by members of the former regime, Saudi and other religious charities or criminal activity – most of it derived from Middle Eastern oil rents. But oil money did not only flow in from outside. Criminal networks, previously honed on the huge infrastructure for illicit oil sales that Saddam Hussein created in order to breach United Nations sanctions, loot Iraqi oil through a smuggling chain that stretches all the way down the Persian Gulf, on the one hand, and through Turkey, on the other. Just as in Saddam's time, the sums of money that disappeared were huge (illegal oil trading was the largest source of illicit revenue for the former regime, estimated at $US9.2 billion from sales to Jordan, Syria and Turkey).

Oil smuggling can take various forms, including siphoning off diesel at source or drilling holes in pipelines. Tribes who were paid to protect pipelines developed a profitable business, siphoning the oil before protecting the pipeline. In addition, competition to gain access to oil rents at local and national levels was an important factor in election-related violence, while other criminal activities like looting, hostage-taking, kidnapping and convoy hijacking can be understood as ways to recycle oil rents. The difficulty with oil as a source of finance is that oil needs to be drilled and this requires, over the long run, a state infrastructure; this may be one reason why Iraq appeared to move away from the brink.[37]

If Iraq was an oil war, then Afghanistan can be described as a drug war. The main sources of finance for the war are external aid and poppy production. Afghanistan is responsible for over 90 per cent of the world's poppy production, largely concentrated in the South and West and based in the most insecure areas.[38] Local Taliban cells are meant to be self-financing; in one area, actually in the North, they are said to receive approximately 30 per cent of their income from Pakistan (raised from wealthy donors in Pakistan and the Persian Gulf), approximately a third from *ushr* ('tax' collected from local communities) and *zakat* (donations), and the rest from drug smuggling.[39] As well as drug smuggling, criminal sources of finance by all groups – warlords, police, etc. – include loot and pillage, timber smuggling, illicit gem smuggling, human trafficking, kidnapping and hostage-taking, and importantly 'protection' for construction and transportation.

Afghanistan is considered almost the most corrupt country in the world. In Transparency International's Corruption Perception index for 2009, Afghanistan ranked 179 out of 180. Yet corruption is almost a misnomer since it is systemic and pervasive, the only way in which people can survive, and it reaches deep into government. Much of the money spent by external donors has passed into the hands of local power-brokers who acted as subcontractors to the coalition forces. Local police are often engaged in illegal activities or are actively tolerant for fear of what might happen. Matthieu Aikins has written a series of articles about Colonel Abdul Razik, a leader of a tribal militia and of the border police force that extends across Kandahar and Helmand where 80 per cent of the poppy is grown. According to Aikins, Razik makes around $US5–6 million a year in drug smuggling. During the 2009 elections, when Karzai won through massive electoral fraud, he personally took the ballot boxes for safe-keeping and ensured a 99 per cent vote for Karzai. People like Razik are appointed by corrupt governors often favoured by the CIA and this is why Western forces are often associated with pervasive criminality and abuse. General Vance, then the Canadian Commander of ISAF in the region, told Aikins:

> We are completely aware that there are a number of illicit activities being run out of that border station ... He runs effective security ops that are designed to make sure that the business end of his life runs smoothly, and there is a collateral effect on public order. Ideally it should be the other way round. The tragedy of Kandahar is that it's hard to find that paragon of virtue.[40]

In other words, in both countries, all sides are engaged in a mutual enterprise of fund-raising that is dependent on continuing violence, whether it is the effort to capture power and thereby control the security forces and the main sources of rent, either oil revenues, as in Iraq, or foreign aid, as in Afghanistan, or whether it is to control territory where illegal activities take place. It is a predatory political economy that is typical of new wars and involves global, national and local connections. In such circumstances, old war behaviour – a focus on the military defeat of enemies – merely helps to sustain and indeed may deepen the mutual enterprise.

Adapting Old War?

According to Thomas Ricks, the 'old war' in Iraq ended on 15 November 2005 when a marine squad went on a killing spree after they had been hit by a roadside bomb in Haditha, killing 24 Iraqis including children. The subsequent report by army Major General Bargewell found that the killings had been carried out 'indiscriminately' and that the leaders of the Marine Command thought it was the right approach. 'All levels of command tended to view civilian casualties, even if in significant numbers, as routine.'[41] This was the event that started a rethinking of the military approach that was to be associated with the surge in Iraq, and later in Afghanistan.

On 10 January 2007, President Bush announced a new military plan for Iraq, known as the surge. The surge in Iraq was not just about an increase in the number of troops, it was a profound change in strategy and tactics, based on, to use the jargon, a 'population-centric approach'. The change in strategy was associated with General Petraeus, who took over the command of the multinational forces in Iraq later the same month. It emphasized the protection of civilians over and above force protection and bottom-up local security over and above technology and firepower.

The ideas and proposals for a change of strategy did not only come from General Petraeus. They had bubbled up from middle-level officers with experience on the ground, as well as defence intellectuals and those involved in civilian affairs. Websites like the Small Wars Journal or blogs from soldiers in the field testified to the change of heart. The ideas did not just come from those frustrated with what was happening in Iraq and Afghanistan. Some of the experience came out of Central America – Panama, Haiti and Colombia – and some came from the Balkans.

Elements of the new strategy in Iraq had already been tried out in Tall Afar by Colonel H.R. MacMaster and in Ramadi by Colonel Sean MacFarlane. The focus was on Baghdad and involved the establishment of Joint Security Stations throughout the cities staffed by US and Iraqi soldiers and Iraqi police. In Sunni areas, the aim was to make it harder for Shi'ite militias to infiltrate. And in Shi'ite areas, 'gated communities' were established with perimeter security measures such as barriers, walls and checkpoints and with hardened markets, shops and public places to prevent Sunni explosive attacks. The Joint Security Stations were also supposed to provide a way of mentoring Iraq forces and to ensure that they performed better; by the same token, the presence of Iraqis may have helped to improve American attitudes towards Iraqi civilians. Petraeus's injunction to 'live amongst the people' was of key importance. And this was not just a matter of improved knowledge and understanding of the situation; it also led to greater empathy and respect for Iraqis.

Despite these efforts, violence continued to intensify up until the middle of 2007. Two factors were responsible for the drop in violence after July 2007. One was the Awakening. This was the change of sides by the Sunni tribes. The Sunni tribes had begun to distance themselves from Al Qaeda as early as 2005. There were plenty of reasons for this. They rejected some of Al Qaeda's more horrific tactics and did not like Al Qaeda's version of Islam. They objected to the way Al Qaeda was muscling in on their communities and, in particular, taking control of their sources of revenue. According to one story, Al Qaeda killed a sheikh who refused to give daughters of the tribe to them in marriage. Some tribes first approached the US marines for help in defeating Al Qaeda in 2005, but it was not until the end of 2006 that the US forces responded to these overtures. Before that, tribal efforts had failed disastrously and led to great brutality and intimidation from Al Qaeda. The first concerted campaign was in Ramadi and it had a dramatic effect on security. Sheikh Sattar al-Rishawi, a smuggler and highway robber, of the Dulaini tribe, joined with Fasal al-Gaoud, a former governor of Anbar whose Hamza forces came from the Albu Mahal tribe, to establish the Anbar Salvation Council. After joining forces with the Americans, Sattar was made 'counter-insurgency coordinator' and the tribal militias were named 'emergency response units'. (Despite, or maybe because of, his efforts, Sattar was assassinated in September 2007.) Local neighbourhood watch organizations were created, which began providing information, protecting their families and patrolling streets along with the Shi'ia-dominated army and police. They were paid $US360 a month by the Americans. The model was copied throughout Iraq using the euphemism 'concerned local citizens' (CLCs) or, as the militias themselves preferred, 'sons of Iraq'.

The other factor was the Sadrist ceasefire of August 2007. The reasons for the ceasefire are various: ethnic cleansing in Baghdad was virtually complete; the decline in Sunni violence weakened Sadrist legitimacy; the Sadrist militias were becoming more undisciplined, acting more and more autonomously, and needed to be reined back; and there was a growing popular backlash against the Sadrist tactics. Moqtada's orders for a ceasefire were largely followed and it led to a dramatic fall in anti-Sunni violence.

What was the role of the new strategy in all this? In the end, it was Iraqis themselves who were substantially responsible for the decline in violence. But the presence of coalition forces on the streets of Baghdad as well as the provision of basic services that helped to lift the 'pall of fear'; the responsiveness to Sunni overtures; the fact that the presence of coalition forces drew Al Qaeda fire away from Shi'ite communities; the readiness of coalition forces to act as local mediators; all these may have been what made these developments possible, creating space in which deals could be made. The decline in violence was the result of local ceasefires made with some 779 militias ranging from 10 to 800 men. As David Kilcullen, General Petraeus's counter-insurgency advisor, put it:

The original concept of the Joint Campaign Plan was that we (the Coalition and the Iraqi government) would create security, which would in turn create space for a 'grand bargain' at the national level. Instead, in 2007, we saw the exact opposite: a series of local political deals displaced extremists, resulting in a major improvement in security at the local level, and the national government then began to jump on board with the program. Instead of Coalition-led top-down reconciliation, this process is Iraqi-led, bottom-up and based on civil society rather than national politics.[42]

Nevertheless, during this period, General Petraeus continued to pound what he called the 'irreconcilables' – largely Al Qaeda. Although violence is considerably reduced since 2006–7, it remains higher than in Afghanistan – both because of attacks from the remnants of Al Qaeda and continuing jokkeying for power, especially during pre-election periods.

A similar approach was supposed to be adopted in Afghanistan. General Stanley McCrystal, then Commander in Afghanistan, produced a comprehensive report in August 2009 proposing an integrated military-civilian campaign plan. The plan went even further than Petraeus's counter-insurgency strategy for Iraq. It put the emphasis on the protection of civilians rather than defeating enemies and even used the term 'human security'. It covered such issues as sustainable jobs, access to justice, governance and communication, and the importance of the Afghan role in all this. It dealt with 'irreconcilables' through isolation rather than direct attack.[43] And it put great emphasis on creating 'population hubs' or 'gated communities'. The report produced an intense debate in Washington about a counter-insurgency approach as proposed by McCrystal or a more limited counter-terror operation focusing on kill and capture, favoured by Vice President Biden. In December 2009, President Obama agreed to the McCrystal proposals and force levels were increased by 30,000 with the proviso that withdrawal would begin in 2011.

In practice, the strategy pursued by McCrystal and his successor General Petraeus was much more 'kinetic', to use the jargon, than the plan. One of the main problems was that the strategy has been led by the military. What McCrystal was proposing required far more civilian inputs for political, developmental and legal assistance. Only a very small proportion of the total Afghan war effort has gone through the State Department as opposed to the Department of Defense. Moreover, it is very difficult to change military mentalities

away from killing enemies and winning towards civilian protection and state-building, and the metrics of killing Taliban
and Al Qaeda leaders play well in the United States. The
entire emphasis of the 'surge' has been on increased offensives
against the Taliban and on an attempt to create something
like the 'Sons of Iraq' through local policing initiatives, which
have frequently been subverted by local armed groups. It
seems as though the counter-terror proponents have won by
default.

The focus on the enemy has meant continuing air strikes
often by unmanned predator drones against suspected Taliban
or Al Qaeda positions, especially in Pakistan. One of the most
significant technological changes that has resulted from the
wars in Iraq and Afghanistan has been the increased use of
robots. US forces had no robots at the time of the invasion of
Iraq. By the end of 2004, there were 150 robots and the
numbers increased to 2,400 in 2005, 5,000 in 2006 and 12,000
in 2008.[44] Robots can search for mines and explosives, greatly
improve surveillance and reconnaissance and also carry out
targeted attacks without risking the lives of American soldiers.
They can vary from the expensive Global Hawk, which will
replace the U-2 spy plane and can stay in the air for 35 hours,
to the small Raven, which can be thrown by a soldier like
a javelin and stay in the air for 90 minutes. As of 2011, the
Pentagon possesses some 7,000 aerial drones and an even
larger number of ground-based robots.

Drones, unmanned aerial vehicles (UAVs) or remotely
piloted vehicles (RPAs), as they are increasingly called, have
been widely used to identify and kill insurgents in both Iraq
and Afghanistan. This was, for example, how Abu Musab al-
Zarqawi was killed. A tip-off from Jordanian intelligence suggested that al-Zarqawi was increasingly listening to the advice
of a certain cleric. US drones followed the cleric 24 hours a
day seven days a week and eventually tailed the cleric to a
farmhouse where he was meeting with al-Zarqawi. 'The farmhouse was then taken out by a pinpoint air strike, guided in by
lasers and GPS coordinates courtesy of the drone.'[45]

Many American policy makers are enthusiastic about the
success of Predator drone attacks destroying Al Qaeda leaders
in Pakistan, Yemen and Somalia. The Predator is a very light
unmanned vehicle that can stay in the air for 24 hours and has

two cameras and a laser designator to lock on to targets. They are operated from drone bases in Nevada and other places in the US as well as Pakistan and Afghanistan. General Tommy Franks described the Predator as 'my most capable sensor in hunting down and killing Al Qaeda and Taliban leadership' and 'critical to our fight.'[46]

Peter Singer of the Brookings Institution, who has written about the growing military use of robots, says that robots are the American answer to suicide bombers. They allow for much more cost-effective attacks. Robots, like suicide bombers, don't have to worry about risking their lives. And this raises many of the same ethical questions about whether war can be carried out remotely. Even if it is the case, and this is not at all clear, that the Predator does not cause civilian casualties, the morality of killing enemies remotely is not only questionable but also highly problematic in political terms. General Barno, former US Commander in Afghanistan, says that 'when we attack like that in the middle of the night, even if we don't kill any civilians we are seen as cowards, hitting from afar in the middle of the night. We should go in there on foot in daylight with Afghan elders and arrest them.'[47] As evidence of this concern, the lyrics of one popular Pakistani song are about the United States viewing Pakistanis as insects.

In a way, the wars in Iraq and Afghanistan have come full circle and the drone attacks can be described as the latest phase of technology-intensive old war. The War on Terror, even if it no longer has that name, seems to have normalized behaviour that would earlier have been considered unethical or illegal such as the long-term detention of terror suspects or long-distance assassination. In October 2011, an American citizen, Anwar al-Awlaki, was for the first time the intended target of a drone attack in Pakistan and this does not seem to have raised serious objection.

Where this new version of old war differs from, say, World War II is that it does not require sacrifice from the American population. They do not have to pay additional war taxes; indeed, the wars were accompanied by tax cuts. Nor are they conscripted to fight in the war, and, unlike the ground warfare in Iraq and Afghanistan, there are no American casualties in drone attacks. All the American public is asked to do is to watch television and applaud.

Was There or is There an Alternative?

All foreign troops have been withdrawn from Iraq except an American training mission; at their peak, the US had 165,000 troops there. In 2011, President Obama announced a reduction of troops by 30,000 in Afghanistan and withdrawal by 2014. The end result could well be a long war in which the United States continues to fight terror through long-distance casualty-free drone attacks, which, in turn, provoke increased recruitment to Islamist armed groups allowing the spread of predation and low-level violence. The occasional showy victory like the killing of Osama Bin Laden helps to sustain the American narrative of a War on Terror.

In the West, there have been big debates about the goals of the war in Iraq, in particular, and the rightness or wrongness of those goals. It is generally agreed that the goal of the war in Afghanistan was to defeat terrorism. In the case of Iraq, those who favoured the war claimed that it was intended to get rid of weapons of mass destruction (WMD) accumulated by Iraq, to defeat terrorism, or to bring democracy to Iraq. Those who opposed the war claimed that this was an imperial war designed to expand American power and, in particular, to control sources of oil.

The argument that I have put forward here is that the technique of 'old war' was a very bad way to achieve any of these goals. Indeed, the war may have achieved the opposite of all of them. In Afghanistan, an assembly of 300 clergy called by Mullah Omar after 9/11, to ask whether he should protect his guest (Al Qaeda), concluded that 'because a guest should not cause his host problems Bin Laden should be asked to leave Afghanistan voluntarily as soon as possible';[48] nevertheless, the air attacks began two days later. And as I have described, the war has recruited hundreds, perhaps thousands, more radicalized Islamists. In Iraq, no one has been able to find any WMD and nor has anyone found any links between Saddam Hussein and Al Qaeda. However, since the war, there have been many attacks by Al Qaeda, and Al Qaeda groups are now present in Iraq and are 'exporting' terrorists. Both Afghanistan and Iraq became magnets for the jihadist movement. As for democracy, the 'new war' is destroying step by step whatever prospects there might have been in both countries, because it has fostered extreme sectarian politics in Iraq, and predatory abusive governance in both countries. And if the American goal in Iraq had been to expand bases and to secure oil supplies, surely a deal with Saddam Hussein would have been an easy and safer option.

My argument is, rather, that the purpose of the war was war; it was designed to keep alive an idea of old war on which American identity is based, to show that old war could be upgraded and relatively pain free in the twenty-first century. I do not want to suggest that this was cynical manipulation; on the contrary, the conservatives in the Bush administration probably believed in American power and their mission to spread the American idea. My point is rather that they were caught up in a narrative of their own making, which resonates well with the American public and is reinforced by the American media. And it can be argued that this belief is mirrored by a similar belief among some elements of the insurgency, particularly those who espouse the idea of a global jihad, of Islam against the West.

So was there and is there an alternative to war? The most important strategy in my type of new war, as I argued in the previous chapter, is the construction of legitimate political authority. This is no less true in Afghanistan and Iraq than in other new wars, both before and after the invasions. Saddam Hussein's regime was one of the most brutal in the world – millions had died from his maniacal foreign adventures, from the suppression of uprisings in the North and the South, and from purges and repression, as well as economic devastation. The Taliban regime was equally brutal, especially in its strict religious injunctions and its treatment of women. There were many moments in both countries when a combination of outside pressure and support for those inside both countries might have contributed to a slower process of opening up. Especially in Iraq, the tragedy is that the country might well have been the first to have its Arab Spring had it not been for the invasion and the war.

There have also been moments in the aftermath of the invasions when there were genuine opportunities to establish legitimate governments. In Iraq, the problem was the reliance on expatriates, the dissolution of the army and the Ba'ath party, and the preoccupation with sectarian politics. In Afghanistan, the problem was the inclusion of commanders, who had previously been defeated by the Taliban and had been totally discredited in the Karzai government. The biggest failure in both countries has been the failure to consult civil society – not just NGOs who are often financed by outsiders, but a range of local people, women's groups, student groups, tribal elders and others. In both countries ordinary people felt marginalized and neglected as people with guns were chosen as the main interlocutors for the outsiders. And in both countries a cosmopolitan form of politics could have been developed by mobilizing those who support a non-sectarian nationalist narrative.

Even today some of these mistakes could be rectified. For example, in Afghanistan, a serious attempt to arrest those involved in corrupt practices, many of whom have American passports, or to condemn fraudulent election practices, would be one way to get rid of predatory commanders and could help to provide a better environment for the emergence of democracy. Moreover, in both countries 'islands of civility' do exist. Greater attention to those islands as opposed to the defeat of enemies could help to spread civility instead of predation.

Legitimate political authority depends on security. In both countries, both outside forces and the newly created national security forces need to see their role in terms of what I have called cosmopolitan law-enforcement as opposed to war-fighting. They have to be used in a way that is neither classic war-fighting nor classic peacekeeping. In new wars, all sides violate the laws of war and human rights law. The task of legitimate security forces is to protect people, provide public security so that a political process can get going, and act in support of the rule of law. For this role, forces are needed that are made up of a combination of soldiers, police, and civilians with the capacity to undertake various humanitarian and legal activities.[49] There also needs to be much more attention to justice mechanisms in general and especially transitional justice.

Finally, of course, there has to be an economic strategy as well. Here, the priority is to create legitimate autonomous ways in which individuals and families can make a living, both as a basis for democratic empowerment and so that they face a material alternative both to criminality and to collaboration (either with the government before the invasion, or with the insurgency now). In Iraq, it is also critical to develop transparent and fair procedures for the distribution of oil revenues. And in Afghanistan legitimate alternatives to the drug economy need to be developed – perhaps through the legalization of drugs.

It is hard to be optimistic at the current juncture. Many Iraqis regard the current situation as worse than in Saddam's day. In Afghanistan, the insurgency continues to escalate and many fear a return to civil war when the Americans leave. The war against civilians in Syria and the growing confrontation between Israel and Iran threatens a regional new war, in which Iraq continues to be torn apart. The financial crisis and the failures of the war have reduced the appetite and interest by outsiders for any kind of help even of the cosmopolitan kind I have proposed. The introverted politics of the United States seems to betoken a continuation of a new form of long-distance warfare. Perhaps the most hopeful development is the Arab Spring and the inspiring way in which protesters in Tahrir Square and elsewhere are reclaiming their dignity despite the efforts of repressive regimes to stop them. The example of Tahrir Square does have reverberations in places like Afghanistan and Iraq. Is it possible that other international actors like the United Nations or the European Union could respond to the demands of civil society and offer some kind of alternative to a global new war along the lines I have outlined?

8

Governance, Legitimacy and Security

Liberal writers of the late eighteenth and nineteenth centuries had a teleological view of history. They believed that the zone of civility would, inevitably, extend itself in time and space. In his book *Reflections on Violence*,[1] John Keane contrasts their optimism with the pessimism of twentieth-century writers such as Zygmunt Bauman or Norbert Elias, who considered that barbarism was the inevitable concomitant of civility. For these writers, violence is embedded in human nature. The cost of allowing the state to monopolize violence is the terrible barbarity of twentieth-century wars and totalitarianism.

The end of the Cold War may have marked the end of statist barbarism on this scale. Certainly, the threat of modern war and, in particular, of nuclear war – the absolute expression of twentieth-century barbarism – has receded. Does this mean that violence can no longer be controlled, that the new type of warfare described in the previous chapters is likely to be pervasive, an ongoing characteristic of the post-modern world? The implication of the argument so far is that it is no longer possible to contain war geographically. Zones of peace and zones of war exist side by side in the same territorial space. The characteristics of the new wars I have described – the politics of identity, the decentralization of violence, the globalized war economy – can be found in greater or lesser degree all over the world. Moreover, through transnational criminal networks, diaspora networks based on identity, the explosive growth of refugees and asylum-seekers, as well as the global media, these characteristics have a tendency to spread. Terrorist attacks in New York, Madrid, London and other cities, conflicts in places such as Bosnia and Somalia, Mexican drug wars and even the virtual old-style wars conducted through air strikes are all manifestations of the new types of organized violence.

But if it is not possible to contain the new wars territorially, is it possible to envisage ways in which they might be contained politically? Globalization, after all, is a process which involves integration and inclusion as well as fragmentation and exclusivism. A new cosmopolitan politics, based on goals such as peace, human rights or environmentalism, is emerging side by side with the politics of particularism. Are the pessimists right? Is violence inherent in human society? Or could the new cosmopolitan politics offer a basis for restoring legitimacy at both local and global levels? Can we conceive of a world in which violence is controlled on a transnational scale, in which the monopoly of legitimate violence is reclaimed by global or transnational institutions, and in which the abuse of power by those same institutions can be checked by an alert and active cosmopolitan citizenry?

As I argued in chapter 2, military power in the post-war period was to a large degree transnationalized. The rigidification of the alliances in Europe and the establishment of integrated command systems, together with a global network of military connections through military assistance, arms sales and training, effectively meant that most countries, apart from the superpowers, abandoned the unilateral capacity to wage wars. Although there was some renationalization of armed forces in the aftermath of the Cold War, a whole set of new arrangements was also put in place – multinational peacekeeping, arms-control agreements involving mutual inspection teams, joint exercises, new or renewed organizations such as the WEU, Partnership for Peace, NATO Coordination Council (NACC) – which constitute an intensification of transnationalization in the military sphere. The promulgation of the 'War on Terror' could be regarded as a reassertion of sovereignty, but the United States is discovering in Afghanistan and Iraq how difficult it is to act unilaterally. During the Cold War, the boundaries of violence were extended to the edges of the two blocs; or, to put it another way, pacification was achieved throughout the bloc system. The question is whether this transnational agglomeration of military power can lead to global pacification. Can we conceive of pacification without territorial boundaries?

There is no self-evident answer. In every era there is a complex relationship between processes of governance (how human affairs are managed), legitimacy (on which the power to govern is based) and forms of security (how organized violence is controlled). On the one hand, the ability to maintain order, to protect individuals in a physical sense, to provide a secure basis for administrative capacities, to guarantee the rule of law, and to protect territory externally are all primary functions of political institutions from which they derive legitimacy. Moreover, the character of these institutions is largely defined in relation to the way in which these functions are undertaken and which aspects of security are accorded priority. On the other hand, it is not possible to provide security in the sense defined above without some underlying legitimacy. There has to be some mechanism, whether it is religious injunction, ideological fanaticism or democratic consent, which explains why people obey rules and why, in particular, agents of organized violence – soldiers or policemen, for example – follow orders.

In chapter 2, I described the way in which the evolution of modern (old) war was linked to the emergence of the European nation-state, in which internal pacification was associated with the externalization of violence and legitimacy derived from notions of patriotism embedded in the actual experience of war. The term 'national security' was largely synonymous with external defence of national borders. In the post-war period, the internal/external distinction extended to bloc boundaries, and ideological identities – notions of freedom and/or socialism – drawn from the experience of World War II supplanted but did not displace national identities as a basis for bloc legitimacy. Bloc security also meant external defence of the blocs.

Today, there is great uncertainty about future patterns of governance and the direction of security policies. The financial crisis, especially in Europe, and the growing wave of protests across the world are associated with a lack of confidence in formal political institutions. To be sure, many countries are introducing new approaches to security to deal with what are known as non-traditional threats like terrorism or organized crime. NATO emphasizes what is known as the comprehensive approach, the Pentagon debates counter-insurgency and population security as opposed to counter-terror. But security capabilities still consist largely of conventional military forces. Moreover, the national monopoly of legitimate organized violence has been eroded from above by the transnationalization of military forces. It has been eroded from below by the privatization of organized violence which is characteristic of the new wars. Under what conditions are existing or new security institutions able to eliminate or marginalize privatized forms of violence and to restore trust in institutions?

My argument is that this depends on political choice and how we choose to analyse the nature of contemporary violence and what conception of security we adopt. Traditional political science rooted in nineteenth- and twentieth-century experience is able to predict only a new variant of the past or else the descent into chaos. Precisely because the dominant stream of political science thinking was directed towards the existing system of governance, providing a form of justification or legitimation of that system and at the same time a basis for offering advice about how to operate within the system, it gives rise to a kind of fatalism or determinism about the future. In contrast, critical or normative approaches to political science allow for human agency. They are based on the assumption that people make their own history and can choose their futures, at least within a certain framework that can be analysed.

In what follows, I outline some possible ways of thinking about security which derive from competing political visions of the future based on differing perceptions of the nature of contemporary violence. One of these visions is a restoration of world order based on the reconstruction of some kind of bloc system in which cleavages based on identity supplant cleavages based on ideology. This approach draws on realist assumptions about international relations in which the main actors are territorially based political authorities and new wars are treated as a variant of old wars – geo-political conflicts. The best-known example of this type of thinking can be found in Samuel Huntington's *The Clash of Civilizations*, where he proposes a variant of the bloc system based on cultural identity instead of ideology.[2] This vision is closest to that put forward by the Bush administration and, perhaps, also by Al Qaeda.

A second vision can be described as neo-medievalism[3] or as anarchy, and draws on a post-modern rejection of realism.[4] Proponents of this line of thought recognize that the new wars cannot be understood in old terms, but at the same time are unable to identify any logic in the new wars. They are treated as a Hobbesian 'warre' against all.[5] This vision is, essentially, a counsel of despair, an admission of our inability to analyse global developments. Finally, a third vision is based on a more normative approach, drawing on the argument put forward for cosmopolitanism in the previous chapter.

The Clash of Civilizations

Huntington's thesis is a variant of the bloc system in which the source of legitimacy is cultural identity – loyalty to what he defines as historic civilizations. His book received so much attention because it expressed what many believe to be the unstated convictions of parts of the political establishment, particularly those whose livelihood depended on the Cold War – an attempt to re-create the comfortable certainties of the bipolar world and to construct a new threat to substitute for communism. The 'War on Terror' could be said to represent a paradigm of the Huntington approach. Islamic terrorism is compared to the totalitarian movements of fascism and communism.[6] The democratic liberal and, implicitly, Christian West has to oppose this movement militarily in the same way as it opposed fascism and communism in World War II and the Cold War in an ongoing confrontation that, according to Donald Rumsfeld, may last for fifty years. By making the 'War on Terror' commensurate with the Cold War, the disparate band of fanatics, criminals and alienated young men that is known as Al Qaeda was elevated into a formidable enemy on a par with Germany or the Soviet Union.

Huntington argues that we are entering a multi-civilizational world in which culture rather than ideology will be the bonding mechanism for societies and groups of states. As many critics have pointed out, he is rather vague about what is meant by culture, although clearly, for him, religion is a key defining element. Thus, the West is Christian, but only Catholic and Protestant. He is adamant that Turkey cannot be allowed to join the EU because it is Muslim, and he considers that the membership of Greece, an Orthodox country, is a mistake; according to Huntington, Greece is definitely not part of Western civilization. It is also clear that, for him, states are the key guarantors of civilizations. He emphasizes the role of 'core states', e.g. the United States for the West and China for Asia.

He defines some six or seven civilizations (Sinic, Japanese, Hindu, Islamic, Western, Latin American and, possibly, African). But he sees the dominant cleavage which shapes global order as running between the West and either Islam or Asia. Islam is viewed as a threat because of population growth and what he sees as the Muslim 'propensity for violence'. Asia is viewed as a threat because of rapid economic growth organized around what he calls the 'bamboo network' of ethnic Chinese. For Huntington, the West is defined as American political creed plus Western culture. He takes the view that Western culture is decaying and must defend itself against alien cultures; in particular, the US and Europe must stick together as they did in the Cold War period.

The main source of violence comes from what Huntington calls 'fault-line wars'. He argues that communal conflicts are a fact of contemporary existence; in other words, he accepts the primordialist conception of the new conflicts. According to him, they are increasing in scale partly because of the collapse of communism and partly because of demographic changes. (He thinks that the war in Bosnia was mainly a consequence of the higher birth rate of Muslims.) When communal conflicts involve different civilizations, as in Bosnia–Herzegovina, they become fault-line wars, calling into being what he calls the kin-country syndrome. Hence, Russia was brought into the Bosnian conflict on the Serbian side, Germany on the Croatian side and the Islamic states on the Bosnian side. (He is a little puzzled by US support for Bosnia, which does not quite fit the thesis, but it can be explained away in terms of the mistaken legacy of a universalizing political ideology.) In other words, the new wars are to be subsumed into a dominant civilizational clash and superpower patrons are to be re-created on a cultural rather than an ideological basis.

Huntington is highly critical of a global universalizing mission, describing himself as a cultural relativist, and, at the same time, deeply opposed to multiculturalism. He argues that the United States no longer has the capacity to act as a global power, citing the overstretch of US forces at the time of the Gulf War, and that its task is to protect Western civilization in a multi-civilizational world. He also considers that human rights and individualism are purely Western phenomena and we have no right to impose Western political values on societies to whom this is alien. At the same time, he argues that the United States has the task of preserving Western culture domestically. Hence, what he envisages is a kind of global apartheid in which relatively homogeneous civilizations held together from above by core states become mutual guardians of international order, helping each other through their mutual confrontation to preserve the purity of their respective civilizations. In other words, he is proposing a form of bloc political mobilization based on exclusive identity: 'In the greater clash, the global "real clash" between Civilization and Barbarism, the world's great civilizations ... will ... hang together or hang separately. In the emerging era, clashes of civilization are the greatest threat to world peace, and an international order based on civilizations is the surest safeguard against world war.'[7]

A major problem for Huntington is the fact that the Muslim world has no core state capable of keeping order. Just as the United States needed the Soviet Union to sustain the bipolar order of the Cold War years, so the Huntington scenario requires a stable enemy. The absence of a core Muslim state is more than just a problem for the argument, for it has something to do with the fragility of the entire theoretical framework. For Huntington, it is geo-politics as usual. In his framework, states retain the monopoly of legitimate organized violence. Civilizational security is provided by core states and, at least implicitly, supplies the basis for the legitimacy of civilizational blocs. But is this realistic?

Huntington does not ask why the Soviet Union collapsed or what are the factors that characterize the current transition period. The Arab Spring, for example, and the passionate commitment to non-violence would be inexplicable within his conceptual framework. Words such as 'globalization' or 'civil society' simply do not enter the Huntington vocabulary. For him, history is about changing state relations; models of state structures can be constructed without any regard to changing state–society relations. Seemingly random developments such as population growth or urbanization are invoked to explain particular phenomena such as the growth of fundamentalism or the strength of China. But there is no questioning of the content of governance, of how political institutions change in character, and little explanation about how the world moves from today's uncertainty to the new civilizational order. It is assumed that territorial defence of civilizations is the way to maintain order; it ignores the complexities of forms of violence which are neither internal nor external, neither public nor private.

The problem has become apparent in the wars in Afghanistan and Iraq. Al Qaeda is not a state and Iraq and Afghanistan were not powerful military enemies but, as became evident afterwards, on the verge of state failure. The defeat of the Taliban or of Saddam Hussein did not mean the defeat of Al Qaeda. On the contrary, even though the training camps were destroyed and some key leaders killed or captured, the Al Qaeda idea is fed by the notion of an ongoing civilizational conflict. The instability in Afghanistan and especially in Iraq provides a fertile environment for terrorism – undermining the notion of civilizational order. Indeed, if the 'War on Terror' has become less central, it is for political reasons, particularly the non-violent protests in Tahrir Square and elsewhere, and is despite rather than because of the continuing military campaigns.

The Coming Anarchy

In contrast to Huntington's thesis, the strength of the anarchy argument is that it takes account of the break with the past and the difference between old and new wars. Robert D. Kaplan's book *The Ends of the Earth: A Journey at the Dawn of the 21st Century* is a good example of this type of thinking. It is a kind of political travel book, which contains compelling descriptions of social life as it exists today on the ground. His conclusions are thus derived from direct experience of contemporary realities. Kaplan draws attention to the erosion of state authority in many parts of the world and the myopia induced by a state-centric view of the world:

> What if there are really not fifty-odd nations in Africa as the maps suggest – what if there are only six, or seven, or eight real nations on the continent? Or, instead of nations, several hundred tribal entities? ... What if the territory held by guerrilla armies and urban mafias – territory that is never shown on maps – is more significant than the territory claimed by many recognized states? What if Africa is even further away from North America and Europe than the maps indicate?[8]

In Sierra Leone, he discovers the breakdown of the monopoly of organized violence, the weakening of the distinction between 'armies and civilians, and armies and criminal gangs'.[9] In Pakistan, he discovers a 'decomposing polity based more on criminal activities than effective government'.[10] In Iran, he speculates about a new type of economy based on the bazaar. His journey gives him scope to describe the growing scarcity of resources, widespread environmental degradation, the pressures of urbanization and the new class of restless, unemployed young urban dwellers attracted to the certainties of religious fundamentalism. He talks about global inequalities of wealth and about the global communications revolution which has made these disparities so visible. He describes the growth of NGOs as 'the international army of the future'.[11] He dwells on the impact of modern technology on traditional societies – on radio, for example, as magic in Africa.

In his original article in the *Atlantic Monthly*, Kaplan coined the phrase the 'coming anarchy' to depict a world in which civil order had broken down. In West Africa, he observed a return to nature and to Hobbesian chaos, which he argued prefigured the future elsewhere in the world. Referring to Africa, Kaplan told a BBC interviewer in March 1995:

> You have a lot of people in London and Washington who fly all over the world, who stay in luxury hotels, who think that English is dominating every place, but yet they have no idea what is out there. Out there is that thin membrane of luxury hotels, of things that work, of civil order, which is proportionately getting thinner and thinner and thinner.[12]

In his book, the thesis is somewhat modified. He also finds islands of civility, in Eritrea, in Risha valley in India, or in the slums of Istanbul, where local people have succeeded in establishing or maintaining new or traditional forms of self-management. He is doubtful about whether these relatively isolated examples can provide models for other regions, arguing that their success depends largely on whether or not they have inherited certain civic-minded traditions, on what is or is not inherent in local culture. He goes on to argue:

> The map of the world will never be static. The future map – in a sense, the 'last map' – will be an ever-mutating representation of cartographic chaos: in some areas benign, or even productive, and in some areas violent. Because the map will be always changing, it may be updated, like weather reports, and transmitted daily over the internet in those places that have reliable electricity or private generators. On this map, the rules by which diplomats and other policymaking elites have ordered the world these past few hundred years will apply less and less. Solutions, in the main, will have to come from within the affected cultures themselves.13

Kaplan's argument is essentially determinist. While he rightly dismisses geo-political solutions of the Huntington type drawn on the state-centric assumptions of the past, he implicitly shares Huntington's hypothesis that the prospects for governance depend on the essentialist assumptions about culture. Because he witnesses collapsing states and because he cannot envisage alternative forms of authority at a global level, his scenario contains no security and no legitimacy except in certain arbitrary instances. Like Huntington, Kaplan laments the passing of the Cold War, suggesting that we may, in future, come to see it as an interlude between violence and chaos, like the Golden Age of Athenian democracy. He concludes his book with an admission of helplessness:

> I would be unfaithful to my experience if I thought we had a general solution to these problems. We are not in control. As societies grow more populous and complex, the idea that a global elite like the UN can engineer reality from above is just as absurd as the idea that political 'science' can reduce any of this to a science.[14]

Cosmopolitan Governance

In contrast to the above approaches, the project for cosmopolitan governance or human governance, as Richard Falk calls it,[15] breaks with the assumption of territorially based political entities. It is a project which derives from a humanist universalist outlook and which crosses the global/local divide. It is based on an alliance, as described in chapter 6, between islands of civility, noted by Kaplan, and transnational institutions. There are no boundaries in a territorial sense. But there are political boundaries – between those who support cosmopolitan civic values and who favour openness, toleration and participation, on the one hand, and those who are tied to particularist, exclusivist, often collectivist political positions, on the other. In the nineteenth century, the dominant international cleavages were national, tied to a territorial definition of nation. These were replaced in the twentieth century by ideological cleavages between left and right or between democracy/capitalism and socialism, which also became tied to territory. The cleavage between cosmopolitanism and particularism cannot be territorially defined, even though every individual particularism makes its own territorial claim.

This is not a project for a single world government. The Kantian notion of cosmopolitan right was based on the assumption of a federation of sovereign states; cosmopolitan right was essentially a set of rules agreed by all the members of the federation. Essentially, what is proposed is a form of 'global overwatch'. It is possible to envisage a range of territorially based political entities, from municipalities to nation-states to continental organizations, which operate within a set of accepted rules and to certain standards of international behaviour. The job of international institutions is to ensure implementation of those rules, particularly as regards human rights and humanitarian law. Just as it is increasingly accepted that governments can intervene in family affairs to stop domestic violence, so a similar principle would be applied on a global scale.

In some senses, a cosmopolitan regime already exists.[16] Transnational NGOs monitor and draw public attention to abuses of human rights, to genocide and other war crimes, and international institutions do respond in different ways. What has been lacking up to now has been enforcement. The argument here is that some form of cosmopolitan law-enforcement, as elaborated in chapter 6, would underpin a cosmopolitan regime. In effect, it would fill the security vacuum and enhance the legitimacy of international institutions, enabling them to mobilize public support and to act in other fields, for example, the environment or poverty. Of course, international institutions would need to increase their accountability and transparency, to develop democratic procedures for authorizing the use of legitimate force. Recent proposals for United Nations reform, including the endorsement of the 'Responsibility to Protect', the establishment of a standing police force and a peace-building commission, agreed at the UN Summit in 2005, are tentative steps in this direction. So is the establishment of the International Criminal Court. Of course all these institutions are as yet biased in favour of dominant states and are rightly accused of double standards but nevertheless their very existence offers openings for alternative approaches. The point is, surely, that, just as the development of the modern state involved a symbiotic process through which war, administrative structures and legitimacy evolved, so the development of cosmopolitan governance and, indeed, democracy is already taking place through a similar, although evidently fragile, process involving growing administrative responsibility for upholding cosmopolitan norms.

What are the implications of this approach for the debate about European security? Any security organization has to be inclusive rather than exclusive. An organization with boundaries is one which implicitly emphasizes external defence against a common enemy rather than cosmopolitan law-enforcement. In the construction of the European Union, there has always been a tension between different conceptions of Europe. One conception is Europe as a superpower in the making. There has always been a strand of Europeanism which sees the project as a way of reversing the decline of Europe's Great Powers. Many European politicians have long favoured a common defence policy because they believed that Europe had the potential to become a superpower rivalling the United States. Such a policy would build European security capabilities on the same model as those of the member states, only bigger and better. Such a conception envisages the strengthening of integrated European military forces on a traditional defence model so that the EU can be either a partner or a competitor to the United States. According to this approach, the main threats to Europe, as for the United States, are states which possess weapons of mass destruction and/or harbour terrorists. The main doctrinal changes required relate to technology, from platform-centric warfare to network-centric warfare.[17] But external defence of the EU, or indeed of NATO, will not protect EU countries from the spread of new wars, rather it will treat those countries outside the boundaries as potential enemies. Those countries that are poorer, with less well-established political institutions, that are perhaps Muslim and/or Orthodox, would be designated as outsiders. This is unlikely to create a new civilizational order on the Huntingtonian model. On the contrary, exclusion is likely to contribute to the conditions that give rise to the new type of warfare which could easily spread and which could nurture terrorism.

The other conception has always been Europe as a 'peace project'. This is an Enlightenment idea – many of the great liberal thinkers (Abbé St Pierre, Jeremy Bentham and Kant) developed perpetual peace projects, which were essentially proposals for European integration. In the same spirit, the founders of what was to become the European Union wanted, in the immediate aftermath of World War II, to preclude another war on European territory. This continues to be a strong motive in the minds of European citizens: when asked what the European Union means to them personally, the third answer that comes up in the Eurobarometer survey, right after the euro and freedom of movement, is 'peace'. Indeed, 8 per cent of respondents consider 'maintaining peace and security in Europe' to be a priority of the EU. It is also considered to be the most effective of EU policies.[18] In a globalizing world, the 'peace project' has to be understood as a process rather than an end goal. The coming together of legal relations and a civil space has had to be reproduced and extended to keep the process going. In the interdependent post-Cold War environment, the peace project can succeed only as a global project and not as a merely European one. Thus this conception of Europe would favour the construction of a European capacity for cosmopolitan law-enforcement as a contribution to global security.[19]

The advantage of NATO was that it became the instrument through which military forces were transnationalized; it provided a basis for transnational pacification. This is probably the most important reason why a war between France and Germany is now unthinkable. The disadvantage was that it kept alive the prospect of bloc war; it now has great difficulty in adapting doctrines to a changed security environment. A cosmopolitan approach to European and, indeed, global security would try to bring together potentially conflicting countries and to spread as far as possible the transnationalization of armed forces. This could be under the umbrella of the United Nations as well as regional organizations such as the EU, NATO or the African Union. The important point is not the name of the organization but how the security task is reconceptualized. A cosmopolitan approach to security encompasses political and economic approaches to security, as described in chapter 6. The task of the agents of legitimate organized violence, under the umbrella of transnational institutions, is not external defence, as was the case for national or bloc models of security, but cosmopolitan law-enforcement.

Conclusion

Table 8.1 provides a schematic description of the relationship between patterns of governance and forms of security and how this relationship would vary according to the competing visions I have described.

Which of the last three scenarios – clash of civilizations, coming anarchy, cosmopolitan governance – will the future hold? It is not possible to predict with any degree of certainty. The answer depends on the outcome of public debates, on the effectiveness of institutions, on political choices being made at various levels of society and in different places – how the war in Afghanistan plays out; the changes taking place in the Middle East and whether a transition to democracy can be achieved in places like Libya, Syria or Yemen; the future of the drone campaign or the campaign against piracy; efforts to solve long-standing conflicts in Israel/Palestine or Kashmir; the future of international administrations in Bosnia or Kosovo; or the commitment to development as an alternative to the globalized war economy. Will Bosnia continue to be divided into Huntington-style statelets or be ruled by an international

Table 8.1 *Patterns of governance*

Patterns of governance	Political institutions	Source of legitimacy	Mode of security
States system	Nation-states	Nation-building, patriotism	External defence, internal pacification
Cold War	Nation-states, blocs, transnational institutions	Ideology – freedom or socialism	Deterrence, bloc cohesion
Clash of civilizations	Nation-states, civilizational blocs	Cultural identity	Civilization defence at home and abroad
Coming anarchy	Pockets of authority	Non-existent	Fortified islands of civility amidst pervasive violence
Cosmopolitan governance	Transnational institutions, nation-states, local government	Humanism	End of modern war, cosmopolitan law-enforcement

administration, or will it eventually be transformed into a functioning democracy? Can the war in Iraq be interpreted as an example of Kaplan's anarchy or a Huntingtonian civilizational war? Has the misuse of Responsibility to Protect in Libya ruled out the possibility of an alternative cosmopolitan intervention that would help to establish democracy and the rule of law? The 'War on Terror', the paradigm of the Huntington visions, is floundering. It has not brought a sense of security either to the Middle East or to Europe and the United States. Yet insecurity does not necessarily lead to a different approach. It may indeed foster more and more extreme positions, leading to a new war on a global scale in which identity politics, attacks on civilians and the shadowy economic underside of globalization are all mutually reinforcing. Will the outcome be a form of anarchy punctured by fortified islands of civility? Or can a cosmopolitan approach offer a way to bridge the gap between zones of war and zones of civility, an alternative to the 'War on Terror'?

Critics of the cosmopolitan approach might argue that it is a modernist/universalist project on an even more ambitious scale than earlier modernist projects such as liberalism or socialism, and thus contains within it a totalitarian claim. Moreover, given the secular character of the concept and the explicit rejection of identity-based forms of communitarianism, it might be argued that the concept is open to more severe charges of utopianism and inconsistency than were earlier modernist projects. I take the view that public morality has to be underpinned by universalist projects, although those projects are periodically changed by circumstances; they always produce unintended consequences and have to be revised. Thus, they can never be universalistic in practice, even if they make universalistic claims. Such projects, like liberalism or socialism, are validated by circumstances, at least for a time, or discredited. The eighteenth-century idea that reason is immanent in nature implied that rational (moral) behaviour can be learned through experience; there is a reality in which there are better or worse ways of living and that how to live in these different ways can be learned through experience – for example, the experience of happy or unhappy families or of war and peace. These lessons are never learned for ever because reality is so complicated and the exact set of circumstances in which a particular rationality seems to work cannot be reproduced. But they can be learned for a while and in approximate circumstances.

In today's reflexive era, a cosmopolitan project is, of its nature, tentative. We are likely to live permanently with contending approaches, although the character and assumptions of the different approaches are bound to keep changing. It may be that no solution will be found in Afghanistan and that Bosnia will be permanently divided and run by an international protectorate, but the wars in Iraq, Afghanistan and Bosnia may well represent for some time to come a new narrative, a way of telling the story of our political differences.

The optimistic view of current developments is the obsolescence of modern war. War, as we have known it for the last two centuries, may, like slavery, have become an anachronism. National armies, navies and air forces may be no more than ritual vestiges of the passing nation-state. 'Perpetual peace', as envisaged by Immanuel Kant, the globalization of civility, and the development of cosmopolitan forms of governance are real possibilities. The pessimistic view is that war, like slavery, can always be reinvented. The capacity of formal political institutions, primarily nation-states, to regulate violence has been eroded and we have entered an era of long-term low-level informal violence, of post-modern warfare. In this book, I have argued that both views are correct. We cannot assume that either barbarism or civility is embedded in human nature. Whether we can learn to cope with the new wars and veer towards a more optimistic future depends ultimately on our own behaviour.

Afterword

The previous editions of this book, along with other works both before and after that put forward versions of the argument,[1] generated a broad-ranging debate about the character of contemporary conflict. A number of other terms were used in this literature – wars among the people, wars of the third kind, hybrid wars, privatized wars, post-modern wars – but it was the term 'new' that seems to have stuck and became the main butt of the critics.

In this afterword, I address the four main thrusts of criticism: whether new wars are 'new'; whether new wars are 'war'; whether existing data confirm or negate the findings; and whether new wars can be described as post-Clausewitzean. Before doing so, it is worth issuing a note of caution. One of the problems with many of the critics is that they lump together the different versions of the argument and treat criticism of one particular aspect contained in one particular version as a criticism of the whole argument. Over and over again, when reading this critical literature, I have found myself wondering how authors came to identify claims about new wars that certainly I have never made. Such claims include the identification of new wars with civil wars, the claim that they are only fought by non-state actors and only motivated by economic gain, or that they are deadlier than earlier wars.[2] In answering the critics I will try not to fall into the same trap.

Are New Wars 'New'?

The most common criticism of the 'new wars' argument is that new wars are not new. It is argued that the Cold War clouded our ability to analyse 'small wars' or 'low-intensity wars', that many of the characteristics of new wars associated with weak states can be found in the early modern period and that phenomena like banditry, mass rape, forced population displacement, or atrocities against civilians all have a long history.

How could I disagree with these points? Of course, many of the features of new wars can be found in earlier wars. Of course, the dominance of the East–West conflict obscured other types of conflict, a point I actually made in chapter 2. But there is an important reason why I stick, at least for the time being, to the adjective 'new'.

What many of the critics of the 'new wars' thesis miss is exactly what they often concede is useful, that is to say, the policy implication of the argument. By describing the conflicts of the 1990s as 'new', I wanted to change the way policy makers and policy shapers perceived these conflicts. In particular, I wanted to emphasize the growing illegitimacy of war and the need for what I called a cosmopolitan policy response – one that put individual rights and the rule of law as the centrepiece of any international intervention (political, military or economic).

Dominant understandings of these conflicts among Western policy makers were of two kinds. On the one hand, there was a tendency to impose a stereotyped version of war, drawn from the experience of the last two centuries in Europe, in which war consisted of a conflict between two warring parties, generally states or proto-states with legitimate interests, what I called 'old wars'. When I used the term 'old war', I was referring to this stylized form of war rather than to all earlier wars. In such wars, the solution is either negotiation or victory by one side, and outside intervention takes the form of either traditional peacekeeping, in which the peacekeepers are supposed to guarantee a negotiated agreement and the ruling principles are consent, neutrality and impartiality, or traditional war-fighting on one side or the other as in Korea or the Gulf War. On the other hand, where policy makers recognized the shortcomings of this stereotypical understanding, there was a tendency to treat these wars as anarchy, barbarism, ancient rivalries, where the best policy response was containment, i.e. protecting the borders of the West from this malady. I wanted to demonstrate that neither of these approaches was appropriate, that these were wars with their own logic, but a logic that was different from 'old wars' and which, therefore, dictated a very different policy response.

As Jacob Mundy puts it, in one of the more thoughtful contributions to the debate:

> Whether we choose to reject, embrace or reformulate concepts such as ... new wars, our justifications should not be based on claims of alleged coherence with particular representations of history. Rather such concepts should be judged in terms of their ability to address the very phenomena they seek to ameliorate.[3]

Even so, I do consider that there are some genuinely new elements of contemporary conflicts. Indeed it would be odd if there were not. The main new elements have to do with globalization and technology.

First of all, the increase in the destructiveness and accuracy of all forms of military technology has made symmetrical war, war between similarly armed opponents, increasingly destructive and therefore difficult to win. The first Gulf war between Iraq and Iran was perhaps the most recent example of symmetrical war – a war, much like World War I, that lasted for years and killed millions of young men, for almost no political result. Hence, tactics in the new wars necessarily have to deal with this reality.

Secondly, new forms of communications (information technology, television and radio, cheap air travel) have had a range of implications. Even though most contemporary conflicts are very local, global connections are much more extensive including criminal networks, diaspora links, as well as the presence of international agencies, NGOs and journalists. The ability to mobilize around both exclusivist causes and human rights causes has been speeded up by new communications. Communications are also increasingly a tool of war, making it easier to spread fear and panic than in earlier periods – hence spectacular acts of terrorism, for example.

Thirdly, I agree with those globalization theorists who argue that globalization has not led to the demise of the state but rather its transformation. But I consider that the state is changing in different ways and that, perhaps, the most important aspect of that transformation is the changing role of the state in relation to organized violence. On the one hand, the monopoly of violence is eroded from above as some states are increasingly embedded in a set of international rules and institutions. On the other hand, the monopoly of violence is eroded from below as other states become weaker under the impact of globalization. There is, I would argue, a big difference between the sort of privatized wars that characterized the pre-modern period, and 'new wars' which come after the modern period and are about disintegration.

Some critics of the 'new wars' argument say the term is too fuzzy – a 'hodgepodge', say Henderson and Singer. Indeed, many similar terms like hybrid warfare, multivariant warfare or complex war-fighting are explicitly about being a mixture. Thus, for example, multivariant warfare refers to a 'spectrum of conflict marked by unrestrained Mad Max ways in which symmetric and asymmetric wars merge and in which Microsoft coexists with machetes and stealth technology is met by suicide bombers.'[4] New concepts are always fuzzy. The problem with existing categorizations of conflict is that they do not easily fit contemporary reality, a point I shall elaborate in the data section, and consequently the policy prescriptions that emerge out of them are confused and distorted. It is to be hoped that the current debate will lead to new categories that may displace the term 'new'.

A typical example of this type of criticism is the article by Sven Chojnacki. Chojnacki argues that the term 'new wars' is too vague and also 'methodologically problematic because the criteria for identifying "new" wars are highly arbitrary, difficult to reproduce inter-subjectively, *and difficult to reconcile with conflict theory*'[5] (italics added). Chojnacki then goes on to establish his own categories based on actors – inter-state, extra-state, intra-state and sub-state, which entirely misses the point of new wars that the actors are both state and non-state, internal and external.

Some critics concede that something like new wars exists. But that does not mean that 'old wars' have gone away. Particularly after the wars in Iraq and Afghanistan, some scholars and policy makers warn of assuming that future wars will look like Iraq and Afghanistan. I hope that future wars will not be like Iraq and Afghanistan because these wars, as I describe in chapter 6, have been exacerbated by outside military interventions. But nor, it is to be hoped, will future wars look like the wars of the twentieth century. Of course, a return to old wars cannot be ruled out. It is possible to imagine continued competitive arming by states, growing inter-state tensions, and a tendency to forget the suffering of previous generations. But failure to deal with the 'new wars' of the present might make that possibility more likely. The reconstruction of militarized states through external wars might come to be viewed as a way of re-establishing the monopoly of violence at national levels. As John Keegan puts it: 'The great work of disarming tribes, sects, warlords and criminals – a principal achievement of monarchs in the 17th century and empires in the 19th – threatens to need doing all over again.'[6] In the present economic crisis, where states are cutting defence budgets, there is a tendency to protect what is seen as the core defence tasks – preparation for 'old war' – and to squeeze the emerging capacity to contribute to global peace enforcement efforts.

Are New Wars 'War'?

Some writers argue that contemporary violence is mainly privatized and/or criminal and cannot therefore be properly described as war. A good example of this kind of thinking is John Mueller's interesting book *The Remnants of War*. He claims that war is becoming obsolescent and what is left are thugs who are the 'residual combatants'.[7] In other words, he defines war as 'old war':

> Thus, most of what passes for warfare to-day is centrally characterised by the opportunistic and improvisatory clash of thugs, not by the programmed and/or primordial clash of civilisations – although many of the perpetrators do cagily apply ethnic, national or ideological rhetoric to justify their activities because

to stress the thrill and profit of predation would be politically incorrect.[8]

I am very sympathetic to this line of argument. In this book I describe new wars as mixtures of war (organized violence for political ends), crime (organized violence for private ends) and human rights violations (violence against civilians). The advantage of not using the term 'war' is that it treats all forms of contemporary violence as wholly illegitimate and demands a policing rather than a political/military response. Moreover, much contemporary violence, like the drugs wars in Mexico or gang warfare in major cities, appears to have a similar logic to new wars but has to be classified as criminal. The same sort of argument has been used in relation to terrorism. There has been widespread criticism of the term 'War on Terror' because it implies a military response to terrorist violence when policing and intelligence methods, it is argued, would be more effective.[9]

But I do think that the political element does have to be taken seriously. It is part of the solution. Articulating a cosmopolitan politics as an alternative to exclusivist identity is the only way to establish legitimate institutions that can provide the kind of effective governance and security that Mueller is proposing as a solution. War does imply organized violence in the service of political ends. This is the way it legitimizes criminal activity. Suicide bombers in their farewell videos describe themselves as soldiers not as murderers. Even if it is the case, and it probably is, that those who frame the violence in ethnic, religious or ideological terms are purely instrumental, these political narratives are internalized through the process of engaging in or suffering from violence. Indeed, this is the point of the violence; it is only possible to win elections or to mobilize political support through the politics of fear. This is a point made strongly by Kalyvas in his *Logic of Violence in Civil Wars*. He quotes Thucydides on 'the violent fanaticism which came into play *once* the struggle had broken out ... society *had become* divided into two ideologically hostile camps, and each side viewed the other with suspicion.'[10] Overcoming fear and hostility does not necessarily come about through compromise, even if that is possible, because compromise can entrench exclusivist positions; rather it requires a different kind of politics, the construction of a shared discourse, which has to underpin any legal response.

A related terminological issue concerns the word 'conflict'. There is a legal difference between 'war' and 'armed conflict', which has to do with whether or not war has been formally declared. Most data sets assume a threshold below which violence cannot be counted as war, say a thousand battle deaths per year as in the Correlates of War database.[11] Without wishing to be overly semantic, the term 'conflict' does seem to imply a contestation around a legitimate grievance that can be resolved either by victory of one side or through compromise; the term used in the Uppsala University Conflict Data Program is 'contested incompatibility'.[12] Actually, conflict is endemic in all societies and necessary for change and adaptation. Democracy is a peaceful mechanism for managing conflict. Violence, as Michel Wievorka contends, tends to be the opposite of conflict. It closes down debates and 'encourages ruptures'.[13] In 'new wars', the 'sides' need an 'incompatibility' in order to justify their existence.

The Debate about Data

The argument in my book was based on qualitative rather than quantitative data. I had developed my ideas through my direct experience of the wars in the former Yugoslavia and the South Caucasus and tested them out both through my own case study of the war in Bosnia–Herzegovina and through comparative case studies of wars in Africa and other places undertaken for the United Nations University project that I directed.[14] This knowledge has since been augmented by research on Iraq and Afghanistan. I did make two quantitative claims to back up my argument that battles are becoming rare and most violence is directed against civilians. I claimed that the ratio of civilian to military casualties has increased dramatically and that the scale of forced population displacement per conflict is increasing.

Nevertheless, the quantitative data, despite claims to the contrary, do seem to confirm my initial intuitive findings. The debate about data covers three broad areas: the numbers and duration of wars; the numbers of casualties; and the levels of forced displacement.

The Numbers and Duration of Wars

There are three main sources for data on numbers of wars. These are:

- the Uppsala Conflict Data Program (UCDP), which is used by the Stockholm International Peace Research Institute (SIPRI) in its annual yearbook, the *Human Security Report* project and the World Bank,[15]
- the Correlates of War project at the University of Michigan, and
- the biennial *Peace and Conflict Survey* produced by the Center for Development and Conflict Management at the University of Maryland.[16]

All three data sets are based on 'old war' assumptions. For violence to be counted as a war, there has to be a state involved at least on one side and there has to be a certain number of battle deaths. Moreover, they all distinguish between intra-state and inter-state war and some have added sub-state or non-state categories. Yet my whole argument about new wars was premised on the difficulty of distinguishing between what is state and what is non-state and what is external or internal. So none of these numbers is really able to capture the nature of new wars.

In particular, the emphasis on battle deaths has the counter-intuitive effect of leaving out major episodes of violence. As Milton Leitenberg puts it: 'There were few "battledeaths" in Cambodia between 1975 and 1978, comparatively few in Somalia in 1990 and 1991, or in Rwanda in 1994: but it would simply be bizarre if two million dead in Cambodia, 350,000 in Somalia and 800,000 or more in Rwanda were omitted from compilations.'[17]

Nevertheless the findings from the three databases do have some relevance to the new wars thesis. They all tend to concur in the following conclusions:

- The virtual disappearance of wars between states.
- The decline of all high-intensity wars, involving more than 1,000 battle deaths.
- The decline in the deadliness of war measured in terms of battle deaths.

- The increase in the duration and/or recurrence of wars.
- The risk factor of proximity to other wars.

In other words, there does seem to be a decline in 'old wars', which is largely what these data measure. There is also a decline in the numbers killed in battles, which is consistent with my argument about the decline of battle. And if some of the conflicts that are included count as 'new wars' there does seem to be evidence for my arguments that new wars are difficult to end and that they tend to spread.

The UCDP has made the most effort to adjust to the new realities and has added data on episodes of one-sided violence and on non-state violent conflicts. Both these numbers seem to be increasing and this again is consistent with my argument that new wars could be treated as cases of mutual one-sided violence and that low-level low-intensity persistent conflicts may be the pattern of the future.

Those who have criticized the new wars argument using these sorts of data have tended to set up straw men to attack. Thus it is argued that new wars are civil wars and the decline in civil wars suggests that new wars are not increasing. But I have always insisted that new wars are not civil wars and I have never made any claim about whether new wars are increasing or decreasing; my argument was always about the changing character of war. Bizarrely, critics have also suggested that the decline of battle severity is a critique of new wars when, on the contrary, it confirms the new wars argument.[18]

Casualties

I calculated the ratio of military to civilian deaths in the first edition of the book based on the numbers that were generated from our case studies of wars in the 1990s in the United Nations University project, which I directed, and from the statistics contained in Ruth Sivard's annual publication *World Military and Social Expenditures*. According to these calculations, the ratio of civilian to military casualties was 20 per cent at the turn of the last century, around 50 per cent in World War II and exactly reversed at 80 per cent in the 1990s.

The problem with this kind of calculation is three-fold. First, figures on civilian casualties are notoriously inaccurate. There are various methods for calculating these numbers – reliance on media and other reports of individual deaths, epidemiological surveys, opinion surveys and, where available, official death certificates. The results vary widely. Thus casualties in the Bosnia war vary from 260,000 (the number I used, which was taken from the Bosnian Information Ministry and widely used by international agencies at the time), of which 60,000 were military, to 40,000 in the World Disasters Report.[19] Similarly, civilian casualties in the Iraq war have been the subject of huge debate; the numbers vary widely from around 100,000 civilian casualties from violence as of 2011 estimated by Iraq Body Count,[20] which relies on media reports and official documents, to the figure of over a million based on an opinion survey in 2007, which asked Iraqis in all 18 governorates whether any member of their family had been killed.[21]

Secondly, it is very difficult to distinguish combatants from civilians. The only figures for which there are accurate statistics are military casualties because these are formally recorded by their governments. Hence we know that as of September 2011, there were some 4,792 military casualties in Iraq, of which 4,474 were American, and some 2,727 military casualties in Afghanistan, of which some 1,776 were American.[22] But, since many combatants in new wars are militia, private contractors, mercenaries, paramilitaries or criminals of various kinds, these are difficult to identify. A good example is the figures produced by the Sarajevo Research and Documentation Centre. They collected death certificates for people killed in the 1992–5 war and estimated that some 97,207 people were killed, of which 39,684 or 41 per cent were civilian and 62,626 or 59 per cent were soldiers. However, the number for soldiers included all men of military age. Since we know that it was mainly men of military age that were killed in ethnic cleansing operations and the majority of displaced people were women, and we also know that participation in the violence was very low, about 6.5 per cent of the population, it is simply not credible that all those men were soldiers. It would presuppose that nearly all the 8,000 men and boys killed in Srebrenica were soldiers, for example.

Thirdly, it is very difficult to distinguish whether civilians were killed as a side effect of battle, as a result of deliberate violence, political or criminal, or as a result of the indirect effects of war – privation and disease. One of the problems with the numbers I used to make my original calculation was that I used figures that related to all these causes of death, whereas my own argument was concerned with the changed pattern of warfare from combat to direct violence against civilians. The *Human Security Report* (HSR) suggests that deaths as an indirect effect of war have declined in contemporary wars. This is because wars are often highly localized and low-level and general improvements in healthcare or in immunization continue during wars. The main method of calculating these indirect effects is through calculating the excess deaths that took place over and above what might have been expected from previous trends. The HSR, for example, criticizes an IRC (International Rescue Committee) report on casualties in the war in the Democratic Republic of Congo, which estimates that 5.4 million people died during the war who would not have died 'had there been no war'; more than 90 per cent were estimated to have died from war-exacerbated disease and malnutrition. The HSR argues that their estimate was based on an estimated infant mortality rate prior to the conflict that was too low and that their surveys were biased in favour of areas with a small population and a high death toll and that the true figure is probably much lower.

So what can be said about the data on casualties? First of all, the data suggest an overall decline in all war-related deaths. One of the misapplied criticisms that have been made of the new wars thesis is that new wars scholars claim that atrocities in new wars are worse than in previous wars. The only claim that the new wars thesis makes is that most violence in new wars consists of violence against civilians rather than combat – it would be mad to claim that violence against civilians is worse than the modernist state-based atrocities like the Holocaust or the Soviet purges. Secondly, there has been a dramatic decline in battle deaths. If we compare all war-related deaths to battle deaths rather than civilian to military casualties, then it is possible to assert that the ratio has increased on a scale commensurate with my original claim.[23] Thirdly, casualties among regular soldiers are a very small proportion of total deaths in wars both because there are fewer regular soldiers taking part in wars and because of the decline in battle.

Finally, what is shocking about this whole debate is the fact that we have good and accurate statistics for the deaths of men in state-based uniforms but information about the vast majority of victims is totally inadequate.

Forced Displacement

The other quantitative claim that I made in the first edition of the book was that forced displacement was increasing. I used the overall numbers provided by UNHCR and the US World Refugee Survey,[24] and I used estimates by Myron Weiner for the number of displaced person per conflict for the years up to 1992.[25]

No one disputes that the overall total displaced population has increased. Indeed, according to UNHCR, the figures for forcibly displaced people in 2010 were at their highest for fifteen years at 43.7 million, including 15.4 million refugees, some 27.5 million internally displaced persons, and 837,500 individuals whose asylum applications had not been processed. But critics suggest that these numbers should be qualified in two respects. First, data collection has greatly improved, especially in relation to internally displaced persons. In particular, the main source of IDP data is the Norwegian Refugee Council's Internal Displacement Monitoring Centre, which has only been collecting data since 1998.[26] Before that date the main source was UNHCR's estimates of those IDPs which were of concern to UNHCR, a much lower figure. Secondly, refugee and IDP data tend to be cumulative since many people do not return to their homes.

Nevertheless, recent conflicts, especially in Iraq, Somalia and Pakistan, do seem to confirm my contention that forcible displacement is a central methodology of new wars. In Iraq, for example, some 4 million people were displaced at the height of the war in 2006–8, roughly half of whom were refugees and half internally displaced. Indeed, it can be argued that one reason for lower levels of deaths in war is that it is easier to spread fear and panic using new communications so that more people leave their homes than formerly. I have added my recent estimates of the increase in the numbers of refugees

and internally displaced persons in countries experiencing conflict in chapter 5 with all the caveats that I have mentioned
above.

One conclusion from this discussion is the need to refine the
displacement data, which could well offer a better indicator of
human insecurity than some of the other numbers that are
used.

The Debate about Clausewitz

The final set of criticisms against the 'new wars' thesis has to
do with the claim that new wars are post-Clausewitzean.[27] I
have addressed this question in a longer article where I conclude that new wars are indeed post-Clausewitzean but not for
the reasons usually attributed to the 'new wars' literature.[28]
Indeed, this question has been very important in helping me
to think through and reformulate the implications of the new
wars argument.

The reasons normally put forward for claiming that new
wars are post-Clausewitzean have to do with the trinitarian
conception of war, the primacy of politics and the role of
reason. Both John Keegan and Martin van Creveld have suggested that the trinitarian concept of war, with its tripartite
distinction of the state, the army and the people, is no longer
relevant.[29] Other authors suggest that war is no longer an
instrument of politics and, indeed, that the 'divorce of war
from politics' is characteristic of both pre-Clausewitzean and
post-Clausewitzean wars.[30] Along with these arguments, critics
have also questioned the rationality of war. Van Creveld, for
example, argues that it is 'preposterous ... to think that just
because some people wield power, they act like calculating
machines that are unswayed by passions. In fact, they are no
more rational than the rest of us.'[31]

In my view all these arguments are rather trivial and, depending on how Clausewitz is interpreted, they can all be refuted.
I agree with Huw Strachan that the trinity refers to 'tendencies'
or motivations rather than empirical categories.[32] The point of
the concept, as I understand it, is to explain how a complex,
social organization, made up of many different individuals
with many different motivations, can become, in his words, the

'personalized state' – a 'side' in or party to war. 'War' says Clausewitz,

> is, therefore, not only chameleon-like in character, because it changes colour in some degree in each particular case, but it is, also, as a whole, in relation to the predominant tendencies which are in it, a wonderful trinity, composed of the original violence of its elements, hatred and animosity, which may be looked upon as blind instinct; the play of probabilities and chance, which make it a free activity of the soul; and of the subordinate nature of a political instrument, by which it belongs to pure reason.[33]

These different 'tendencies' – reason, chance and emotion – are mainly associated with the state, the generals and the people respectively, but the word 'mainly' or 'more' suggests that they are not exclusively associated with these different components or levels of warfare.

Clausewitz argues that war is what unites the trinity. The trinity was 'wondrous' because it made possible the coming together of the people and the modern state. Obviously, the distinction between the state, the military and the people is blurred in most new wars. New wars are fought by networks of state and non-state actors and often it is difficult to distinguish between combatants and civilians. So if we think of the trinity in terms of the institutions of the state, the army and the people, then it cannot apply. But if we think of the trinity as a concept for explaining how disparate social and ethical tendencies are united in war, then it is clearly very relevant.

A second issue is the primacy of politics. Among translators of Clausewitz, there is a debate about whether the German word *politik* should be translated as 'policy' or 'politics'. I believe it applies to both if we roughly define policy as external, in terms of relations to other states, and politics as the domestic process of mediating different interests and views.

New wars are also fought for political ends and, indeed, war itself can be viewed as a form of politics. The political narrative of the warring parties is what holds together dispersed loose networks of paramilitary groups, regular forces, criminals, mercenaries and fanatics, representing a wide array of tendencies – economic and/or criminal self-interest, love of adventure,

personal or family vendettas, or even just a fascination with
violence. It is what provides a licence for these varying tendencies. Moreover, these political narratives are often constructed
through war. Just as Clausewitz described how patriotism is
kindled through war, so these identities are forged through fear
and hatred, through the polarization of us and them. In other
words, war itself is a form of political mobilization, a way of
bringing together, of fusing the disparate elements that are
organized for war.

Understood in this way, war is an instrument of politics
rather than policy. It is about domestic politics even if it is a
politics that crosses borders rather than the external policy of
states. If, for Clausewitz, the aim of war is external policy and
political mobilization is the means, in new wars it is the other
way round. Mobilization around a political narrative is the aim
of the war and external policy or policy vis-à-vis the proclaimed enemy is the justification.

So if new wars are an instrument of politics, what is the role
of reason? 'New wars' are rational in the sense of instrumental
rationality. But is rationality the same as reason? The Enlightenment version of reason was different from instrumental
rationality. As used by Hegel, who was a contemporary in
Berlin of Clausewitz, it had something to do with the way the
state was identified with universal values, the agency that was
responsible for the public as opposed to the private interest.
The state brought together diverse groups and classes for the
purpose of progress – democracy and economic development.
Clausewitz puts considerable emphasis on the role of the
cabinet in formulating policy and argues that the Commander-
in-Chief should be a member of the cabinet. The cabinet,
which in Clausewitz's time was a group of ministers advising
the monarch, was thought to play a role in bringing together
different interests and motivations and providing unifying publicly justifiable arguments for both war and the conduct of war.
Of course, members of the cabinet had their own private motivations, as do generals (glory, enrichment, jealousy, etc.), but
it is incumbent on them to come to some agreement, to provide
the public face of the war and to direct the war, and this has
to be based on arguments that are universally acceptable (universal, here, referring to those who are citizens of the state).
In his description of the evolution of warfare and the state,

which echoes Hegel's stadial theory of history, Clausewitz argues that only in the modern period can the state be regarded as 'an intelligent being acting in accordance with simple logical rules'[34] and that this is associated with the rise of cabinet government where the 'cabinet had become a complete unity, acting for the state in all its external relations.'[35]

The political narratives of new wars are based on particularist interests; they are exclusive rather than universalist. They deliberately violate the rules and norms of war. They are rational in the sense of being instrumental. But they are not reasonable. Reason has something to do with universally accepted norms that underpin national and international law.

However, there is another argument about why new wars are post-Clausewitzean. This has to do with the fundamental tenets of Clausewitzean thought – his notion of ideal war. This is derived from his definition of war. 'War', he says,

> is nothing but a duel on an extended scale. If we would conceive as a unit the countless number of duels which make up a war, we shall do so best by supposing to ourselves two wrestlers. Each strives by physical force to compel the other to submit to his will: each endeavours to throw his adversary, and thus render him incapable of further resistance. *War therefore is an act of violence intended to compel our opponent to fulfil our will.*[36] (italics in the original)

Violence, he says, is the means. The ultimate object is the 'compulsory submission of the enemy to our will' and, in order to achieve this, the enemy must be disarmed.

He then goes on to explain why this must lead to the extreme use of violence:

> Now philanthropists may easily imagine there is a skilful method of disarming and overcoming an enemy without causing great bloodshed ... However plausible this may appear, still it is an error, which must be extirpated; for in such dangerous things as war, the errors which proceed from a spirit of benevolence are the worst. As the use of physical power to the utmost extent by no means excludes the co-operation of intelligence, it follows that he who uses forces unsparingly, without reference to the bloodshed involved, must obtain a superiority if his adversary uses less vigour in its application. *The former then*

dictates the law to the latter, and both proceed to extremities to which the only limitations are those imposed by the amount of counteracting force on each side.[37] (my italics)

In other words, the inner nature of war – Absolute War – follows logically from the definition as each side is pushed to make fresh efforts to defeat the other – a proposition that Clausewitz elaborates in chapter 1 through what he calls the three reciprocal actions according to which violence is 'pushed to its utmost bounds'.[38] For Clausewitz, combat is the decisive moment of war.

Real war may depart from ideal war for a variety of reasons, but as long as war fits his definition, it contains the logic of extremes, and in chapter 2 of my book I describe how that logic applied to 'old wars'. It is this logic of extremes that I believe no longer applies in 'new wars'. I have, therefore reformulated the definition of war. I have defined war as 'an act of violence involving two or more organized groups framed in political terms'. According to the logic of this definition, war could either be a 'contest of wills', as is implied by Clausewitz's definition, or it could be a 'mutual enterprise'. A contest of wills implies that the enemy must be crushed and therefore war tends to extremes. A mutual enterprise implies that both sides need the other in order to carry on the enterprise of war and therefore war tends to be long and inconclusive. This does not necessarily imply conspiracy; indeed the two sides may themselves view the conflict as a contest of wills. Rather it is a way of interpreting the nature of war.

My argument is that 'new wars' tend to be mutual enterprises rather than a contest of wills. The warring parties are interested in the enterprise of war rather than winning or losing for both political and economic reasons. The inner tendency of such wars is not war without limits but war without end. Wars, defined in this way, create shared self-perpetuating interest in war to reproduce political identity and to further economic interests.

As in the Clausewitzean schema, real wars are likely to be different from the ideal description of war. The hostility that is kindled by war among the population may provoke disorganized violence or there may be real policy aims that can be achieved. There may be outside intervention aimed at suppressing the mutual enterprise. Or the wars may produce unexpectedly an animosity to violence among the population undermining the premises of political mobilization on which such wars are based.

In redefining war in this way, I am offering a different interpretation of war, a theory of war, whose test is how well it offers a guide to practice. Since my definition of war is, as it were, an ideal type, I can use examples to support the theory but it is, in principle, unprovable. The question is whether it is useful. Take the example of the 'War on Terror'. Antulio Echevarria defines the 'War on Terror' in classic Clausewitzean terms. 'Both antagonists seek the political destruction of the other and, at this point, neither appears open to negotiated settlement.'[39] Understood in this way, each act of terrorism calls forth a military response, which in turns produces a more extreme counter-reaction. The problem is that there can be no decisive blow. The terrorists cannot be destroyed by military means because they cannot be distinguished from the population. Nor can the terrorists destroy the military forces of the United States. But if we understand the 'War on Terror' as a mutual enterprise, whatever the individual antagonists believe, in which the US administration shores up its image as the protector of the American people and the defender of democracy and those with a vested interest in a high military budget are rewarded, and in which extremist Islamists are able to substantiate the idea of a global jihad and to mobilize young Muslims behind the cause, then action and counterreaction merely contribute to 'long war' which benefits both sides. Understood in Clausewitzean terms, the proposed course of action is total defeat of the terrorists by military means. Understood in post-Clausewitzean terms, the proposed course of action is very different; it has to do with both the application of law and the mobilization of public opinion not on one side or the other but against the mutual enterprise.

The contrast between new and old wars, put forward here, is thus a contrast between ideal types of war rather than a contrast between actual historical experiences. Of course, the wars of the twentieth century, at least in Europe, were close to the old war ideal, and the wars of the twenty-first century are closer to my depiction of new wars. I am not sure that all contemporary wars actually conform to my description any more than earlier wars conformed to the old war description. Perhaps another way to describe the difference is between realist interpretations of war as conflicts between groups, usually states, that act on behalf of the group as a whole, and interpretations of war in which the behaviour of political leaders is viewed as the expression of a complex set of political and perhaps bureaucratic struggles pursuing their particular interest or the interests of their faction or factions rather than the whole. It can be argued that in the Westphalian era of sovereign nation-states, a realist interpretation had more relevance than it does today.

This conceptual distinction is not quite the same as the way I describe 'new wars' in earlier work, which referred to the involvement of non-state actors, the role of identity politics, the blurring of the distinction between war (political violence) and crime (violence for private interests) as well as the fact that in new wars battles are rare and violence is mainly directed against civilians.[40] But it is not inconsistent with that earlier description; it merely involves a higher level of abstraction.

Conclusion

The debate about new wars has enabled me to refine and reformulate my arguments. The debate about Clausewitz has facilitated a more conceptual interpretation of new wars while the debate about data has led to the identification of new sources of evidence that have helped to substantiate the main proposition.

The one thing the critics tend to agree upon is that the new war thesis has been important in opening up new scholarly analysis and new policy perspectives.[41] The debate has taken this further. It has contributed to a burgeoning field of conflict studies. And it has had an influence on the intensive policy debates that are taking place, especially within the military and ministries of defence – the debate about counter-insurgency, for example, in the Pentagon, or about human security in the European Union and indeed about non-traditional approaches to security in general. A good example of the extent to which the discourse is changing is the World Bank's World Development Report of 2011. Its main argument is that:

Global systems in the 20th century were designed to address interstate tensions and civil wars. War between nation-states and civil war have a given logic ... 21st century violence does not fit the 20th-century mold ... Violence and conflict have not been banished ... But because of the successes in reducing interstate war, the remaining forms of violence do not fit neatly either into 'war' or 'peace', or into 'political' or 'criminal' violence.

Many countries and subnational areas now face cycles of *repeated* violence, weak governance, and instability ... The new forms of violence interlinking local political conflicts, organized crime, and internationalized disputes mean that violence is a problem for both the rich and the poor.[42]

What I still think is lacking in the debate is the demand for a cosmopolitan political response. In the end, policing, the rule of law, justice mechanisms and institution-building depend on the spread of norms at local, national and global levels. And norms are constructed through politics. The struggles going on in the Middle East as I write are an extraordinary example of what I am talking about – where secularists and Islamists, men and women, different communities, refuse to be drawn into sectarian politics. But the huge significance of what is happening and its potential for other situations seems to have very little resonance among the very policy makers who are debating these issues.

Notes

Preface to the Third Edition

1 Steven Pinker, *The Better Angels of Our Nature*, London: Allen Lane, 2011; John Mueller, *The Remnants of War*, Ithaca and London: Cornell University Press, 2004; Human Security Report 2009/10, http://www.hsrgroup.org/human-security-reports/human-security-report.aspx.

2 Mary Kaldor, *Human Security: Reflections on Globalisation and Intervention*, Cambridge: Polity Press, 2008; Shannon D. Beebe and Mary Kaldor, *The Ultimate Weapon is No Weapon: Human Security and the New Rules of War and Peace*, New York: Public Affairs Books, 2010.

Chapter 1   Introduction

1 The research project was undertaken for the United Nations University's World Institute for Development Economics Research (UNU/WIDER). The results are published in Mary Kaldor and Basker Vashee (eds), *Restructuring the Global Military Sector*, Volume I: *New Wars*, London: Cassell/Pinter, 1997.

2 David Keen, 'When war itself is privatized', *Times Literary Supplement* (December 1995).

3 Mark Duffield, 'Post-modern conflict: warlords, post-adjustment states and private protection', *Journal of Civil Wars* (April 1998); Michael Ignatieff, *The Warrior's Honor: Ethnic War and the Modern Conscience*, London: Chatto & Windus, 1998.

4   Chris Hables Gray, *Post-Modern War: The New Politics of Conflicts*, London and New York: Routledge, 1997.

5   Frank Hoffman, *Conflict in the 21st Century: The Rise of Hybrid Wars*, Potomac Institute for Policy Studies, 2011.

6   John Mueller, *The Remnants of War*, Ithaca and London: Cornell University Press, 2004.

7   See, for example, the various chapters including my own chapter 'Elaborating the "new war" thesis', in Jan Angstrom and Isabelle Duyvesteyn, *Rethinking the Nature of War*, London and New York: Frank Cass, 2005; see also Errol A. Henderson and David Singer, ' "New wars" and rumours of "new wars" ', *International Interactions*, 7/2 (2002); Stathis N. Kalyvas, ' "New" and "old" civil wars: a valid distinction?', *World Politics*, 54 (October 2001).

8   Martin Shaw, 'War and globality: the role and character of war in the global transition', in Ho-Won Jeong (ed.), *Peace and Conflict: A New Agenda*, Aldershot: Ashgate, 2000.

9   See David Jablonsky, *The Owl of Minerva Flies at Night: Doctrinal Change and Continuity and the Revolution in Military Affairs*, US Army War College, Carlisle Barracks, PA, 1994; Elliott Cohen, 'A revolution in warfare', *Foreign Affairs* (March/April 1996); Robert J. Bunker, 'Technology in a neo-Clausewitzean setting', in Gert de Nooy (ed.), *The Clausewitzean Dictum and the Future of Western Military Strategy*, The Hague and London: Kluwer Law International, 1997.

10 Jean Baudrillard, *The Gulf War*, London: Power Publishers, 1995.

11 See Malcolm Waters, *Globalization*, London: Routledge, 1995; David Held, *Democracy and the Global Order: From the Modern State to Cosmopolitan Governance*, Cambridge: Polity, 1995.

12 See Mary Kaldor, Ulrich Albrecht and Asbjörn Eide, *The International Military Order*, London: Macmillan, 1978.

13 Anthony Giddens makes a similar argument about the new political cleavage between cosmopolitanism and fundamentalism. See Anthony Giddens, *Beyond Left and Right: The Future of Radical Politics*, Stanford, CA: Stanford University Press, 1994.

14 On the concept of the mode of warfare, see Mary Kaldor, 'Warfare and capitalism', in E.P. Thompson et al., *Exterminism and Cold War*, London: Verso, 1981.

15 See, for example, David Keen, *Conflict and Collusion in Sierra Leone*, Oxford: James Currey, 2005.

16 The Responsibility to Protect: Report of the International Commission on Intervention and State Sovereignty, 2001. http://responsibilitytoprotect.org/ICISS%20Report.pdf.

17 In addition to the research project undertaken for UNU/ WIDER, I and my colleagues at the Sussex European Institute undertook a research project in 1995 on Balkan reconstruction for the European Commission. See Vesna Bojičić, Mary Kaldor and Ivan Vejvoda, 'Post-war reconstruction in the Balkans', *SEI Working Paper*, Brighton: Sussex European Institute, 1995. A shorter updated version is published in *European Foreign Affairs Review*, 2/3 (Autumn 1997). See also the report of the UNDP project, 'Evaluation of UNDP support to conflict-affected countries', http://www.undp.org/evaluation/documents/thematic/ conflict/ConflictEvaluation2006.pdf.

Chapter 2   Old Wars

1 According to Clausewitz: 'War belongs not to the province of Arts and Sciences but to the province of social life ... It would be better instead of comparing it with any Art, to liken it to business competition, which is also a conflict of human interests and activities.' *On War* (first pubd 1832), Harmondsworth: Penguin, 1968, p. 202.
2 Clausewitz, *On War*, p. 101.
3 Martin van Creveld, *The Transformation of War*, New York: Free Press; Oxford: Maxwell Macmillan International, 1991.
4 John Keegan, *A History of Warfare*, London: Hutchinson, 1993, p. 12.
5 Michael Roberts, 'The military revolution 1560–1660', in David B. Ralston, *Soldiers and States: Civil–Military Relations in Modern Europe*, Boston: Heath & Co., 1966, p. 18.
6 Max Weber, *The Theory of Social and Economic Organization*, trans. and ed. A. M. Henderson and Talcott Parsons, New York: Free Press, 1947, p. 326.
7 Van Creveld, *Transformation of War*, p. 41.
8 I am indebted to Robert Neild for some of these points. See *Public Corruption: The Dark Side of Social Evolution*, London: Anthem Press, 2002.
9 See Charles Tilly, *Coercion, Capital and European States AD 990–1990*, Oxford: Blackwell, 1990; Michael Mann, *States, War and Capitalism*, Oxford: Blackwell, 1988.
10 Anthony Giddens, *The Nation-State and Violence*, Cambridge: Polity, 1985.
11 Theda Skocpol, *States and Social Revolutions*, Cambridge: Cambridge University Press, 1979.
12 'Abstract and judgment of Saint-Pierre's project for perpetual peace' (1756), in Stanley Hoffman and David P. Fidler, *Rousseau*

    on International Relations, Oxford: Oxford University Press, 1991, pp. 90–1.

13 'Perpetual peace' (1795), in *Kant's Political Writings*, ed. Hans Reiss, Cambridge: Cambridge University Press, 1992.

14 Clausewitz, *On War*, pp. 119–20.

15 See Richard Simpkin, *Race to the Swift: Thoughts on Twenty-First Century Warfare*, London: Brasseys, 1985.

16 Clausewitz, *On War*, p. 102.

17 The St Petersburg Declaration of 1868, which limited weapons that cause unnecessary suffering, reads as follows:

> Considering that the progress of civilization should have the effect of alleviating as much as possible the calamities of war;
> That the only legitimate object which states should endeavour to accomplish during war is to weaken the military forces of society;
> That for this purpose it is sufficient to disable the greatest possible number of men;
> That this object would be exceeded by the employment of arms which uselessly aggravate the sufferings of disabled men or render their death inevitable;
> That the employment of such arms would therefore be contrary to the laws of humanity.

    Quoted in Michael Howard, 'Constraints on warfare', in Michael Howard, George J. Andreopoulos and Mark R. Shulman (eds), *Constraints on Warfare in the Western World: The Laws of War*, New Haven, CT, and London: Yale University Press, 1994.

18 This crime against humanity, as it was labelled after the war, did not technically count as a violation of the nineteenth-century laws of war, as Adam Roberts points out, since it took place in occupied territory. See Adam Roberts, 'Land warfare: from Hague to Nuremberg', in Howard, Andreopoulos and Shulman, *Constraints on Warfare*.

19 See Ernest Gellner, *The Conditions of Liberty: Civil Society and its Rivals*, London: Hamish Hamilton, 1994.

20 This is explored in my book *The Baroque Arsenal*, London: Andre Deutsch, 1982.

21 See, for example, Lawrence Freedman, *The Evolution of Nuclear Strategy*, London: Macmillan, 1981.

22 The issue has been extensively discussed in the pages of the American journal *International Security*. Key studies include Michael Doyle, 'Liberalism and world politics', *American Political Science Review*, 80/4 (December 1986); and Bruce Russett, *Grasping the Democratic Peace: Principles for a Post-Cold War World*, Princeton, NJ: Princeton University Press, 1993.

23 Claus Offe, 'Western nationalism, Eastern nationalism, and the problems of post-communist transition', *Europe and the Balkans International Network*, Bologna, 1996.
24 Van Creveld, *Transformation of War*, p. 16.
25 Edward N. Luttwak, 'Towards post-heroic warfare', *Foreign Affairs*, 74/3 (1995).

Chapter 3   Bosnia–Herzegovina: A Case Study of a New War

1 He said: 'I understand your frustration but you have a situation that is better than ten other places in the world ... I can give you a list.' Quoted in David Rieff, *Slaughter House: Bosnia and the Failure of the West*, New York: Vintage, 1995, p. 24.
2 *Final Report of the Commission of Experts Pursuant to Security Council Resolution 780 (1992)*, S/1994/674, 27 May 1994, vol. I, annex IV, par. 84.
3 The story is contained in a collection of Ivo Andrić's short stories published in *The Damned Yard and Other Stories* (London and Boston: Forest Books, 1992). At the end of the story, the young man volunteers to fight in the Spanish Civil War, where he is killed in an air raid. 'Thus ended the life of a man who ran away from hatred', writes Andrić. Does this mean that hatred is everywhere? Or that, in volunteering to fight in Spain, he had some hopes of overcoming hatred?
4 Perhaps this was because the perception corresponded to the world view of European politicians themselves. David Owen's book is peppered with remarks that suggest that he himself categorizes people in national terms. Thus, for example, Cosić, the then Yugoslav president, is described as showing 'some of the qualities that have made and will in future make Serbs a substantial people'. The challenge for the negotiations, he says, is to devise a structure which preserves the integrity of Bosnia–Herzegovina but allows the Serbs to 'preserve and safeguard their national identity'. See David Owen, *A Balkan Odyssey*, London: Victor Gollancz, 1995, pp. 48, 67.
5 'Croats belong to a different culture – a different civilisation from the Serbs. Croats are part of Western Europe, part of the Mediterranean tradition. Long before Shakespeare and Molière, our writers were translated into European languages. The Serbs belong to the East. They are Eastern people, like the Turks and Albanians. They belong to the Byzantine culture ... Despite similarities in language, we cannot be together.' Quoted in Leonard J. Cohen, *Broken Bonds: Yugoslavia's Disintegration and*

Balkan Politics in Transition, Oxford and Boulder, CO: Westview Press, 1995, p. 211.

6   See for example, A.D. Smith, *Theories of Nationalism*, London: Duckworth, 1971.

7   According to Sead Fetahagić, a member of Circle 99, the association of independent intellectuals in Sarajevo: 'Many of us are opposed to this multiculturalism because multiculturalism has accepted the manner in which the West has accepted it – one culture alongside another culture alongside a third culture. But we in Bosnia–Herzegovina have always had one culture. I have been brought up within the Serb, Croat, Muslim, Jewish, Czech, European and American culture. We think that one culture exists and not several which are developed one next to the other.' 'The Force of Irreality', *hCa Quarterly*, 15/16 (Winter/ Spring, 1996). Likewise, according to a sociological study undertaken in 1939, 'a feeling of real ethnic and characterological unity remains alive alongside all the historical and national-political differentiation'; quoted in Cohen, *Broken Bonds*, pp. 19–20.

8   See Ernest Gellner, *Nations and Nationalism*, Oxford: Blackwell, 1983.

9   See Ivan Vejvoda, 'Yugoslavia 1945–91 – from decentralisation without democracy to dissolution', in D.A. Dyker and I. Vejvoda, *Yugoslavia and After: A Study in Fragmentation, Despair and Rebirth*, London and New York: Longmans, 1996.

10   For a more extensive discussion of this, see Susan Woodward, *Socialist Unemployment: The Political Economy of Yugoslavia 1945–90*, Princeton, NJ: Princeton University Press, 1995; Vesna Bojičić and Mary Kaldor, 'The political economy of the war in Bosnia–Herzegovina', in Mary Kaldor and Basker Vashee (eds), *Restructuring the Global Military Sector*, Vol. 1: *New Wars*, London: Cassell/Pinter, 1997.

11   See David Dyker, 'The degeneration of the Yugoslav Communist Party as a managing elite – a familiar East European story?', in Dyker and Vejvoda, *Yugoslavia and After*.

12   See Mark Thompson, *Forging War: The Media in Serbia, Croatia, and Bosnia–Herzegovina*, London: Article XIX, 1994.

13   See James Gow, *Legitimacy and the Military: The Yugoslav Crisis*, London: Pinter, 1992.

14   See Milos Vasić, 'The Yugoslav Army and the post-Yugoslav armies', in Dyker and Vejvoda, *Yugoslavia and After*.

15   Rieff, *Slaughter House*, p. 103.

16   'To invite the émigrés back to the homeland for a great meeting was risky to the point that even those people who were later in

my leadership waited till the last minute to see whether we would be arrested or not. This is why that was a turning point in my life in terms of decision-making ... Great deeds, both in individual creative terms, and especially in social innovation, and even militarily, are created on the razor's edge between the possible and the impossible.' Quoted in Laura Silber and Alan Little, *The Death of Yugoslavia*, London: Penguin, 1995, p. 91.

17 Xavier Bougarel, 'Etat et communautarisme en Bosnie–Herzegovina', unpublished MS; English version in Dyker and Vejvoda, *Yugoslavia and After*.

18 Private interview with the author.

19 For example, one of its editorials said: 'Instinctively every Muslim would wish to save his Serb neighbour instead of the reverse, however, every Muslim must name a Serb and take an oath to kill him.' 1 April 1993, quoted in Mazowiecki Report E/CN.4/1994/3, 5 May 1993.

20 I am indebted to my doctoral student Neven Andjelić for detailed information about the pre-war peace movement. See *Bosnia–Herzegovina: The End of a Legacy*, London: Frank Cass, 2003.

21 According to one of his fellow students:

> Many people will tell you now that they saw the war coming then, but I didn't and I don't think Suada [the student who died] did either ... As a medical student scheduled to graduate in May, Suada could easily have stayed away from the demonstration that day. She wasn't from Sarajevo. She wasn't even Bosnian ... It was not an angry crowd ... The people around us, most of them young, were good-humoured and eager to make their point in a peaceful way. I was about fifty metres from the bridge when a few shots – maybe five or six – rang out. Everybody began to run. Once we got to cover behind a building, I was incredibly angry. It had never occurred to me that someone would open fire on a group of unarmed demonstrators. Strange to say, war still didn't seem inevitable. It was only a few days later that there seemed no turning back, that we began to speak of Suada as the first person killed in the Bosnian war. What had seemed a random act of violence, a great personal tragedy, slowly took shape in our minds as the first incident in a far greater drama: Europe's worst war in fifty years.

Quoted in Silber and Little, *The Death of Yugoslavia*, pp. 251–2.

22 'Dans un ultime sursault, la société civile bosniaque naissante a tenté d'évincer le communautarisme de la sphère politique. Un moment déstabilisées, les parties nationalistes se vengent en faisant entrer la guerre dans la vie quotidienne.' Bougarel, 'Etat et communautarisme'.

23 *Report on the Situation of Human Rights in the Territory of Former Yugoslavia*, United Nations, E/CN.4/1992/S–1/9, New York, 28 August 1992, par. 17.

24 Stockholm International Peace Research Institute, *SIPRI Yearbook 1992: World Armaments and Disarmament*, Oxford: Oxford University Press, 1992.

25 Ibid.

26 The same company has been used since the Dayton Agreement to train the army of the Federation of Bosnia–Herzegovina. See David Shearer, *Private Armies and Military Intervention*, Adelphi Paper 316, London: International Institute for Strategic Studies, 1998.

27 *Final Report of the Commission of Experts.*

28 This was a point generally missed by those who advocated lifting the arms embargo on Bosnia–Herzegovina as a solution to the war. Whatever symbolic significance this may have had, it would have had little practical significance, since whether or not the Bosnian army received arms depended on the attitude of the Croatian government. Perhaps the most positive consequence would have been the circumventing of illegal arms dealers in Zagreb.

29 Reports in both the Croatian and the Serbian press refer to cooperation between the JNA and Croat factories to produce M-84 tanks. There were also reports that all three sides in Bosnia–Herzegovina cooperated in the production of ammunition because even the 7.62mm rifle bullet contained components that were produced by the different sides. See Milan Nikolić, 'The Burden of the Military Heritage', unpublished paper produced for WIDER, Helsinki, 1993.

30 *Final Report of the Commission of Experts*, Annex IV, 'Ethnic Cleansing', par. 238.

31 His doctoral thesis, which he completed in 1976, was on Marxist justifications for war.

32 *Final Report of the Commission of Experts*, Annex IV, 'Ethnic Cleansing', par. 103.

33 Ibid., Annex III A, 'Special Forces', par. 68.

34 See Vasić, 'The Yugoslav Army', p. 129.

35 Silber and Little, *The Death of Yugoslavia*, p. 270.

36 Shems Hadj-Nassar, 'Has Rape been Used as a Systematic Weapon of War in the Conflict in the Former Yugoslavia?', unpublished Master's thesis, University of Sussex, 1995.

37 Ethnic cleansing continued in Banja Luka and in Bijeljina and Janja right up to the end of the war. UNHCR reported one man arriving in Tuzla at the end of 1994: 'There are no more

children, no more friends, no more information, no more life, no more Mosques and no more graveyards.' UNHCR, *Information Notes on Former Yugoslavia*, 11/1994, Zagreb, November 1994.

38 Mazowiecki Report E/CN.4/1994/3, 5 May 1993.

39 *Final Report of the Commission of Experts*, Annex III A, 'Special Forces', par. 70.

40 At Dretelj, 'Victims stated that they were subjected to sexual torture, beaten with truncheons and sticks, burned with cigarettes and candles, and forced to drink urine and eat grass. One victim reported that she was held in a room with three other professional women for ten days during which time women in the room were raped repeatedly.' Ibid., par. 67.

41 Vasić, 'The Yugoslav Army', p. 134.

42 *Final Report of the Commission of Experts*, Annex III, par. 239. Interestingly, during the war in Croatia, an internal JNA memo stated that Arkan and Šešelj were dangerous to 'military morale' and that their 'primary motive was not fighting against the enemy but robbery of private property and inhuman treatment of Croatian citizens'. Ibid., par. 100.

43 Xavier Bougarel, *L'Anatomie d'un conflit*, Paris: La Découverte, 1995.

44 *Final Report of the Commission of Experts*, Annex III, par. 102.

45 Ibid., Annex IV, par. 142.

46 Alex de Waal, 'Contemporary warfare in Africa', in Kaldor and Vashee (eds), *Restructuring the Global Military Sector*.

47 This was a German initiative supported only reluctantly by the other European countries. In fact, under German pressure, the EU appointed the Badinter Commission to report on the criteria for recognition for all Yugoslav successor states. In the event, only Macedonia and Slovenia met the criteria for satisfactory arrangements for minorities, but Macedonia's recognition was delayed because of Greek objections.

48 Owen himself suggests that a settlement could have been reached much earlier had the international community been more united and had the negotiators had the full backing of the Americans. He blames the lack of American support for the failure to impose the Vance–Owen Plan in the summer of 1993. It is certainly true that when the Americans took charge much more was achieved, as in the case of the Washington Agreement and the Dayton Agreement. But this argument misses the politics of the period; there was great reluctance to impose partition. A different proposal, say a protectorate, might have mobilized international support. By the time the Dayton Agree-

ment was reached, most people had given up on the alternatives to partition.

49   See Pierre Hassner, 'Ex-Yougoslavie: le tournant?', *Politique Internationale* (Autumn 1995).

50   As Carrington recalls: 'When I talked to Presidents Tudjman and Milošević, it was quite clear to me that both of them had a solution which was mutually satisfactory, which was that they were going to carve it up between them. They were going to carve Bosnia up. The Serb [areas] would go to Serbia and the Croat [areas] to Croatia. And they weren't worried too much, either of them, about what was going to happen to the Muslims.' Quoted in Silber and Little, *The Death of Yugoslavia*, p. 210.

51   Owen insists that he did treat Izetbegović differently because he was the president, but this was not the public impression, and that, after all, was what mattered.

52   UN Department of Public Information, *United Nations Peace-Keeping Information Notes: Update December 1994*, DPI/1306/Rev.4, New York, March 1995, p. 104.

53   SCR 836 extended the mandate of UNPROFOR 'to deter attacks against the safe areas ... to promote the withdrawal of military and para-military units other than those of the Government of the Republic of Bosnia and Herzegovina and to occupy some key points on the ground.' It authorized UNPROFOR 'acting in self-defence, to take all the necessary measures, including the use of force, in reply to bombardments against the safe areas by any of the parties or to armed incursion into them or in the event of any deliberate obstruction in or around those areas to the freedom of movement of UNPROFOR or of protected humanitarian convoys.' And it decided that 'Member States, acting nationally or through regional organisations or arrangements [i.e. NATO], may take, under the authority of the Security Council and subject to close coordination with the Secretary-General and UNPROFOR, all necessary measures through the use of air power, in and around the safe areas in Bosnia and Herzegovina to support UNPROFOR.' UN Department of Public Information, *The United Nations and Former Yugoslavia*, DPI/1312/Rev.2, New York, 15 March 1994, p. 136.

54   This was a proposal put forward at the beginning of the war by the Bosnian peace movement. It was discussed as a proposal for negotiation; the idea was that Izetbegović would have been satisfied by preserving the integrity of Bosnia and Herzegovina and that the Serbs would have been satisfied by the removal of the SDA from power. It was considered seriously in the autumn of

1992 but rejected on the grounds that it would have been too costly in both military and financial terms.

55 Mazowiecki Report, E/CN 4/1994/110, 21 February 1994, par. 347.

56 Quoted in Rieff, *Slaughter House*, p. 211.

57 Owen, *A Balkan Odyssey*, p. 354. This was not the case for men on the ground whom I talked to.

58 Allied Forces Southern Europe, Public Information, *Fact Sheet: Operation Deliberate Force*, Naples, 6 November 1995.

59 Formally, Bosnia was divided into two entities – Republika Srpska and the Federation of Bosnia and Herzegovina – but the latter was partitioned between the Croats and the Muslims.

60 Gerald Knaus and Felix Martin, 'Lessons from Bosnia and Herzegovina: Travails of the European Raj', *Journal of Democracy*, 14/3 (2003), http://www.journalofdemocracy.org/articles/KnausandMartin.pdf. See also the website of the European Stability Initiative: www.esiweb.org.

Chapter 4   The Politics of New Wars

1 Ernest Gellner, *Nations and Nationalism*, Oxford: Blackwell, 1983.

2 Paul Hirst and Grahame Thompson, *Globalization in Question: The International Economy and the Possibilities of Governance*, Cambridge: Polity, 1996.

3 C. Freeman, J. Clarke and L. Soete, *Unemployment and Technical Innovation: A Study of Long Waves and Economic Development*, London: Frances Pinter, 1982; C. Perez-Perez, 'Micro-electronics, long waves, and world structural change', *World Development*, 13/3 (1985).

4 See Margit Mayer, 'The shifting local political system in European cities', in Mick Dunford and Grigoris Kafkalas (eds), *Cities and Regions in the New Europe: The Global–Local Interplay and Spatial Development Strategies*, London: Belhaven Press, 1992; also Manuel Castells and Peter Hall, *Technopoles of the World: The Making of Twenty-First-Century Industrial Complexes*, London: Routledge, 1994.

5 For information on transnational movements and NGOs, see the annual publication *Global Civil Society*, published by Oxford University Press from 2001 to 2003, Sage from 2004 to 2009, and currently by Palgrave Macmillan. See also www.gcsknowledgebase.org

6 Nikolai Bukharin, *Economics of the Transformation Period*, New York: Bergman, 1971.

7 Robert Reich, *The Work of Nations: Preparing Ourselves for 21st Century Capitalism*, London: Simon & Schuster, 1993, p. 97.

8 Alberto Melucci, *Nomads of the Present: Social Movements and Individual Needs in Contemporary Society*, London: Hutchinson Radius, 1989.

9 Alain Touraine, *The Post-Industrial Society*, New York: Random House, 1971.

10 Reich, *The Work of Nations*, p. 178.

11 Giddens calls these symbols 'disembedding mechanisms'. The key characteristic of modernity was what he calls 'time–space distantiation', in which social relations can be constructed with 'absent' others. He defines globalization as a stretching of time–space distantiation. See Anthony Giddens, *The Conditions of Modernity*, Cambridge: Polity, 1990.

12 This definition was developed by Radha Kumar. See Mary Kaldor and Radha Kumar, 'New forms of conflict', in *Conflicts in Europe: Towards a New Political Approach*, Helsinki Citizens' Assembly Publication Series 7, Prague, 1993.

13 See Mary Kaldor and Diego Muro, 'Religious and nationalist militant networks', in Mary Kaldor, Helmut Anheier and Marlies Glasius, *Global Civil Society 2003*, Oxford: Oxford University Press, 2003.

14 In his analysis of conflicts involving political Islam, Mohamed El-Sayed Said distinguishes between Islam based on missionary politics and Islam based on identity politics. The Iranian revolution is an example of the former, while Islamic movements in India are an example of the latter. See 'Conflicts involving Islam', in Mary Kaldor and Basker Vashee (eds), *Restructuring the Global Military Sector*, Vol. 1: *New Wars*, London: Cassell/ Pinter, 1997.

15 I am indebted to Ivan Vejvoda for this point.

16 The term is used by Katherine Verdery in 'Nationalism and national sentiment in post-socialist Rumania', *Slavic Review*, 52/2 (1993).

17 Ibid., p. 82. See also Robert M. Hayden, 'Constitutional nationalism in the formerly Yugoslav republics', *Slavic Review*, 51/4 (1992).

18 This argument is also developed by Katherine Verdery. See, in particular, 'Ethnic relations, economies of shortage and the transition in Eastern Europe', in C.M. Hann (ed.), *Socialism: Ideals, Ideology and Local Practice*, London: Routledge, 1993.

19 See, for example, Andrei Amalrik, *Will the Soviet Union Survive Until 1984?*, London: Penguin, 1970; or Hélène Carrère d'Encausse, *Decline of an Empire: The Soviet Socialist Republics in Revolt*, New York: Newsweek, 1979.

20 Teresa Rakowska-Harmstone, 'The dialectics of nationalism in the USSR', *Problems of Communism*, 23/1 (1974).
21 In many cases, these titular nationalities were artificial. Tadjikistan, for example, is an invented territorial unit. The Tadjik language is a Persian dialect spoken in parts of Iran and Afghanistan which was given a Cyrillic alphabet. The main Tadjik centres of civilization, Samarkand and Bukhara, ended up outside the borders of Tadjikistan, in Uzbekistan.
22 Victor Zaslavsky, 'Success and collapse: traditional Soviet nationality policy', in Ian Bremmer and Ray Taras (eds), *Nations and Politics in Soviet Successor States*, Cambridge: Cambridge University Press, 1993.
23 See, for example, Peter Lewis, 'From prebendalism to predation: the political economy of decline in Nigeria', *Journal of Modern African Studies*, 34/1 (1996); Obi Igwara, 'Holy Nigerian nationalisms and apocalyptic visions of the nation', *Nations and Nationalism*, 1/3 (1995); and Kisangani N.F. Ermizet, 'Zaire after Mobutu: a case of a humanitarian emergency', *WIDER Research for Action 32*, Helsinki: UNU/WIDER, 1997.
24 See Cynthia Brown and Farhad Karim (eds), *Playing the 'Communal Card': Communal Violence and Human Rights*, London and New York: Human Rights Watch, 1995.
25 For a description of this phenomenon in various places, see the Médecins Sans Frontières report on world crisis intervention, *Life, Death and Aid*, London: Routledge, 1993. In Liberia, Charles Taylor's National Patriotic Front of Liberia is described as marching on the capital: 'Constantly drunk or high on Marijuana, wearing wigs, wedding dresses or welder's goggles, they acted out the profound identity crisis in which their shattered world has led them' (p. 56).
26 Rakiya Omaar and Alex de Waal, *Rwanda: Death, Despair and Defiance*, London: Africa Rights, 1994, p. 35.
27 Šumit Ganguly, 'Explaining the Kashmir insurgency: political mobilisation and institutional decay', *International Security*, 21/2 (1996).
28 Radha Kumar, 'Nationalism, nationalities and civil society', in *Nationalism and European Integration: Civil Society Perspectives*, Helsinki Citizens' Assembly Publication Series 2, Prague, 1991.
29 See Oliver Roy, *The Failure of Political Islam*, London: Taurus, 1994; see also Ernest Gellner, *Postmodernism, Reason and Religion*, London and New York: Routledge, 1992.
30 A.D. Smith, *Nations and Nationalism in a Global Era*, Cambridge: Polity, 1996.

31 Kwame Anthony Appiah, 'Cosmopolitan patriots', *Critical Inquiry* (Spring 1997), p. 618.
32 See Robert D. Kaplan, 'The coming anarchy', *Atlantic Monthly* (February 1994).

Chapter 5   The Globalized War Economy

1 Jeffrey Herbst, 'Responding to state failure in Africa', *International Security*, 21/3 (1996–7), pp. 121–2.
2 Cynthia Brown and Farhad Karim (eds), *Playing the 'Communal Card': Communal Violence and Human Rights*, London and New York: Human Rights Watch, 1995.
3 Maggie O'Kane, 'The terrible day when Frenki's Boys came calling', *The Guardian* (19 June 1999).
4 David Keen, 'When war itself is privatized', *Times Literary Supplement* (December 1995).
5 For details on this story, see David Shearer, *Private Armies and Military Intervention*, Adelphi Paper 316, London: International Institute for Strategic Studies, 1998.
6 International Institute for Strategic Studies, *Military Balance 1996–7*, London: Brasseys, 1997, p. 237.
7 Quoted in Richard Simpkin, *Race to the Swift: Thoughts on Twenty-First Century Warfare*, London: Brasseys, 1985, p. 311.
8 The great exception, widely quoted, was the British experience in Malaya. However, the revolutionary movement was quite limited, consisting mainly of the Chinese minority. Nevertheless, what is interesting is the way in which, in contrast to other counter-insurgency practices, the British copied revolutionary tactics by trying to win 'hearts and minds' through the promise of independence and using similar military tactics to the guerrillas. See ibid.
9 Brown and Karim, *Playing the 'Communal Card'*, p. 9.
10 Bethany Lacina and Nils Petter Gleditsch, 2005. 'Monitoring Trends in Global Combat: A New Dataset of Battle Deaths', *European Journal of Population* 21/2–3 (2005).
11 UNHCR, *The State of the World's Refugees: In Search of Solutions*, Oxford: Oxford University Press, 1995. UNHCR, *Global Refugee Trends*, Geneva, 17 June 2004. See also http://www.unhcr.org/pages/4a0174156.html; http://www.refugees.org/resources/refugee-warehousing/archived-world-refugee-surveys/2009-world-refugee-survey.html.
12 Internal Displacement Monitoring Centre, Geneva. http://www.internal-displacement.org/

13   Myron Weiner, 'Bad neighbours, bad neighbourhoods: an inquiry into the causes of refugee flows', *International Security*, 21/1 (1996).

14   Mark Duffield, 'The political economy of internal war: asset transfer, complex emergencies and international aid', in Joanna Macrae and Anthony Zwi (eds), *War and Hunger: Rethinking International Responses*, London: Zed Press, 1994.

15   David Keen has described the way in which the famine in Southern Sudan was caused by cattle-raiding by Baggara militiamen in the North supported by the Sudanese government as a way of weakening the SPLA (Sudan People's Liberation Army) which operated from the South: 'For young Baggara men, particularly those severely hit by economic marginalisation and drought, raiding offered the prospect of increasing their meagre capital stock.' David Keen, 'A disaster for whom? Local interests and international donors during famine. Among the Dinka of Sudan', *Disasters*, 15/2 (1991), p. 155.

16   'Central Asia's narcotics industry', *Strategic Comments*, 3/5 (1997); 'Colombia's escalating violence: crime, conflict and politics', *Strategic Comments*, 3/4 (1997).

17   See Mary Kaldor, Terry Lynn Karl and Yahia Said, *Oil Wars*, London: Pluto Press, 2007.

18   Duffield, 'Political economy of internal war', p. 56.

19   Keen, 'When war itself is privatized'.

20   John Simpson, *In the Forests of the Night: Encounters in Peru with Terrorism, Drug-running and Military Oppression*, London: Arrow Books, 1994.

21   Mats R. Berdahl and David M. Malone, *Greed and Grievance: Economic Agendas in Civil Wars*, International Peace Academy, Boulder, CO: Lynne Rienner, 2000.

22   Keen, 'When war itself is privatized'.

23   A Norwegian psychologist describes a session with 'Ivan', a boy from Bosnia–Herzegovina:

> How can one talk to a nine year old child about the fact that his father shot his best friend? I asked him for his own explanation, and he looked me right in the eyes and said 'I think they have been drinking something that has been poisoning their brains.' But he suddenly added, 'But now they are all poisoned, so I'm sure it is in the drinking water, and we really have to find out how to clean the polluted water reservoirs.' When I asked him if children were as much poisoned as adults he shook his head and said 'No, not at all. They have smaller bodies, so they are less contaminated, and I have discovered that small children and babies who mostly drink milk, they are not poisoned at all.' I asked him if he had ever heard the word politics. He almost jumped and looked at me and said, 'Yes. That's the name of the poison.'

Quoted in Dan Smith, *The State of War and Peace Atlas*, Harmondsworth: Penguin, 1997, p. 31.

24 Several writers refer to the predatory character of contemporary war economies. See Xavier Bougarel, *L'Anatomie d'un conflit*, Paris: La Découverte, 1995, whom I quote in chapter 3. See also R.T. Naylor, 'The insurgent economy: black market operations of guerrilla organizations', *Crime, Law and Social Change*, 20 (1993); and Peter Lewis, 'From prebendalism to predation: the political economy of decline in Nigeria', *Journal of Modern African Studies*, 34/1 (1996).

25 Michael Cranna (ed.), *The True Cost of Conflict*, London: Earthscan, 1994.

26 See Vesna Bojičić, Mary Kaldor and Ivan Vejvoda, 'Post-war reconstruction in the Balkans', *European Foreign Affairs Review*, 2/3 (1997).

27 UNHCR, *The State of the World's Refugees*.

28 By the end of 1986, the United States had supplied some $3 billion worth of aid. Some was diverted by the CIA to Nicaragua and Angola; some was diverted by Pakistani military intelligence for its own use and for the black market; some was sold by political leaders; and some was diverted by the arms suppliers through inflated invoices and pilfered cargoes. According to Naylor ('The insurgent economy', p. 19): 'The result was that not only did international aid organizations have to scour the bazaars to buy back the diverted food, clothing, tents and medicine, but those Afghan rebel chiefs who actually did fight sometimes had to use the profits of the heroin traffic to buy weapons that had already been paid for by the US and Saudi Arabia.'

29 Duffield, 'Political economy of internal war', p. 57.

Chapter 6   Towards a Cosmopolitan Approach

1 http://responsibilitytoprotect.org/ICISS%20Report.pdf.

2 Noam Chomsky, *The New Military Humanism: Lessons from Kosovo*, London: Pluto, 1999.

3 See Michael Walzer, *Just and Unjust Wars: A Moral Argument with Historical Illustrations*, Harmondsworth: Penguin, 1980.

4 Hannah Arendt, *Reflections on Violence*, London and New York: Harcourt, Brace, 1979, pp. 50–1.

5 'Perpetual Peace' (1795), in *Kant's Political Writings*, ed. Hans Reiss, Cambridge: Cambridge University Press, 1992.

6 See Rudi Teitel, *Humanity's Law*, Oxford: Oxford University Press, 2011.

7 'The law of armed conflict had the purpose of restricting the uses of violence between states and, in the case of civil wars, between governments and rebels. Human rights law had (among other things) the purpose of averting and restricting the uses of violence by governments towards their subjects whether formally in rebellion or not; a field of conflict for which international law, by definition, brought no remedies.' Geoffrey Best, *War and Law Since 1945*, Oxford: Clarendon Press, 1994.

8 On the references to humane or cosmopolitan law, see J. Pictet, 'International humanitarian law: a definition', in UNESCO, *International Dimensions of Humanitarian Law*, Dordrecht: Martinus Nijhoff, 1988.

9 Teitel, *Humanity's Law*.

10 For good introductions to the literature, see Oliver Ramsbotham and Tom Woodhouse, *Humanitarian Intervention in Contemporary Conflict: A Reconceptualization*, Cambridge: Polity, 1996; Ian Forbes and Mark Hoffman, *Political Theory, International Relations and the Ethics of Intervention*, London: Macmillan, 1993.

11 Adam Roberts, *Humanitarian Action in War*, Adelphi Paper 305, Oxford: Oxford University Press for the International Institute for Strategic Studies, 1996.

12 See Radha Kumar, 'The troubled history of partition', *Foreign Affairs*, 76/1 (1997).

13 Mary Kaldor, 'A decade of humanitarian intervention: the role of global civil society', in Helmut Anheier, Marlies Glasius and Mary Kaldor (eds), *Global Civil Society 2001*, Oxford: Oxford University Press, 2001.

14 http://www.afpam.org/2011/09/nulla-dolore-amet-blandit-wisi/.

15 Davin Bremmer, 'Local peace and the South African transition', *Peace Review*, 9/2 (1997).

16 William Warfield, 'Moving from civil war to civil society', *Peace Review*, 9/2 (1997).

17 Ed Garcia, 'Filipino zones of peace', *Peace Review*, 9/2 (1997).

18 *Times Literary Supplement* (21 February 1997).

19 Quoted in ibid., p. 30.

20 Alex de Waal, *Famine Crimes: Politics and the Disaster Relief Industry in Africa*, Bloomington and Indianapolis: Africa Rights and the International African Institute/Indiana University Press, 1997, p. 178. See also Mohamed Sahnoun, *Somalia: The Missed Opportunities*, Washington, DC: US Institute for Peace, 1994.

21 See, for example, William J. Durch (ed.), *The Evolution of UN Peacekeeping: Case Studies and Comparative Analysis*, New York: St Martin's Press, 1993; Ministry of Defence, *Wider Peacekeep-*

ing, London: HMSO, 1995; Mats R. Berdal, *Whither UN peace-keeping?*, Adelphi Paper 281, London: International Institute for Strategic Studies, 1993.

22 See, for example, John Mackinlay and Jarat Chopra, *A Draft Concept of Second Generation Multinational Operations*, Providence, RI: Thomas J. Watson Jr. Institute for International Studies, 1993.

23 Charles Dobbie, 'A concept for post-Cold War peace-keeping', *Survival* (Autumn 1994).

24 'Torture, rape, pillage and even cannibalism by ECOMOG supported factions hurt ECOMOG's general political acceptance.' Herbert Howe, 'Lessons of Liberia: ECOMOG and regional peace-keeping', *International Security*, 21/3 (1996–7), p. 163.

25 Quoted in African Rights, *Somalia and Operation Restore Hope: A Preliminary Assessment*, London: African Rights, 1993, p. 28.

26 Roberts, *Humanitarian action*, p. 51.

27 John Mackinlay, 'Improving multifunctional forces', *Survival* (Autumn 1994). In fact, Mackinlay is himself confused. He goes on to say: 'Where force is used, impartiality [here he means neutrality] may seem to have been lost, especially by the party concerned. If legitimacy is intact, however, the appearance of impartiality can be restored.' What is important here is legitimacy in the eyes of the local population. It may not be possible to restore neutrality, which he refers to as impartiality, since the warring parties are no respecters of rules. The point is to retain impartiality from the point of view of the victims.

28 Quoted in Dobbie, 'A concept', p. 137.

29 Ioan Lewis and James Mayall, 'Somalia', in James Mayall (ed.), *The New Interventionism 1991–4: United Nations Experience in Cambodia, Former Yugoslavia, and Somalia*, Cambridge: Cambridge University Press, 1996, p. 117.

30 I discuss at length the idea of human security forces in Shannon D. Beebe and Mary Kaldor, *The Ultimate Weapon is no Weapon: Human Security and the New Rules of War and Peace*, Public Affairs, New York, 2010.

31 There have been reports of human rights abuses by UN personnel in Cambodia, Bosnia–Herzegovina, Somalia and Mozambique. Abuses have included rape, killings and involvement in child prostitution in Mozambique. See, for example, African Rights, *Somalia: Human Rights Abuses by the UN Forces*, London: African Rights, 1993.

32 *Doctrine of the International Community*, speech by Tony Blair at the Economic Club, Chicago, 24 April 1999, http://www.pm.gov.uk/output/Page1297.asp.

33 http://daccess-dds-ny.un.org/doc/UNDOC/GEN/N11/268/39 /PDF/N1126839.pdf?OpenElement.

34 The number of deaths is widely disputed. These figures represent the best estimate of the Independent International Commission on Kosovo based on the collation of a wide range of reports from NGOs and other sources. See Annex 1, 'Documentation on human rights violations', *The Kosovo Report: The Report of the Independent International Commission on Kosovo*, Oxford: Oxford University Press, 2000.

35 Mark Duffield, 'Relief in war zones: towards an analysis of the new aid paradigm', *Third World Quarterly* (1997).

36 Alvaro de Soto and Graciana del Castillo, 'Obstacles to peacebuilding', *Foreign Policy*, 94 (Spring 1994).

37 African Rights, *Somalia and Operation Restore Hope*.

38 Frances Stewart and Valpy Fitzgerald, *War and Underdevelopment*, Oxford: Oxford University Press, 2001.

39 See the annual *Conversion Survey* on *Global Disarmament, Demilitarisation and Demobilization* of the Bonn International Conversion Centre, www.bicc.de.

40 Alex de Waal, 'Contemporary warfare in Africa', in Mary Kaldor and Basker Vashee (eds), *Restructuring the Global Military Sector*, Vol. 1: *New Wars*, London: Cassell/Pinter, 1997, p. 331.

41 http://web.undp.org/evaluation/documents/thematic/conflict/ SierraLeone.pdf.

Chapter 7   The New Wars in Iraq and Afghanistan

1 George W. Bush, 'President Bush announces major combat operations in Iraq have ended: remarks by President Bush from the USS *Abraham Lincoln*', 1 May 2003.

2 Ibid.

3 Max Boot, 'The new American way of war', *Foreign Affairs* (July/ August 2003).

4 See Mary Kaldor, *Imaginary War: Understanding the East–West Conflict*, Oxford: Blackwell, 1990.

5 Ibid., chapters 11 and 12.

6 See Lawrence Freedman, *The Revolution in Strategic Affairs*, Adelphi Paper 318, London: International Institute of Strategic Affairs, 1998.

7 In the aftermath of 9/11, the military recruited the University of Southern California's Institute of Creative Technology to involve Hollywood in imagining terrorist worst-case scenarios. See James Der Derian, '9/11: Before, After and Between', in Craig Calhoun, Paul Price and Ashley Timmer (eds),

Understanding September 11, New York: New Press, 2002, p. 180.

8   According to Max Boot, the *New York Times* report left out the phrase 'a bit', thereby exaggerating American difficulties. See Boot, 'The new American way of war'.

9   Elliott A. Cohen, 'A tale of two secretaries', *Foreign Affairs* (May/June 2002), p. 39.

10 Donald H. Rumsfeld, 'Transforming the military', *Foreign Affairs* (May/June 2002), p. 21.

11 Donald H. Rumsfeld, Testimony to the Senate Armed Services Committee, 9 July 2003.

12 Kersti Hakansson has demonstrated this point in a comparison of tactics in Vietnam and Afghanistan. See 'New wars, old warfare? Comparing US tactics in Afghanistan and Vietnam', in Jan Angstrom and Isabelle Duyvesteyn, *The Nature of Modern War: Clausewitz and his Critics Revisited*, Stockholm: Swedish National Defence College, Department of War Studies, 2003.

13 George W. Bush, West Point graduation speech, 1 June 2002.

14 Bush, 'Major combat operations in Iraq have ended'.

15 See Ahmed S. Hashim, *The Sunni Insurgency in Iraq*, Center for Naval Warfare Studies, 15 August 2003, http://www.mideasti. org/articles/doc89.html.

16 Thomas Barfield, *Afghanistan: A Cultural and Political History*, Princeton, NJ: Princeton University Press, 2010, p. 238.

17 Ibid., p. 6.

18 See Yahia Said, 'Civil society in Iraq', in Helmut Anheier, Marlies Glasius and Mary Kaldor, *Global Civil Society 2004/5*, London: Sage, 2005, p. 6.

19 Ashraf Ghani and Clare Lockhart, *Fixing Failed States: A Framework for Rebuilding a Fractured World*, Oxford and New York: Oxford University Press, 2008.

20 Quoted in Lawrence Freedman, 'The transformation of strategic affairs', Adelphi Paper 379, London: International Institute for Strategic Studies, 2006.

21 'Campaign 2000: Promoting the National Interest', *Foreign Affairs* (January/February 2000).

22 Hashim, *The Sunni Insurgency in Iraq*. See also Samir Haddad and Mazin Ghazi, 'An inventory of Iraqi resistance groups: "Who kills hostages in Iraq?"', *Al Zawra* [Baghdad] (19 September 2004).

23 Hashim, *The Sunni Insurgency in Iraq*.

24 A Jordanian militant, Abu Musab al-Zarqawi, who had fought with the *Mujahidiin* in Afghanistan, had established a small group, Ansar Al-Islam, which had a camp in the autonomous

Northern part of Iraq. Al-Zarqawi joined with the more extremist Islamist groups in Iraq after the invasion, and in 2004, he pledged allegiance to Osama Bin Laden and renamed his organization Al Qaeda in Mesopotamia or Al Qaeda in the Land of Two Rivers.

25 See Austin Long, 'The Anbar awakening' *Survival*, 50/2 (2008).
26 Florian Broschk, 'Inciting the believers to fight': A closer look at the rhetoric of the Afghan jihad', *Afghan Analysts Network* (February 2011).
27 Anand Gopal, 'The Battle for Afghanistan: Militancy and Conflict in Kandahar', Counterterrorism Strategy Initiative Policy Paper, Washington, DC: New America Foundation, November 2010, p. 14.
28 Quoted in Andrew F. Krepinevich, 'How to win in Iraq', *Foreign Affairs* (September/October 2005).
29 Kate Clark, 'The Takhar attack: Targeted killings and the parallel worlds of US intelligence and Afghanistan', *Afghan Analysts Network* (May 2011).
30 Gopal, 'The Battle for Afghanistan'.
31 UNAMA, *Protection of Civilians in Armed Conflict*, Kabul, Afghanistan, annual report 2011.
32 Gilbert Burnham, Riyadh Lafta, Shannon Doocy and Les Roberts, 'Mortality after the 2003 invasion of Iraq: a cross-sectional cluster sample survey', *The Lancet*, 368/9545 (2006).
33 Opinion Research Business, 'Revised Casualty Data, press release', 28 January 2008. London: ORB. http://www.opinion.co.uk/Documents/Revised%20Casulaty%20Data%20%20Press%20release.doc.
34 UNAMA, 'Afghanistan, Annual Report 2010 – Protection of Civilians in Armed Conflict', http://unama.unmissions.org/Portals/UNAMA/human%20rights/March%20PoC%20Annual%20Report%20Final.pdf.
35 UNAMA, 'Afghanistan, Midyear Report 2011 – Protection of Civilians in Armed Conflict', http://unama.unmissions.org/Portals/UNAMA/Documents/2011%20Midyear%20POC.pdf.
36 Internal Displacement Monitoring Centre, *Afghanistan: Need to Minimise New Displacement and Increase Protection for Recently Displaced in Remote Areas*, 11 April 2011. www.internal-displacement.org.
37 Mary Kaldor, Terry Lynn Karl and Yahia Said, *Oil Wars*, London: Pluto Press, 2007.
38 http://www.unodc.org/documents/crop-monitoring/Afghanistan/Afg_opium_survey_2010_exsum_web.pdf.

39 Antonio Gustiozzi and Christof Reuter, 'The insurgents of the Afghan north: The rise of the Taleban, the self-abandonment of the Afghan government and the effects of ISAF's "capture-and-kill" campaign', *Afghan Analysts Network* (April 2011).

40 Matthieu Aikins, 'Letter from Kandahar: The Master of Spin Boldak: Undercover with Afghanistan's drug-trafficking border police', *Harpers Magazine* (December 2009).

41 Thomas E. Ricks, *The Gamble: General Petraeus and the Untold Story of the American Surge in Iraq 2006–8*, London: Allen Lane, 2009, p. 7.

42 David Kilcullen, *The Accidental Guerilla: Fighting Small Wars in the Midst of a Big One*, Oxford and New York: Oxford University Press, 2009, p. 182.

43 *United States Government Integrated Civilian-Military Campaign Plan for Support to Afghanistan*, 10 August 2009. http://www.comw.org/qdr/fulltext/0908eikenberryandmcchrystal.pdf.

44 Peter Singer, *Wired for War: The Robotics Revolution and Conflict in the 21st Century*, Washington, DC: Brookings Institution, 2009.

45 Ibid., p. 223.

46 Ibid., p. 34.

47 Interview with author.

48 Barfield, *Afghanistan*, p. 269.

49 For a detailed discussion of what this might mean, see *A Human Security Doctrine for Europe: The Barcelona Report of the Study Group on European Security Capabilities* (15 September 2004).

Chapter 8   Governance, Legitimacy and Security

1 John Keane, *Reflections on Violence*, London: Verso, 1996.

2 Samuel P. Huntington, *The Clash of Civilizations and the Remaking of World Order*, New York: Simon & Schuster, 1996; also 'The clash of civilizations?', *Foreign Affairs* (Summer 1993).

3 The neo-medievalism thesis is usually accredited to Umberto Eco, *Travels in Hyperreality*, London: Picador, 1987. For a description, see Barry Smart, *Postmodernity*, London: Routledge, 1996. It should be distinguished from Bull's New Medievalism, which referred to the idea of overlapping political sovereignties and is closer to the cosmopolitan governance approach. Hedley Bull, *The Anarchical Society: A Study of Order in World Politics*, London: Macmillan, 1977.

4 Robert D. Kaplan, 'The coming anarchy', *Atlantic Monthly* (February 1994); and Robert D. Kaplan, *The Ends of the Earth: A*

Journey at the Dawn of the 21st Century, London: Papermac, 1997.

5   According to Martin van Creveld: 'Truth to say, what we are dealing with here is neither low-intensity conflict nor some bastard offspring of war. Rather it is WARRE in the elemental Hobbesian sense of the word, by far the most important conflict of our time.' Van Creveld, *The Transformation of War*, New York: Free Press; Oxford: Maxwell Macmillan International, 1991, p. 22.

6   For an elaboration of this argument, see Paul Berman, *Terror and Liberalism*, London: Norton, 2003.

7   Huntington, *The Clash of Civilizations*, p. 321.

8   Kaplan, *The Ends of the Earth*, p. 6.

9   Ibid., p. 45.

10 Ibid., p. 329.

11 Ibid., p. 432.

12 Quoted in David Keen, 'Organized chaos: not the new world we ordered', *World Today* (January 1996).

13 Kaplan, *The Ends of the Earth*, p. 337.

14 Ibid., p. 436.

15 Richard Falk, *On Humane Governance*, Cambridge: Polity, 1995.

16 David Beetham, 'Human rights as a model for cosmopolitan democracy', in Daniele Archibugi and David Held (eds), *Reimagining Political Community: Studies in Cosmopolitan Democracy*, Cambridge: Polity, 1998.

17 See *European Defence: A Proposal for a White Paper Report of an Independent Task Force*, Paris: European Union Institute for Strategic Studies, May 2004.

18 European Commission, *Eurobarometer 60: Public Opinion in the European Union, Autumn 2003*, http://europa.eu.int/comm/public_opinion/archives/eb/eb60/eb60_rapport_standard_en.pdf (2004).

19 *A Human Security Doctrine for Europe: The Barcelona Report of the Study Group on Europe's Security Capabilities*, Barcelona, September 2004, http://www.lse.ac.uk/Depts/global/Publications/HumanSecurityDoctrine.pdf

Afterword

1   See Martin van Creveld, *The Transformation of War*, 1991; Kalevi J. Holsti, *The State, War and the State of War*, Cambridge: Cambridge University Press, 1996; Donald Snow, *Uncivil Wars: International Security and the New Internal Conflicts*, Boulder, CO: Lynne Rienner, 1996; Mark Duffield, *Global Governance and*

the New Wars: The Merging of Development and Security, London: Zed Books, 2001; Herfried Munkler, *The New Wars*, Cambridge: Polity, 2005; Erhard Eppler, *Vom Gewaktmärkte zum Gewalt-markt?* Berlin: Suhrkamp, 2001; Rupert Smith, *The Utility of Force: The Art of War in the Modern World*, New York: Alfred A. Knopf, 2007.

2 Stathis N. Kalyvas, ' "New" and "old" civil wars: a valid distinc-tion?', *World Politics*, 54 (2001), pp. 99–118; Bob de Graaff, 'The wars in Former Yugoslavia in the 1990s: Bringing the state back in', in Jan Angstrom and Isabelle Duyvesteyn, *The Nature of Modern War: Clausewitz and his Critics Revisited*, Stockholm: Swedish National Defence College, Department of War Studies, 2003; Patrick A. Mellow, 'Review Article: In search of new wars: The debate about the transformation of war', *European Journal of International Relations*, 16 (2010) p. 297; Mats Berdal, 'How "new" are "new wars"? Global economic change and the study of civil war', *Global Governance*, 9 (2003), pp. 477–502.

3 Jacob Mundy, 'Deconstructing civil wars: Beyond the new wars debate', *Security Dialogue*, 42 (2011), p. 289.

4 Michael Evans, 'From Kadesh to Kandahar: Military theory and the future of war', *Naval War College Review* (Summer 2003). See also Frank Hoffman, 'Hybrid warfare and challenges', JFQ, 52 (2009), pp. 34–9.

5 Sven Chojnacki, 'Anything new or more of the same? Wars and military intervention in the international system, 1946–2003', *Global Society*, 20/1 (2006), pp. 25–46.

6 Quoted in John Mueller, *The Remnants of War*, Ithaca, NY: Cornell University Press, 2004, p. 172.

7 Ibid., p. 2.

8 Ibid., p. 115.

9 See Michael Howard, 'What's in a Name?: How to fight terror-ism', *Foreign Affairs* (January/February 2002).

10 Stathis N. Kalyvas, *The Logic of Violence in Civil Wars*, Cambridge: Cambridge University Press, 2006, p. 78.

11 http://www.correlatesofwar.org/.

12 http://www.pcr.uu.se/research/ucdp/definitions/definition_of_armed_conflict/.

13 Michel Wievorka, *Violence: A New Approach*, Thousand Oaks, CA: Sage, 2009.

14 Mary Kaldor and Basker Vashee (eds.), *New Wars*, London: Pinter, 1997.

15 http://www.pcr.uu.se/research/ucdp/program_overview/.

16 http://www.cidcm.umd.edu/pc/.

17   Milton Leitenberg, 'Deaths in War and Conflicts in the 20th Century', Cornell University Peace Studies Program Occasional Paper 29, 3rd edn, 2006.

18   Erik Melunder, Magnus Oberg and Jonathan Hall, 'Are "new wars" more atrocious? Battle severity, civilians killed and forced migration before and after the end of the Cold War', *European Journal of International Relations*, 15 (2009), p. 505.

19   Adam Roberts, 'Lives and statistics: Are 90% of war victims civilians?', *Survival*, 52/3 (2010), pp. 115–36.

20   http://www.iraqbodycount.org/.

21   http://www.opinion.co.uk/Documents/Revised%20 Casulaty%20Data%20-%20Press%20release.doc.

22   http://icasualties.org/.

23   See Bethany Lacina and Nils Petter Gleditsch, 'Monitoring trends in global combat: A new dataset of battle deaths', *European Journal of Population*, 21 (2005), pp. 145–66.

24   http://www.unhcr.org/pages/4a0174156.html;   http://www. refugees.org/resources/refugee-warehousing/archived-world-refugee-surveys/2009-world-refugee-survey.html.

25   Myron Weiner, 'Bad neighbours, bad neighbourhoods: an inquiry into the causes of refugee flows', *International Security*, 21/1 (1996).

26   http://www.internal-displacement.org.

27   See, for example, Hew Strachan and Andreas Herbeg-Rothe, *Clausewitz and the Twenty First Century*, Oxford: Oxford University Press, 2007; Bart Schurman, 'Clausewitz and the "New Wars" Scholars', *Parameters* (Spring 2010).

28   Mary Kaldor, 'Inconclusive wars: Is Clausewitz still relevant in these global times?', *Global Policy*, 1/3 (2010).

29   John Keegan, *A History of Warfare*; Martin van Creveld, *The Transformation of War*.

30   Donald Snow, quoted in Jan Angstrom, 'Introduction', in Angstrom and Duyvesteyn, *The Nature of Modern War; Clausewitz and his Critics Revisited*, p. 8.

31   Van Creveld, *The Transformation of War*, p. 10.

32   Huw Strachan, *Carl von Clausewitz's On War: A Biography*, London: Atlantic Books, 2007.

33   Clausewitz, *On War*, p. 24.

34   Ibid., p. 342.

35   Ibid., p. 344.

36   Ibid., p. 5.

37   Ibid., p. 6.

38   Ibid., p. 7.

39   Antulio Echevarria, *Clausewitz and Contemporary War*, Oxford: Oxford University Press, 2007, p. 211.

40　Mary Kaldor, *New and Old Wars: Organised Violence in a Global Era*, 2nd edn, Cambridge: Polity, 2007.

41　Edward Newman, 'The "new wars" debate: a historical perspective is needed', *Security Dialogue*, 35/2 (2004), pp. 173–89; Errol A. Henderson and David Singer, '"New wars" and rumours of "new wars"', *International Interactions*, 28/2 (2002).

42　*World Development Report 2011: Conflict, Security and Development: Overview*, Washington, DC: The World Bank, 2011, pp. 4–5.

Index